PEACE WILL HAVE
THE LAST WORD

SISTER EMMANUEL MAILLARD

PEACE WILL HAVE
THE LAST WORD

children
of
Medjugorje

© 2015 Children of Medjugorje, Inc.

TRANSLATOR: Anne Laboe, USA 2015
EDITOR: Christine Zaums, USA 2015
GRAPHIC ARTIST: Nancy Cleland, USA 2015
COVER PHOTO © Shutterstock
BOOK DESIGN: Catholic Way Publishing

Ordering Information:
Orders by trade bookstores and wholesalers.
Please contact Ingram Content at www.ingramcontent.com

ISBN-13: 978-0-9980218-1-2

11 10 9 8 7 6 5 4 3 2

Available in eBook.

Children of Medjugorje
www.childrenofmedjugorje.com

Contents

To my brothers and sisters of "The Family of Mary"* who allowed me to draw a few stories from their wonderful magazine "The Triumph of the Heart."

To my assistant Gabriel, without whom this book would not exist.

To all those, known or unknown who prayed that this book will be for the greatest glory of God.

* The Family of Mary:
contact@familledemarie.com/www.familledemarie.org

PREFACE

S R. EMMANUEL IS SOMEONE whom I have known for many years. Her personal testimony made a profound impression upon me. She has served Our Blessed Mother and the Church in a wonderful way through her apostolate in Medjugorje, and her many travels around the world, anxious to preach the Gospel and disseminate the messages of Our Lady.

This book provides relief for a weary world.

Everywhere Sister Emmanuel travels people share with her their expectations, their struggles, their sufferings and their questions. As an outstanding wellspring of grace within the Church, unique in our time, they expect Medjugorje to offer light and hope from heaven.

Sister Emmanuel's writings have always conveyed this sense of hopeful expectation, and so it is with this book, *Peace Will Have the Last Word.* Some of these stories concern her own life; others are drawn from the lives of saints, such as Padre Pio or Mother Teresa; while others depict men and women who have literally escaped from hell to proclaim the Good News. Gathered from all over the world, these accounts are not only real, but they are also captivating, because they respond to the pre-eminent question of our troubled world: 'How can we find peace, true peace?'

When you take up this book, be prepared for a late night because you will not be able to put it down. But read it in small doses, a chapter a day, so as to allow all the riches it contains to sink in. It is a modern day Gospel!

I hope you enjoy reading it as much as I have, and I ask you to join me in praying for Sr. Emmanuel and for all those who have contributed to this excellent work.

SR. BRIEGE MCKENNA*

---

* Sister Briege McKenna O.S.C. is a Sister of Saint Clare from Ireland, of international renown. She travels the world calling priests and lay faithful back to a Christ-centered life. Endowed with gifts of prophecy and healing, she preaches excellent spiritual retreats. Jesus has entrusted His priests to her in a special way, for whom she exercises a remarkable ministry. She authored the bestselling book *Miracles Do Happen,* which has been translated in 25 languages, and *The Power of the Sacraments,* both published by Servant Books. Find out more about Sr. Briege on her website: www.sisterbriege.com, or you can email her apostolate: prayer@sisterbriege.com.

INTRODUCTION

"Dear children! I desire to place all of you under my mantle and protect you from all satanic attacks. Today is a day of peace, but in the whole world there is a great lack of peace. That is why I call you all to build a new world of peace with me through prayer. This I cannot do without you, and this is why I call all of you with my motherly love and God will do the rest. So, open yourselves to God's plan and to His designs to be able to cooperate with Him for peace and for everything that is good. Do not forget that your life does not belong to you, but is a gift with which you must bring joy to others and lead them to eternal life. May the tenderness of the little Jesus always accompany you! Thank you for having responded to my call."

(MESSAGE OF DECEMBER 25, 1992)

Dear Readers!

I FELT COMPELLED TO write this book, because I have looked at you. I have looked at you deeply and at length. I have seen you arrive with your luggage, your questions, your hopes, your desires, and your struggles. I have penetrated your gaze and found there both light and darkness. I have observed you in your streets, your shopping centers, and your traffic jams. I have listened to you in your homes, and I have seen your tears. I have traveled to the ends of the earth to find you. I ate and drank with you in lonely country dwellings as well as in the high-rise buildings of your cities. I have prayed in your churches and I have wept with your sick … And I said to myself, "But there is a luminous response from God to all of this!"

And so I raised my hands heavenwards for you, but that wasn't enough. You have asked me to speak, to write, to recount, to "say something." But what can I say? Am I going to add my own messages to the sublime messages that the Queen of Heaven is giving us? No, not add to, but illustrate, yes! Because in looking at you, a great desire has been kindled in my heart: that of collaborating with her, for your happiness! I believe that it is she who has allowed me to recognize in such and such an event, or in such and such a testimony, little presents gift-wrapped for you! How I would love them to renew your hope and lighten your hearts, which are created to soar very high! How I wish that this tremendous potential of love that you carry within you be realized a little more and a little better, with the help of these simple little stories gleaned from our world, which so desperately yearns for peace.

With God, everything—even the worst—can be transformed into happiness. If today it seems that the world is falling into the hands of the enemy in many respects, if the Evil One is enjoying his hour, deafening us with incessant noise, using every electronic means possible; let's not forget the one who has been chosen, together with her offspring, to crush the head of the Serpent, and who is already at work. "This is MY time … It is a time of grace," she says in Medjugorje. The prophecy she made at Fatima flashes across our modern world like a bolt of lightning in a dark sky. "In the end, my Immaculate Heart will triumph and there will be a time of peace." *(July 13th, 1917).* During a private apparition she said to little Jacinta; "The peace of the world has been entrusted to the Immaculate Heart of Mary, and it is from her that we should ask for it."

The triumph of the Immaculate Heart is not going to fall from heaven unexpectedly, with special effects like in a Hollywood movie. It will come about quietly, through the hearts of her children, her 'apostles,' who are following her faithfully and who will have overcome Satan. We can see the first glimmer of it, or rather, we can breathe in the first ocean spray, like travelers, who after being on the road for days, smell the sea even before it comes into view.

The marvels of God are rarely published in the secular media. By contrast, we have become targets for all the rest, and especially for the noise that is cunningly orchestrated to prevent man from thinking and from knowing the depths of his heart. And so, in my little patchwork of stories that is somewhat impressionistic in style, through people like Carolina, Tony Daud, Claude Newman, Ivona and many others, I invite you to discover the hidden beauties and magnificent victories that God weaves into our lives and which deserve to be proclaimed from the rooftops. Allow yourselves to be captivated by the reality of these accounts so that joy might flow like a river within you! In the midst of the gnawing anxieties and chaos of atheism, may a new courage come to inhabit your daily life when you discover what God dreams of doing for you, too! May a new enthusiasm enrich your heart, as you adopt these new friends who will become members of your spiritual family! And then, jump, dance, and weep for joy before the One who loves you too much not to reveal to you His splendid face, or let you explore His Heart!

Yes, our God is peace, and for you, too, peace will have the last word!

1

Take Hold of the Blessed Mother's Hands

A T THE AGE OF 7, Dave was sexually abused by a neighbor in the parking garage of his apartment building in the United States. He remained deeply traumatized by this experience, as one can imagine. Utterly bewildered and filled with rage, his little child-like heart was unable to make sense of anything. The wound bled in silence, because the child in his shame told no one what had happened. This unbearable secret affected his entire childhood and adolescence.

Later on, as an adult, he became involved in certain perverse sexual practices. Even though he was very successful in his professional life, Dave felt that he was being destroyed from within little by little, so disgusted was he by his behavior. His attempts to break free were in vain, because his good intentions never lasted more than a few days. He was on an inescapable slippery slope, which gradually led him into depression and then despair. From a Jewish background, he had had a personal encounter with Christ and had asked to be baptized, after which a great light had illuminated his way for several months. But his lack of willpower gained the upper hand, so that Dave fell even lower than before.

He saw himself as something despicable, a human wreck, the worst kind of scum. His whole identity had sunk into a black hole, as if he had already passed into a world of darkness with no way out. His life had become a nightmare.

One day, he couldn't take anymore, so he decided to commit suicide. As he worked out his plan and prepared to act upon it, with the attention to detail of someone truly in despair, a friend knocked on his door and announced out of the blue:

"Dave, I'm organizing a trip to Medjugorje and I've come to invite you! Come on, come with us, it will do you good!"

"Medjugorje? What's that?"

His friend explained in a few words the impact that this village had had on him, told him briefly about some of the things he had experienced, and finished by saying, "It's a place of grace, when you go there, you don't come back the same."

"Where is it?"

"In Bosnia and Herzegovina."

Dave had no idea where Bosnia-Herzegovina was, but he thought to himself, 'Okay, why not? This is my last chance! If things don't work out there, I'll kill myself.'

It was on a warm summer's day that Dave's group arrived in Medjugorje. Haunted by his dark thoughts, Dave was feeling too miserable to be able to appreciate the activities offered by his group. He was so caught up in his inner hell that he wasn't taking in anything.

One night, unable to sleep, he got up at 2 o'clock in the morning to take a walk through the town, or rather, to wander around like a lost soul. In his wanderings he found himself in the piazza in front of the church of Saint James and noticed a statue of Mary nearby, surrounded by a small fence. He decided to go closer. There, in front of his Heavenly Mother, he finally broke down and, falling to his knees, began to sob like a child. Between sobs he cried out his misery, "I want to die! I can't go on living like this! Everything I do is wrong! I want out! I can't take anymore!"

Suddenly, he heard a female voice that was both gentle and purposeful, "Dave, give me your hand and allow me to lead you to my Son Jesus!" Shocked at seeing he wasn't alone, Dave turned around to see who had spoken. But at this late hour of the night, there wasn't a living soul around. "Oh great! So now I'm hearing voices, too? That's all I need! Am I going crazy, or what?" But the mysterious voice repeated the same message a second time with the same tone, "Dave, give me your hand and allow me to lead you to my Son Jesus." The sound was like music. Only then did Dave understand that it was the Virgin Mary talking to him, inviting him to give her his hand.

Overwhelmed, he decided to do what the voice told him: he jumped over the little fence, and going up close to the statue, he placed his hand in that of Mary's. She was, in fact, holding one hand on her heart and the other was extended. Dave stayed like that for a long time, hand in hand with the Blessed Virgin, but he continued crying out and shouting in despair. "I've got too many problems. I want to die. I'm done with life!" Then the Lady's voice was heard again, "Dave, give me all your problems and allow me to present them to my Son Jesus with the heart of a mother." Dave was silent. The Lady repeated this message and once again, Dave decided to do what she told him. He launched into a long description of all his problems, down to the last detail: every struggle, all his hang-ups, failures, and his countless emotional disappointments. His list seemed endless, but each time he named a problem, Dave placed it in Mary's Heart, as if to let it go forever. After reciting his long list, Dave experienced a deep peace, and felt as though he had off-loaded his heavy burden and put it in a safe place. He returned to his hotel feeling released from all these worries, went to bed and slept like a baby.

Seven years later, I met him in Medjugorje. As it turned out, he had listened to one of my CDs and wanted to talk to me. It's then that he told me his whole story, and at the end he added these moving words, "Sister Emmanuel, you probably won't believe me, but I can tell you that since that night, when I held Mary's hand and handed over all my problems to her, I have never fallen back into those horrible sins that I committed so often. I have never stopped holding that hand! The Mother of God is holding on to me, and I am holding on to her! I have no intention of letting go, because I know myself too well. If I let go, I'm lost! Every summer I come back to Medjugorje to thank Jesus and Mary for having saved my life. They've turned me into a man who is happy to be alive, imagine that, after all the horror of my life! I'm happy to bear witness to their love to those who find themselves in a dead-end situation, like the one I was in before."

Dave did not know back then that the two words he had received from Our Lady's own lips had already been given by her several times in Medjugorje, to all her "dear children." In truth, she is speaking to each one of us!

Is Our Lady Going to Send Us an Email?

I love telling Dave's testimony, because those words of Mary touch all those who are suffering. In addition, it often happens that after having heard Dave's story, one or two men in the crowd will come up to me and tell me: "Sister Emmanuel, I am another Dave, but Dave in the time prior to his conversion. I want to break free and today you've given me hope again; pray for me!"

Taking hold of Mary's hand is our best option. Mary is the only Mother who knew ahead of time the identity of the child she was going to conceive, through what the Angel Gabriel revealed, as well as his mission on earth. In the same way, as Mother of the Creator, Mary knows God's unique plan for each one of us. To take her hand is a way of being secure. Amid the trials and tribulations of this world, she leads us along a safe path and isn't afraid of the thorns that seem to block our way.

How can we really hold Mary's hand? Nothing could be more simple! Whenever we are faced with a choice, have a decision to make, or have to discern what direction to take, instead of just thinking about it or calling our friends to see what they think, all we need to do is take a moment of silence and recollection, and ask Our Lady: 'What would you do, dear Mother, if you were in my position? What would you choose?' This question can be just as valid for the choice of a partner as it is for where to go on vacation, which movie to watch, what words to speak or which dress to buy.

For sure, Our Lady is not going to give us an answer over the phone, or send us an email![1] No, she has another means by which to answer us, one that is much more profound and effective. It can happen that, when we are silent, when we are open to her inspiration, she gives our heart an inclination towards the will of God. In fact, she is an expert in this field! She acts, therefore, in a way that is very delicate and often imperceptible to our senses. Even if we do not feel the work that she is doing within us, our heart mysteriously adjusts to it and we are much more likely to make the decision that most pleases God. I have often experienced this myself. How many times have I made a decision about something I had to do and how many times have I asked the Heavenly Mother, "What do you think about that? What would you do if you were me?" Very often, after this time of silence, I have had to

---

[1] Although it is true that the two monthly messages of Our Lady are transmitted through the internet, thus reaching millions of people in a matter of minutes. To receive these by email, send your email address to: contact@sisteremmanuel.org.

concede that it would be better to forget my plan and do something else.

Yes, holding Mary's hand is not just a token gesture, but is to engage our entire being with the demands that go with this. As spouse of the Holy Spirit, Mary will always point us along a path that will help us to grow, as opposed to always taking the easy way, which at first seems to require less effort. Let us keep a tight hold of her hand and if ever we were to let go, to run along our own dead-end paths, may she rush to snatch us back like any good mother would do when some danger threatened her child.

Holding Mary's hand also means that we can be sure of the constant assistance of the Holy Spirit. Saint Louis de Montfort wrote, "When the Holy Spirit has found the love for Mary in a soul, He flies there!"[2]

If Mary succeeded in this feat of changing Dave's entire existence when he was a complete wreck, how could she not also change the life of each one of us?

---

[2] St. Louis De Montfort, *True Devotion to Mary,* (Baronius Press, 2012), Chap. 1 § 36.

Mother Teresa's Testimony

One day, the late Bishop Paolo Maria Hnilica of Slovakia, asked Mother Teresa what was the secret behind her success with the poor. She recounted the following episode from her childhood, "I owe this grace to my mother! When I was seven, or eight years old, my mother took me for a walk in a park, holding me by the hand, and she said, 'My daughter, just as you have held my hand today, during all your life, always hold the hand of your Heavenly Mother, the Virgin Mary. She will be the one to guide you to Jesus and to heaven. With her, you will never lose your way, and never take the wrong path. Never let go of the Blessed Mother's hand!' That is the secret of my success!"

2

Angels They Exist!

"No evil will befall you, nor will any plague come near your tent, for He will give His angels charge concerning you, to guard you in all your ways. They will bear you up in their hands, that you do not strike your foot against a stone. You will tread upon the lion and the cobra, the young lion and the serpent you will trample down."

(PSALM 91)

WHEN FACED WITH THE natural catastrophes that have multiplied over recent years, a sense of powerlessness could take hold of us. The enormity of the needs and the depth of the suffering—sometimes—endured by certain populations, overwhelms us. Are we without any possibility of coming to their aid? Certainly not! We have a wonderful means of aid at our disposal, which we don't think about enough. To illustrate this, here is something that was told to me by my brother Pascal, who is a permanent deacon:

"Before his conversion, the Russian writer, Alexander Ogorodnikov, had run the gamut of all the nihilistic and destructive philosophies of the 20th century. He was a professor of philosophy, who had also surrendered to a great and secret passion: breaking into apartments at night with his partners in crime—an activity that paid off considerably! But, grace was at work and he converted in the 70s, at the same time as another Russian intellectual, Tatiana Goritcheva.

"He then created a soup kitchen to feed the poor in Moscow, and he founded a 'seminary': it was a sort of community of intellectuals who were believers, who gathered together to pray, to reflect about the faith, to study the faith in depth, and to evangelize, but in a clandestine way. However, it really wasn't as clandestine as all that, because Alexander was arrested several times, until finally he was given a choice: exile or prison. Alexander refused exile and was sent to prison.

"Over a ten-year period, he was subjected to several types of detention: first, as a political prisoner, then with common criminals, the worst criminals and several others. But it was his last detention that was the most terrible for him, when he was thrown completely naked into a freezing cell (the walls were covered with ice) in total solitude. An atrocious torture!

"He knew he was dying. I don't know how, but he succeeded in getting a letter to his mother in which he described the conditions of his detention, his agony, the psychological tortures, etc. He begged his mother to have his letter smuggled out to the West. That is how the letter came to be published in Germany and France in the spring of 1986. Thousands of petitions were subsequently gathered, and Alexander was finally freed."

When my brother Pascal discovered the letter in France, he wept with sorrow over it and decided with his fiancée to offer all their hardships and their prayers for Alexander. Each day, their prayers at each moment were carried by their guardian angels to Alexander's horrible cell, to comfort him and to help him survive.

After his liberation in 1986, Alexander was able to make a pilgrimage to Lisieux, France, in 1987 with Sister Tamara, a missionary in Russia, who organized a bus of 50 Russian pilgrims to help them discover Saint Therese, the Little

Flower.[1] My brother, Pascal, was leading the pilgrimage that weekend. During a meal, he found himself seated opposite a Russian, a very dignified man with a small beard. They introduced themselves, and it was Alexander Ogorodnikov! I will not attempt to describe the emotion they both felt when Pascal recounted how he and his fiancée had faithfully accompanied him during his ordeals! It was then that Alexander confided to him that, in the squalid dungeon, where he had been thrown and left to die, he had been visited by the angels of Christians in the West who were praying for him. He had felt the warmth of the angels surrounding him like a cloak, and he sensed that this favor was linked to the prayer of those Christians. He owed his survival both to the angels and to the warmth of the prayers, which came to comfort him in his solitude.[2]

This fervent Russian Orthodox, who still lives in Moscow, had numerous mystical experiences while he suffered in prison, cut off from everything. Now he has almost come to

---

[1] Lisieux is the location of the Carmel monastery where St. Therese spent her years as a religious. Lisieux is becoming one of the premier pilgrimage places in the world, currently receiving more than two million pilgrims a year and the number continues to grow. The city is well established for receiving pilgrims, with a number of places related to the life of St. Therese. The most prominent are the Carmelite convent, her home (Les Buissonets), the Cathedral, and the Basilica. For more information see: http://www.saint-therese.org/lisieux-france/ or http://therese-de-lisieux.catholique.fr.

[2] See § 328 to 336 on angels in the *Catechism of the Catholic Church,* which can be accessed here: http://www.vatican.va/archive/ccc_css/archive/catechism/p1s2c1 p5.htm

regret regaining his liberty, because he fears losing that closeness with the divine.

Wars and arbitrary arrests are not lacking today: thousands of victims cry out their pain in the dark night of their prison cells. So many men and women are in despair on our planet! They need our angels, all of our angelic friends! We will never regret sending them our angels, just as Padre Pio did, St. Faustina, St. Pope John XXIII, and so many others. We will see in heaven all the good they will have done in the course of these "special missions" that we entrust to them![3]

---

[3] Pope Pius XII wrote; "Familiarity with the angels gives us a feeling of security. Our invisible companions communicate to us something of the peace that they draw from God. Our guardian angel also works for our sanctification, putting everything in place to facilitate our spiritual ascension and to develop our intimacy with God."

3

Rosie's Wasps

"SISTER, COME RIGHT AWAY! You don't have a minute to lose, take your own car, ours isn't here, hurry!" I hung up the phone, and that voice, with a hint of a German accent, allowed no hesitation. This doctor was adamant. I returned to the living room and I announced to my American assistant, Rosie, that we were leaving right away. Slumped on the couch, with her head back, she murmured in an almost inaudible voice, "It's not that bad, I'll be okay, don't worry."

It was the 2nd of August in 2011, right in the middle of the Youth Festival, and there were tens of thousands of young people there. Just like every second of the month, Our Lady appeared to the visionary Mirjana at around 8:30am near the Blue Cross. Crowds of people had assembled there to participate in the long prayer to prepare for her coming.

After the apparition I directed my path, as usual, towards the parish office, to translate Mary's message from Croatian into French with the team of translators created by Fr. Slavko Barbaric. While I was walking towards the church on the little red path that winds through the fields, a thought invaded my mind,

'I'm not going!'

Just then, another thought, this time more logical, replied, 'What do you mean, I'm not going? I have to go!' But the first thought imposed itself anew with even more force. 'I'm not going, and that's that!'

'Why? They're going to wonder why I didn't come to translate, and I have no valid reason!'

'No, I'm not going! End of story!'

The thought was so strong that I returned to the house without another thought for the message to be translated and without even an ounce of scruples. On the little patio in front of the house I encountered five nice young girls, who were waiting impatiently, because they wanted to speak to me. But I answered them without thinking, "No, not now, sorry!" And I disappeared into the house. Closing the door behind me, I asked myself why I had said no to them so abruptly. I could at least have seen what they wanted! But I let it go and went into the living room where I saw Rosie, slumped on the couch, obviously in a bad state.

"What's the matter?"

"I was stung by wasps," she murmured feebly. I looked at her fingers. They were swollen and in a lot of pain.

"I'm calling the Order of Malta!" (They are a group of workers who offer medical aid in Medjugorje.)

When I explained to them on the telephone that Rosie had received seven wasp bites and that she was a very petite girl, they were extremely concerned. I put Rosie in the car, and five minutes later, we arrived at their medical center.

I was astounded! Five doctors and nurses were waiting at the door, lined up side by side! They rushed towards Rosie and took her immediately into a room that was already prepared. They laid her on a bed and began to slap her face violently, entreating her not to go to sleep. But she was already half unconscious. They couldn't find veins to inject her. Several of them made attempts, on the left arm, the right arm, and the neck. They jabbed and jabbed her again, doubling their efforts in grave silence, all the while continuing to slap her. It hurt me to watch!

Finally, they managed to give the injection! They let out a cry of relief, and only then did they tell me the cause of their anxiety, "Sister, if you had arrived five minutes later, she would have been dead!"

When she heard the young girls ringing our doorbell, Rosie leaned out of the window and was stung seven times on her hands. Wasps nests were concealed under the windowsill, and she had crushed them with her fingers. The wasps avenged themselves! What would have happened if our guardian angels hadn't taken action? If they hadn't swerved me off my course and imposed on my mind that refusal to go translate the message, I would have found my sister in the house, dead! But they managed to make themselves heard and to guide the hands of the first aiders with that astonishing mastery which only they possess. May they be very blessed, and may they continue their marvelous role as heavenly companions!

We all have our own guardian angel, and if we bind ourselves to them in friendship, if we speak to them each day as we would with a very intimate and very dear friend, we will never regret it![1] Theology teaches us that one guardian angel alone is more powerful than all the demons in hell. He has God with him! So, each day in prayer, we should entrust our

[1] See also Thomas Aquinas, *My Way of Life: Pocket Edition of St. Thomas [Aquinas]: The Summa Simplified for Everyone* eds. Walter Farrell & Martin Healy (Confraternity of the Precious Blood, 1952). Cardinal Jean Danielou, *The Angels and Their Mission: According to the Fathers of the Church* (Thomas More Publishing, 1987); Fr. Pascal Parente, *The Angels in Catholic Teaching and Tradition,* (TAN Books, 1994); George Huber, *My Angel Will Go Before You,* (Christian Classics, 1983); Fr. Paul O'Sullivan, *All about Angels* (TAN Books, 1991).

needs to our angels, entreating them to act powerfully and to bring us always into line with God's will.[2] What could be sadder than an unemployed guardian angel?

An Angel at the Pools of Lourdes

Since the time of my arrival in Lourdes, I had already received three SMS messages from my friend Chantal. She was suffering greatly and sick with cancer. She would have come with me, but her doctor had not allowed her to, since, in her extreme weakness, she would not have been able to withstand the shock of such a journey. I promised that I would go and bathe for her in the pools of Lourdes.[3] She was longing for that moment like a watchman waiting for the dawn!

[2] St Thomas Aquinas teaches that, "From the time of birth, every human person benefits from the assistance of an angel, who, all along the path of life, with all its pitfalls, is the sure and watchful guide. At the end of our earthly life, he will also be our companion for eternity in heaven."

[3] The pools at Lourdes are large baths filled with water coming from the miraculous spring indicated by Mary to St. Bernadette. You go down three steps to get into them. There, two people dress you in a damp, white tunic, which is used for everyone. You cross the pool and kiss a statue of the Virgin on the other side while praying a Hail Mary. Afterwards, you are clothed in a blue tunic in which you return to the locker room. There, you get dressed again, but without drying yourself, because one of the "miracles" of Lourdes is that this water dries up by itself, without the help of a towel. Thousands of people go to bathe there each year. The miracles of interior and physical healing are countless, as well as cases of deliverance from evil spirits.

But there was a problem! It was the middle of summer, and besides the fact that thousands of pilgrims of every nation and language were swarming around every corner of the town, it was also the 40th anniversary of my community (The Beatitudes), and I was supposed to give a number of talks during the course of the day. Standing in line at the baths was out of the question! As for the baths themselves, most were closed for renovation, because of the previous spring's powerful floods, which had ravaged the entire area around the Gave River. That was truly the cherry on the cake!

There was no question of disappointing Chantal either! When it is humanly impossible to overcome some obstacle, it is then that heaven has to come to the rescue! To each his own grace!

That morning, a Sister invited me to go with her to the baths, because she had been given the job of taking a group of children there. That way I would be there as her "assistant." But with or without this magic label, I realized that even Sister had to wait in line for several hours, and I decided that waiting would be impossible! However, after a while I was drawn by the idea of overcoming the obstacle, so I decided to wander around in the vicinity of the baths for a while. Then, I saw the Sister on the other side of the railings, calmly seated with her young ones on the bench designated for those getting ready to enter the baths! She had waited her turn for a very long time. It was impossible for me to join her because at Lourdes, the guards are strict, and entry into the baths is carefully controlled.

But since nothing is impossible with God, I was not going to give up! So I sent a very clear message to my great heavenly friend, my guardian angel, calling out to him with these words: "I can't not go into the baths, you know that. The person I'm going in for would be so disappointed! So, you have a job to do: get me in! Please make it happen, you're an angel, you can do it!" I continued to walk along the railings when all at once I saw something that would normally never happen in Lourdes: the two guards had disappeared from in front of the door! I didn't have a minute to lose. I seized the opportunity and passed through the gate with an unconcerned air to go and sit near my Sister. Twenty minutes later, I was in the (freezing) water! Bravo to my guardian angel! I knew I could count on him! As for Chantal, you can imagine the joy she felt knowing I had prayed for her there!

I have to add that, when getting out of the water, the same phenomenon occurs each time for me: getting into that unclean and freezing cold water is a real penance, but the grace which accompanies the plunge is overwhelming! When coming out of the water, I feel wrapped in Mary's maternal mantle, and this makes tears come to my eyes, so much so, that I have to run and hide so that no one can see me cry … tears of joy! To everyone's astonishment, I can say that, for me, this experience is as powerful as being present at an apparition of Our Lady with the visionaries in Medjugorje. And to be perfectly honest, I must admit that it is at times even more powerful!

If ever you go to Lourdes, don't miss the pools!

4

How I Ended Up in Medjugorje

*Visionary Marija receives the apparition of Our Lady
on August 22, 2013, in Sister Emmanuel's garden.*

O N DECEMBER 5ᵀᴴ 1989, I left for Medjugorje for the third time, full of enthusiasm despite the freezing weather; this time I was going to stay.

Here's a little flashback to my two previous visits:

In June of 1984, when the village was still in its primitive but very endearing state, my pilgrimage coincided with the third anniversary of the apparitions. I stayed only a short time, but I'm happy that I got to know Medjugorje during that particular period, as it will never again be as it was then.

In September 1989, I returned to Medjugorje with two Sisters from my community, this time on a reporting assignment for the magazine *Fire and Light*.[1] I had scarcely put one foot on that burning soil of Medjugorje when Our Lady began to pursue me and to work on my heart, which she knows so well how to do! One of her messages haunted me, "Without you, dear children, I cannot help the world. I need you. Each one of you is important," (8/28/1986). She wanted to achieve a great plan, and I was burning with the desire to collaborate with her.

Each of us needs her motherly aid; that much is clear. But here she was, she who is the mother of the Creator, the Queen of Heaven and Earth, in need of us! In other words, she was short of helpers! The realization that she was in need moved me deeply, and I told her, "If you need me, here I am! I would be more than happy to help you, if I can!" I wanted to be an instrument in her hands for whatever she wanted. The more I opened my eyes, the more I understood the vehemence of her call for help. I had a great desire to spread her messages—these pearls of great price—and to allow them to reach a great number of hearts.

Upon my return to France, I shared this call with the founder of my Community. After praying for a long time, he confirmed the authenticity of the call and said to me, "You leave in one month, get ready! Take another Sister with you."

---

[1] The magazine *feu et lumiere* is still in existence in France. It is a publication of the Beatitudes Community, and is dedicated to spreading the joy of the Gospel by promoting the truth, beauty and goodness of the Christian faith. To learn more, in French, log on to: www.feuetlumiere.org. Facebook: www.feuetlumiere.org.

For the first year, that Sister was Marie-Raphaël, who proved to be a marvelous companion.

We lodged in a small, freezing room, about a kilometer from the church, found for us by Fr. Petar Ljubicic. We had only two beds, no other furniture, and since we didn't have a closet, we kept our suitcases under our beds. And what can I say about the thing we used for a bathroom down the hall that we shared with the whole floor! There was mold on the walls, and the tiny cold water faucet only worked sporadically. But what did all that matter when joy reigned! We were so happy to be in Medjugorje! It was the grace of all graces!

Medjugorje was still in its golden age. Before the businesses and hotels appeared on the scene, the whole village prayed in the church when the evening program started. In those first years, even for affluent pilgrims, the joy was simply to be there, to allow oneself to be wrapped in Mary's maternal mantle, she who came from heaven each day for us. So what did the uncertain living conditions matter? They were the least of our worries.

The only thing of value that we owned was a car, a Peugeot, that we received from a man named Joseph, from Lourdes, at the end of a novena that we had made to his patron saint. When it was too cold in our room, we took refuge in the running car to sing morning prayer. We did our shopping in the little village of Citluk, ten minutes away, because at that time, under the communist regime, the food at the general store near the Medjugorje post office left a lot to be desired. Old blocks of butter oozed orange-colored blobs through their half-opened wrappings. Flies shamelessly feasted on pieces of meat and deli products. In makeshift crates, parts of the fruit were rotten, threatening the rest with contamination and a foreshortened expiration date. Some of the walls were covered with saltpeter. As for the garbage cans outside … Well, that was the problem, there were no garbage cans! So, naturally, many undesirable things were strewn in the street to the great joy of dogs, cats, rats, and other unidentifiable creatures! Simply put, every man for himself!

The workers, who were poorly paid, and therefore discontented, weren't rushing to come to our aid, to make a sale, or to outdo one another in zeal. It has to be said that the store belonged to the government and at that time there were no privately owned businesses.

We spent a lot of time on the mountains, asking the "Gospa" to help us understand what she expected of us and how to work in concert with her. We were like those people gathered around the apostles at Pentecost, who said to Peter, "*What must we do?*" This period of searching in the dark didn't last long, Mary knew very well how to show us. Marie-Raphaël was saying to me, "I'm overdosing on inactivity!" An historic statement, which she never had to reiterate!

Throughout the 25 years that followed, the Lord guided us step by step, in spite of our blunders and imperfections. But enthusiasm has never been lacking in us, nor has gratitude, which was renewed each day, for being able to serve this extraordinary divine plan played out in Medjugorje for the salvation of our peace-starved world.

On March 25th, 1990, we founded the French organization *Les Enfants de Medjugorje* (Children of Medjugorje), which later grew to become international, and through which we have been able to put into place an apostolate, which is still active today, that publishes a little quarterly newsletter of the same name. Its goal is to make the Gospa known to many people by spreading her words, her actions, and her blessings.[2]

In April of 1992, the Balkan war broke out in our region, after having left a trail of destruction through Croatia. Our little community of the Beatitudes made a decision to remain in Medjugorje, and I too made a decision to remain the shepherd of our house there. I have already recounted this sorrowful and unforgettable episode in my book, *Medjugorje, the War Day by Day.*[3]

I cannot thank God enough for all these years of happiness, struggles, divine intimacy as well as all the crosses we had to bear! I want to sing with David, King of Israel, "What can I render the Lord for all his goodness to me?" (Ps. 116:12).

Gabriel, Sister's Assistant in Medjugorje.

---

[2] Sr. Emmanuel founded *Les Enfants de Medjugorje* in France in 1990. In 1995, *Children of Medjugorje—Children of Fatima United for the Triumph of the Immaculate Heart* was created as a branch of Sister Emmanuel's French apostolate. The apostolate is now known as *Children of Medjugorje, Inc.,* a not-for-profit 501 (c) 3 organization. For more information log on to: www.sremmanuel.org.

[3] Now out of print in English. If you would like to sponsor another printing of this book, please contact Sister Emmanuel's organization by writing an email to: contact@sisteremmanuel.org.

5

Padre Pio Hears the
Confession of a Free Mason

JESUS SAID TO SR. FAUSTINA, *"Tell souls that they must look for consolation at the tribunal of the Divine Mercy. There, the greatest miracles will keep repeating without ceasing. It is sufficient simply to cast oneself in faith at the feet of the one who is taking my place and tell him his wretchedness, and the miracle of the Divine Mercy will manifest itself in all its fullness. Even if that soul is like a decomposing cadaver and even if, humanly speaking, there is no longer any hope of returning to life and all seems lost, it is not that way with God. The miracle of Divine Mercy will bring that soul back to life in all its fullness. Oh! Unhappy are those who are not profiting now from this miracle of the Divine Mercy. In vain will you call; it will be too late!"*[1]

While he was still a seminarian in Italy, Pierino Galeone was healed by Padre Pio in 1947. He became the spiritual son of Padre Pio, and was blessed to be very close with him, in heart. With his own eyes, he witnessed many of the events of the life of Padre Pio, and in 1986 he gave his testimony

[1] Maria Faustina Kowalska, *The Diary of Saint Maria Faustina Kowalska: Divine Mercy in my Soul,* (Massachusetts: Marian Press, 3rd Edition, 2005), §1448.

during Padre Pio's diocesan process of beatification.[2] In 2010, to mark the 100th anniversary of Padre Pio's ordination, he published his most precious memories in a book entitled *Padre Pio, My Father*.[3] From this gold mine of information, I wish to draw a testimony, which reveals a very touching aspect of Padre Pio's spirituality: the extent to which he dedicated his life to help many sinners recover their peace.

I will let Father Pierino, himself, describe his unforgettable encounter with a freemason named Del Fante.

"We met for the first time in a hotel. Out of the blue, he introduced himself to me saying, 'I am Alberto Del Fante, a lawyer from Bologna, a former Freemason of the thirty-third degree. I was converted a short time ago by Padre Pio and I am writing books about him.' Although I did not ask him anything, he immediately started to praise Padre Pio with

---

[2] The process of documenting the life and virtues of a holy man or woman is called the beatification and canonization process. In the initial phases, the Bishop of the diocese in which the person has died, petitions the Holy See to allow the initialization of a Cause for Beatification and Canonization. If nothing stands in the way of the individual proceeding to the next step, the person is called a Servant of God. During this first phase, the religious institute charged with promoting the Cause must gather testimony about the life and virtues of the Servant of God, as well as the Servant's public and private writings. This documentary phase of the process concludes with the judgment of a diocesan tribunal and the decision of the bishop, that the heroic virtues of the Servant of God have or have not been demonstrated. The results are then communicated to the Congregation for the Causes of the Saints.

[3] Pierino Galeone, *Padre Pio, mio padre,* (Italy: San Paolo Edizioni, 2009).

enthusiasm for giving him back his faith, and he expressed his joy at being able to live a new life completely dedicated to the service of others.

"Del Fante shared, 'My wife had cancer and she was close to death. There was no more hope. A friend told her about Padre Pio, a humble Capuchin Priest in San Giovanni Rotondo, because she heard that many people had been healed by him and had returned home healthy. I was standing at her deathbed as she begged me in tears to go to Padre Pio and ask him for her healing. She knew that I was a Freemason and a terrible enemy of the Church. At first, I rejected and mocked the idea. 'Science is powerless; such a poor monk will surely not be able to do anything either,' I thought to myself. However, as I saw her crying in this deplorable condition, I wanted to fulfill her wish and said, *All right, I'll go! Not because I believe in him, but because I can try my luck, as in the lottery.*

'I left and I arrived that same evening in San Giovanni Rotondo. The following morning, I stood in line for confession after I had participated in the lengthy Holy Mass. When it was my turn, I did not kneel down right away but remained standing in front of Padre Pio. I asked him if I could speak with him briefly. Padre Pio yelled at me, *Young man, don't waste my time! What are you here for? To try your luck in the lottery? If you want to make a confession then kneel down; otherwise, let me hear the confessions of these poor people who have been waiting.* Astounded to hear the same expression that I had used with my wife and shaken by his unexpected rudeness I knelt down, not out of conviction, but somehow automatically. I was completely unprepared for a confession and could not even say two words! I was even less able to recall any of my sins. As soon as I knelt down, however, Padre Pio's tone of voice changed and he became mild and fatherly. By asking me questions, he gradually unveiled all the sins of my former life. And the sins I had committed were numerous! With my head lowered, I listened to his questions and always answered, *Yes.* Overwhelmed, and at the same time moved, I remained petrified. Finally, Padre Pio asked me, *Do you have any other sins that you would like to confess?* I answered, *No.* I was certain that he had already said all my sins, and since he obviously knew my life in detail, I was sure I did not have anything else to confess.

'Then Padre Pio said with surprising sternness, *Aren't you ashamed? The young lady, whom you had return to America a short time ago, gave birth to a son. This child is your flesh and blood, and like a raven you abandoned mother and child.* It was all true. I did not answer. I broke into tears and cried bitterly. I was crushed. As I cried, bent over the kneeler, covering my face with my hands, Padre Pio gently placed his arm around me, drew close to my ear and whispered with a sniffle, *My child, I redeem you with the price of my precious blood.*

'At those words, I felt as if my heart were cut in two with a fine blade. Bent over, I cried. Several times I lifted my head, my face overrun with tears, and repeated, *Father, forgive me, forgive me, forgive me!* Padre Pio, who had already put his arm around me, drew me closer still, and began to cry with me. A wonderfully sweet peace filled my spirit. 'I suddenly felt how this indescribable pain was transformed into an unbelievable joy. *Padre,* I said. *I belong to you! Do with me what you will!* He wiped away his own tears and whispered to me, *Support me by helping others.* Then he added, *Give my greetings to your wife!* When I arrived at home, my wife had been healed.'"

At the time, Alberto Del Fante did not understand the full depth of these surprising words, which Padre Pio, crying, whispered in his ear during this Confession, 'My child, I redeem you with the price of my precious blood.'" Of course, it was Jesus himself who said this through this simple Capuchin father, because no one other than the Divine Redeemer had shed his Precious Blood once and for all, for the forgiveness of sins. No one other than Jesus Himself offers the infinite treasures of His grace through the priest in the Sacrament of Confession. Padre Pio's words may also be figuratively applied to Padre Pio, himself, since it was through his stigmata that he intimately participated in the Passion of the Lord and did, in fact, shed his blood for the conversion of Alberto Del Fante, and for all of his 14 million spiritual children.

A Prayer for Mercy

Jesus, like the Good Samaritan, You do not close your eyes to our sin, as though it does not exist. You put it into the very gentle light of Your mercy, and you fill us with that "sorrow born of the Holy Spirit, which leads us to repentance," (Corinthians 2:7–9). Our tears of bitterness then become tears of joy and gratitude. You long to lift from us the cruel burden of our un-confessed sins, which deprive us of Your Heavenly peace. What you did for Alberto, Oh Jesus, do it for me, do it for us all, sinners!

6

Don Bosco and the Snake

"Dear children! Today, like never before, I invite you to prayer. Let your prayer be a prayer for peace. Satan is strong and desires to destroy not only human life, but also nature and the planet on which you live. Therefore, dear children, pray that through prayer you can protect yourselves with God's blessing of peace. God has sent me among you so that I may help you. If you so wish, grasp for the rosary. Even the rosary alone can work miracles in the world and in your lives. I bless you and I remain with you for as long as it is God's will. Thank you for not betraying my presence here and I thank you because your response is serving the good and the peace."

(MESSAGE OF JANUARY 25, 1991)

DON BOSCO IS ONE of the most likeable saints in history! He had a number of arrows in his quiver: he knew how to win the hearts of the young people with his magic tricks;

he spoke with passion and with a great deal of humor; he brought about spectacular conversions; he helped the poor; he worked miracles; God's Providence provided divinely for the needs of 'his children'; and he obtained all that he wanted from the Mother of God, to name just a few.

But there was one rather rare feature that characterized Don Bosco, a trait he had in common with St. Joseph. God visited him and provided instructions to him through his dreams. His dreams were collected for posterity, and today they still offer us precious insights for our Christian life. Let's look at one of the most astonishing dreams from his collection: the one about the snake.

On the Vigil of the Assumption, during the night of the 14th to the 15th of August, 1862, Don Bosco, in a dream, found himself in his brother's house at Castelnuovo d'Asti, which from then on was called *Colle Don Bosco.* All his young people were with him. Suddenly, his "guide" appeared to him. At this point I would like to mention that, in his dreams, a person whom he called "the guide" would explain to Don Bosco the meaning of what he saw, making his dream crystal clear through his teaching. This guide was none other than the Virgin Mary. That night, she invited him to come into the meadow beyond the courtyard of the farm. There, in the grass, she showed him an extraordinarily large snake, 7 to 8 meters in length. Don Bosco was horrified and turned to flee. However, the "guide" asked him to stay, reassuring him that there was no cause for alarm. She went to get a rope, came back to Don Bosco and said to him, "Take the end of this rope and keep it pulled tight. I will hold the other end, and the two of us are going to tie the rope to the snake."

"What then?" The still fearful Don Bosco asked. "We'll beat him to the ground."

"Not on your life!" Exclaimed Don Bosco. "Woe to us if we do such a thing! The snake will turn on us and rip us to pieces!"

"No he won't, let me do it," insisted the guide. "I don't want to risk my life!"

Don Bosco recounted, "She assured me that the snake would do us no harm." He said that while his guide was reassuring him, he consented to do what she asked. Then, from her end, she lifted up the rope and inflicted a wound on the back of the reptile. The snake did an about-face. It turned its head to try to bite what had touched the back of him, but he couldn't reach it and found himself strung up in a slipknot. "Hold the rope tight!" The guide cried out to Bosco, adding, "Whatever you do, don't let go!"

She ran to tie the end of the rope she was holding to a nearby pear tree. Successful, she then went to attach the other end of the rope to bars on a window of the house. During this time, the snake was struggling furiously and was banging itself against the ground as much with its head as with its terrible coils. Its flesh came off in shreds, and pieces of it were projected far and wide, until nothing was left of it but skin and bones.

Once the snake was dead, the guide untied the rope from the tree and the window, and coiled it into a box. She reopened the box several moments later. Don Bosco said that he looked into the box with his young people at his side and they were astonished to see how that rope was arranged. It had formed the words *Ave Maria*. Then the guide explained to me,

"The snake represents the devil, and as for the rope, these are the *Hail Mary's*, or more precisely, it is the rosary, which is a succession of *Hail Marys,* thanks to which we can fight, conquer, and destroy all the demons of hell."[1]

At this point, a very sad scene developed before the eyes of Don Bosco: he saw some young people gathering the pieces of scattered snake flesh, eating them, and being poisoned. In his own words, Don Bosco wrote, "I was totally helpless and distraught. Despite my warnings, they continued to eat. I cried out to one of them, and called to another. I slapped one across the face, threw a punch at another, and tried to prevent them from eating, but everything was useless. I was beside myself, seeing all around me a great number of young people lying on the ground in a wretched state."

He continued recounting that when he saw this, he turned to the guide and asked, "Is there no remedy for such evil?"

"Of course there is." "What is it?"

"There's only one solution: the anvil and the hammer." "But how? Must I put them on the anvil, and hit them with the hammer?"[2]

"That's it," answered the guide. "The hammer stands for Confession, and the anvil, Holy Communion. You must use these two means."

---

[1] *Il Serpente e il Rosario,* (Italy: Editrice Elledici, 1995) p. 57–58.

[2] In the Italian countryside, young agricultural workers use the forge, the anvil, and the hammer to craft good work tools. Applied to the sacraments of confession and communion, this means that confession is not about an easy way to clear your conscience, and neither is communion a simple form of devotion. These are vigorous ways the priest possesses to guide the faithful along the right path.

The "Saint of Young People" was, without a doubt, one of the most fervent saints in the practice of the rosary.[3] One day, a distinguished guest came to visit Don Bosco. Bosco showed him the work he was doing with young people, their daily routine and curriculum. The guest was delighted by it, but he made this remark: "Why dedicate so much time to the daily recitation of the rosary? It's a waste of time for these young people, precious time that could be used for important things!" Don Bosco replied, "The last thing I would cut out is the rosary! It's the surest way to be saved from attacks of the devil, to enliven the faith and purity of the young people, to be defended against error, and to help the Church." Then, referring to the vision of his guide conquering the serpent using a rope, he said, "The rosary is the *rope of salvation* with which we can fight, conquer, and destroy all the demons of hell!"

Don Bosco and Saint Dominic Savio

Why did Jesus send His Mother to Medjugorje? I believe that, when He looked at the world, submerged as it is in sin and crushed by infidelities of every kind, the Lord saw that we couldn't get by without her. By appearing among us in such a concrete way and by speaking to us so clearly, she comes in order to win us back! She is taking us under her

---

[3] The visionary Marija asked the Virgin Mary the following question, "What do you want to recommend to priests?" "I ask you to call priests to the prayer of the Rosary. Through the Rosary you will overcome all the misfortunes that Satan wants to inflict upon the Catholic Church. Pray the Rosary, all you who are priests. Consecrate time to the Rosary." (June 25, 1985).

maternal mantle to restore peace that has been lost, and to offer us to God. She offers us great security!

St. Dominic Savio, the famous student of Don Bosco who died at an early age, came one night to visit his friend in a dream. Don Bosco asked him, "What was your greatest consolation when you were at the point of death?"

"What do *you* think it was?"

"To have lived such a pure life? To have amassed so many treasures in heaven with all your good deeds?"

To each proposed option, Dominic just shook his head, with a smile.

"So, tell me," insisted Don Bosco, rather disconcerted by his lack of success, "What was it?"

"What helped me the most and gave me the greatest joy when I was dying was the loving attention and the help of the marvelous Mother of God. Tell your sons to make sure they stay close to her during their lives. But hurry, the time has almost come!"[4]

---

[4] Adapted from St. John Bosco, *Forty Dreams Of St. John Bosco: From St. John Bosco's Biographical Memoirs,* (North Carolina: St. Benedict Press, LLC & Tan Books, 2009).

7

The Rosary of Mother Teresa

ACCORDING TO WHAT SHE revealed about herself to her confessors, Mother Teresa lived through a long dark night of the soul that lasted more than 40 years.[1] Yet, in no way did her dark night alter her missionary activity, which was extraordinarily fruitful. In the midst of this long trial that was permitted by the Lord, Mother Teresa looked for and always found refuge in the Blessed Mother, as a little child does with his mother. When her suffering became almost unbearable, she would pray the rosary and place herself before the Blessed Sacrament. "One Hail Mary after another," she would often say, thus tightly gripping the hand of her Heavenly Mother. Trusting in Our Lady's presence, Mother Teresa drew from her the strength to endure this utterly incomprehensible suffering and say, "Yes" one more time to the will of God.

To Fr. Picachy, her Bishop, she wrote, "Often I wonder what God really gets from me in this state—no faith, no love—not even in feelings. The other day I can't tell you how bad I felt—There was a moment when I nearly refused to accept—Deliberately I took the rosary and very slowly without even meditating or thinking—I said it slowly and

---

[1] Mother Teresa, *Mother Teresa: Come Be My Light: The Private Writings of the "Saint of Calcutta,"* Ed. Brian Kolodiejchuk (New York: Doubleday, 2007).

calmly. The moment passed—but the darkness is so dark, and the pain is so painful—But I accept whatever he gives and I give whatever He takes."[2]

In the life of Mother Teresa, Mary became the lighthouse by which she directed herself when discerning her way through the darkness. Even if she herself was not enjoying the Divine light in a tangible way, the work she left in her wake is witness to the reality of that light within her. No matter how black the darkness became, with the suffering that only those who go through it can imagine, all she had to do was take out her rosary, and peace returned to her little by little, even in the midst of the waves. She repeated: "My God, give me courage now to fight self and the tempter. Let me not draw back from the sacrifice I have made of my free choice and conviction. Immaculate Heart of my Mother, have pity on thy poor child. For love of thee I want to live and die a Missionary of Charity."[3]

Along her way, miracles both small and great happened. Sometimes, when she saw someone in difficulty, she would say to them: "Here, take my rosary. Our Lady will help you!" One of the most beautiful examples is that of Bishop Paul Hnilica. In March of 1984, he had a deep desire go to Moscow and consecrate Russia to the Immaculate Heart of Mary, in communion with Pope John Paul II and all the bishops of the world! But he wasn't able to go because, at that time, the iron curtain made it impossible to cross the border. But Mother Teresa said to him, "Take my rosary. Our Lady will open the doors of Russia for you!" And so he succeeded in

---

[2] Ibid., 251, Letter to Bishop Picachy, September 21, 1962.

[3] Ibid., 147, Journal, February 28, 1949.

this masterstroke and consecrated Russia in a former chapel in the Museum of Atheism![4]

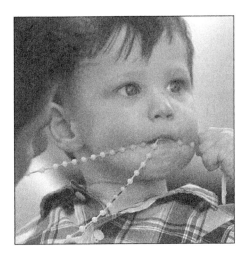

8

A Cry in the Prison

"Today, bring to me the souls who honor and glorify my mercy in particular and immerse them in my mercy. These souls have empathized with the suffering of my passion in the most profound way and have penetrated the most deeply into my spirit. They are the living reflection of my compassionate heart. These souls will shine with special brilliance in their future life; none will go into the fire of Hell; I will defend each one of them, particularly at the hour of death."

(JESUS TO ST. FAUSTINA)[1]

MANY YEARS AGO I had a wonderful French assistant in Medjugorje who later became a religious nun. She was sent by her community in France to live and work on the East coast of the United States, and she found that she has a particular charism: to visit prisoners. But not just any prisoners! She visits the hardest of the hardened, those who are likely to spend hundreds of years in prison because their offenses were so great, and each offense corresponds to a certain number of years. She told me the following story from her experience:

"The first time I went to visit a jail in the United States was in November 2008. I was sent first into protective custody, where the guys are alone, and there are eight cells on

---

[1] Jesus to St. Faustina. Maria Faustina Kowalska, *Diary,* §1224.

each side of the hallway. When I arrived a black male prisoner yelled, 'Hey guys, a nun!' I felt very uncomfortable! All the guys came to the door of their cells, where there was protective glass. I turned around and went to that guy, and when I got to his door, I saw that he had six tears tattooed on his face. I knew that a tear is a gang sign, which means either that the prisoner shot somebody dead, or that somebody close to them had been shot—it's one or the other. Most of the time it's because they killed somebody though, and I knew that, so when I saw the six tattooed tears I kind of froze.

"He looked at me and said very seriously, 'What is a nun doing in this hell?' Inspired by the Holy Spirit, I answered, 'Because Jesus came to wipe away all our tears.' That happened to be the reading at Mass that day. He froze for a while and gazed right into my eyes and said, 'You'd better not joke with that!' 'You know, I'm here because the first man who made it to heaven was a criminal.' 'What?'

'Yes, the first man who made it to heaven was a criminal.' I told him about the 'good thief' but in the original Greek text, the word is 'criminal.' I said, 'You know he recognized that his sentence was just, that being crucified was just, because of what he'd done. He didn't just steal an apple. He really was a criminal. At first he was against Jesus just like the other criminal, but at one point he understood something and he turned to Jesus and said, *Lord, remember me when you come into your kingdom.* And Jesus said, *Today you will be with me in paradise.* So the first guy who made it to heaven was a criminal and that's why I'm here.'

'Are you really telling me I have a chance?' 'Have a chance for what?'

'That I'm not doomed to hell. Do I have a chance for heaven?' 'Of course, that's why I'm here—Jesus came to wipe away all the tears from our eyes, and even the tears that you have tattooed on your face.'

"He was very emotional and he said, 'Are you sure of what you are telling me?'

'I guarantee! If you really ask for forgiveness from God for what you have done, and do your best not to do it again, the Lord will forgive you and take you to Himself in heaven.' 'My name is HB,' (we'll never know his real name) 'please pray for me, that I can make it to heaven like that criminal.'

"I assured him of my prayers and went to the next cell. HB had a friend on the opposite side of the hallway and his friend called out to him, 'So, what did she say, what did she say?' To be able to hear one another they had to yell. So HB yelled from his cell, 'Mo,' that was the nickname of the other guy. 'The nun told me that I can still make it to heaven, man! She told me I can make it to heaven. Can you believe it? She told me I can make it to heaven! I'm not doomed to hell. I can make it to heaven!' He couldn't stop saying it. So I went back to his cell and said, 'Yeah, please keep spreading the good news!'

"And that was the first and the last time I saw him. I returned to that jail every week but he was transferred to a state prison because the jail I was visiting was one where they were awaiting trial. So sometimes a guy would disappear. Sometimes I would see a guy for two or three years and another time I'd see a guy just once.

"In general, when I arrive in front of their doors, I offer to pray with them. There was one guy, and he never wanted to pray, Nashon. I saw him for six months in a row, going in front of his cell I'd always say, 'Do you want to pray?' and he would say, 'No, I don't pray.' And so one day I said, 'Hey, I've seen you for so many weeks, even months, and you never pray.'

'No, I don't pray. I don't want to be a hypocrite and pray, while I know perfectly well that as soon as I'm out of here I'm going to do the same thing.'

'Well, that's honest, but maybe if you pray, the desire to do the same thing will go away.' He gave me a weird look, and then I said, 'Get on your knees.' He got on his knees and we started to pray. After that we prayed every week together.

"Most of the guys I visited were guys who started to pray. Many guys, especially in protective custody, at first would say 'no,' once, twice, and then the next time they would pray. I was telling them, you know Jesus said, 'When two or three are gathered in my name, I am in their midst.' When there were two in the same cell, I said, 'I know you didn't choose one another, but now you can choose one another as brothers in Christ and you'll have Christ's presence in yourself.' And I'm a witness that some of them started to pray together. There are two of them that I actually saw outside. And you know what they said, 'Prayer bound us together so much that we have the same apartment and we help each other.'

"There's another guy—I can't say his name because he's known worldwide because of what he did—but he had satanic drawings in his cell, it was full of drawings. I knew about his crime. Most of the time I don't know about the crimes, but in his case I did. I went in front of his cell each time, and one day the Lord inspired me just to write down from scripture on a piece of paper,

> We are ambassadors for Christ, as if God were appealing through us, we implore you on behalf of Christ, be reconciled to God. We appeal to you not to receive the grace of God in vain, for He said, in an acceptable time I heard you, and on the day of salvation I helped you. Behold now is the very acceptable time, behold now is the day of salvation. (2 Co 5:20).

"So I wrote that on a piece of paper and I asked one of the lay visitors to put the paper under the door and leave it with him. "A week later he called us to pray with him, and he continued to pray for a long time, but after that I lost track of him. He went to a state prison and he lost contact with everybody, even his mother. He refused to see her. He had three life sentences so I don't know what became of him. But I was very impressed. I guess he was 30 or 31.

"In some States of the US, they convict even kids for the rest of their life. They give life sentences to kids who are, 12, 14, 15 years old. When they are 15 years old at the time of the crime, they convict them and give them life sentences. Most of the time it's far away from where their family lives. At the beginning they receive visits but after a while they are forgotten, out of sight, out of mind. In the protective custody section of the prison, for example, there were 120 inmates and no more than 15 to 20 received visitors.

"I met some prisoners whose crime was committed when they were 15 or 16, and when they turn 18 they will be sent to the adult jail. To protect them from the others they would be locked up in their cell on their own for 23 ½ hours a day. They were allowed out of their cells for half an hour each day. During that time they had the opportunity to make a phone call, ($5.00 for 15 minutes) or they could walk in the hallway. They couldn't even go outside. The only time they breathed fresh air was when they were going to court. When they were going to court they were chained to one another, treated like animals, and put in a big van. One of them said to me, 'Here, it's like you are dead, except that you don't turn cold.'

"I went to a cell in the psychiatric section of the prison and the guard who was accompanying me said, 'Not that one, Sister, there's no point.' The guy was standing right behind his door without moving at all. I tried to talk to him.

I asked his name, but he wouldn't even blink an eye, nothing, nothing! So I started to pray as there was nothing I could do. I made the sign of the cross and when I made the sign of the cross, the guy made the sign of the cross, too. The guard said, 'See … look at him.' So I did it a second time and the guy did it a second time. Then, I prayed out loud, I said an *Our Father*, a *Hail Mary* and prayed for a minute or two. I told him, 'I'll come next week. I'll come and see you again.' The following week he was in a different cell, still in the psychiatric section. He called out to me, 'Oh thank you, thank you.'

'What?'

'Thank you for spending time with me last week.' 'What happened to you?'

'They drugged me. I didn't know who I was anymore. But I remember you. I know you spent time with me. Thank you for spending time with me.'

"There, the detainees nicknamed me "Sister OG" for *Original Gangster*. OG signifies that you have status in a gang. They called me *Sister OG* to show me the extent to which they had adopted me. There, it's a sign of nobility! I'm not kidding! They call each other OG among themselves, in the same way that a consecrated person would say *sister or father* to their fellow consecrated friends. As a matter of fact, when I introduced myself to the guys, I would say: 'Hi! My name is Sister OG!' They couldn't get over it; but it did the trick. It was an instant icebreaker! It was an extraordinary tool for evangelization.

"What I drew from my experience with these visits is that when the mercy of God is proclaimed, it is received!"

9

The Little Flower Strikes Again!

"I feel that I am going to enter into my rest … But I feel above all, that mission is going to begin, my mission to make God loved the way I love Him, to give my little way to souls. If the Good Lord grants me my desire, I will spend my Heaven on earth until the end of time. Yes, I want to spend my Heaven doing good on earth."

(ST. THÉRÈSE OF LISIEUX)[1]

SISTER BRIEGE MCKENNA SPENT a few days in Medjugorje with us, and it was a great joy to be with her.[2] The last evening of her stay, October 1st, was the feast of St Thérèse,

---

[1] Taken from *St. Thérèse of Lisieux: Her Last Conversations,* trans. John Clarke, OCD (Washington: ICS Publications, 1977), 102.

[2] Sister Briege McKenna, see footnote number 1 in the preface.

the Little Flower. Sr. Briege told us the following very moving story to commemorate the feast, and it can help us to make better use of the assistance coming from Heaven:

"One day," said Sr. Briege. "Jesus spoke to my heart and told me, 'Go and talk to the priests and bishops.' My answer was, 'What are you talking about Lord? I am a simple elementary school teacher.' A few months later I met a Jesuit priest who told me, 'You know, Briege, the Lord put something in my heart—to invite you to give a priests' retreat.'

'I'm afraid you didn't hear correctly, Father. You know I teach children.'

'Don't worry,' he said. *These priests are like children, they are very open and charismatic.*' That retreat was for about 60 priests, and I had to lead it without him because he had to be hospitalized the next day! Never in my life had I stood before priests. They couldn't see them, but my knees were shaking. So I prayed to St. Therese, and to make a long story short, the retreat was very blessed.

"Not long after that a bishop from California, who had heard about the retreat, invited me to preach another one in San Diego. I felt a little bit more secure, seeing that the Lord had worked well during the first retreat. As soon as I arrived at the second retreat, the Trappist priest who organized the retreat confided to me, 'There are 50 parish priests on this retreat. They do not want to be here. Their bishop forced them to come. They are absolutely mad that there is a nun giving the keynote address, and they want to tear you apart!' Then, I had an inner battle and I said to Jesus, 'It's not me who invited myself here, it is YOU Lord who brought me here, so do something!'

"The next day, I learned that this Trappist brother had to leave so he put me in charge of all the conferences! Then I recalled all the horrible things these priests had said about me. On the morning of the retreat I got up very early and prayed for several hours. Then, knowing that there was a statue of St. Therese in the campus grotto, I bought the biggest candle I could find for her, and I went to pray to her. I said, 'Listen, Saint Therese! For me, leading this retreat is worse than going into the lions' den. Please help me, please come with me, and help me talk to these priests!' "When I walked into the conference room, all these priests had their arms folded, and you could see by their body language that they were not very happy to be there. Anyway I started to give my first talk. I gave three talks that day, and I knew I had them because you could see a transformation.

"After supper I went back to the grotto with another candle that I lit in front of St. Therese and I said to her, 'I really want to thank you for being with me today.'

"Later I met an Irish Monsignor who told me, 'I never in my life listened to a nun. I was very resentful. You know, this morning, when you were talking to us, you told us to close our eyes, but I did not close my eyes. I had my head down for a moment and then I looked up to see what you were doing.' Then he asked me, 'Do you have a special devotion to St. Therese?'

'Why?' I asked.

'Because, you know, I'm not the type to see visions, but St. Thérèse was standing by your side, in front of us, while you were talking to us, and I realized that she was there to help you.'

"This taught me a lot about the saints!" She continued, "I often tell that story to parents when they are choosing a name for their child. I tell them, 'Ask that saint to give your child his own gifts, so that your child can continue to glorify Jesus in the manner that this saint glorified Him! When you have the name of a saint, that saint loves to accompany you.

He helps you to accomplish what you have to do in your life to be a saint.' When we invite the saints, they will actually come and accompany us in our work and in our ministries!"

This testimony from Sister Briege attests to the strong invitation of the Gospa to read the lives of saints, and to pray to them. Spiritually speaking, most Catholics live below their spiritual means and miss huge graces offered to them by the elected ones in Heaven. Before Halloween, rather than collect pumpkins, let us discover the life of a saint, either our patron saint or another one of our choice, and ask him to come and help us. Of course, the point is not to expect a vision like the one the bishop had of St. Therese, but we can be assured of the fruitful care of the saint because in Heaven, angels and saints love us with the very love of God.[3]

---

[3] Let's be practical. Go to www.sremmanuel.org to download a list of saints. The list can then be cut apart and used to find the saint who chose you as a companion, to accompany you for the year!

10

Janet's Walk in Siroki-Brijeg

JANET CAME TO VISIT us from Ireland. She had saved her money for a long time to be able to return to Medjugorje, the land of her happiness and her salvation. When she rang our doorbell, I noticed right away a sort of peaceful light in her eyes, the kind of light that emanates from those who pray a lot. That day, busy with urgent business, I didn't have the time to sit down with her as she was hoping. However, later in the week I made time because I was curious to find out what made her so beautiful, so filled with joy. She certainly had some secret. She was both shy and humble. At first she didn't want to share too much about her personal experience, saying that she was only one pilgrim among so many others. So, I had to convince her to tell her story by using the magic words: "Think of all those who will be touched by God and consoled in reading about what happened to you; you can't deny them that!" The argument changed her mind, and with great simplicity she began to tell her story:

"I was a cradle Catholic. I went to Mass every Sunday, but I was so bored. My husband was not a Catholic—in fact he was a Hindu, but we both decided that we wanted to raise our three children as Catholics, and for us that meant that I always took them to Mass on Sundays, and sent them to Catholic schools. I thought that this was all I was obliged to do as a parent. I had no taste for religion and I had not understood anything about prayer. I never prayed, or even taught my children about God! The reality was that I was practicing my faith superficially, not living it with my heart, and it didn't even cross my mind that there might be another way. Because of my ignorance and spiritual laziness, I was vulnerable to anything that contradicted my faith. Then a Christian man told me that Jesus is not present in the host, and that to believe in the real presence was ridiculous. So I doubted. I was bored during Mass and couldn't wait for it to be over. I was thinking about everything except God!

"I have a very good friend who had often been to Medjugorje. She kept pleading with me, 'Come with me to Medjugorje!' Finally, despite great protest in my heart, in May of 1997 she convinced me to come with her and a group of other friends. As far as I was concerned, I was going for a girls' vacation in the sun, to enjoy nature in good company and to chat together. It would be cool! I didn't think for one second that I would go there to pray.

"The first days went as planned, and they were very pleasant. I enjoyed the food, fresh air, sunshine, and was happy to get a little tan. I thought, 'This is the best holiday ever!' On the third day, we went off with John, our Irish guide, in an old ratty van to a Mass being celebrated by Fr. Jozo at Siroki-Brijeg, where 30 Franciscan priests were martyred during World War II. Going there didn't please me at all, but everyone else seemed so excited by this event. It was as if we were going to see the Pope himself! When we arrived, even though the church was very large, it was already packed. All the pews were occupied and pilgrims were crowded into the aisles in such great numbers that moving through the throng of people was impossible. This situation proved providential for me. I decided with a clear conscience to remain outside where I could stay in the sun and chat with my friends. Mass was about to begin and it was then that the most surprising thing happened.

"A man, whom I had never met before, very gently took my hand and walked me through the crowds. I didn't even feel as though we were pushing; it was as if the space opened up and we simply walked through. He took me to the steps of the sanctuary and placed me right in front of the priest who was about to start the Mass. Then he suddenly disappeared. I had the best spot in the church! I thought I was dreaming, as it was very surreal, but at the same time everything seemed as though what was happening was completely normal. I don't remember anything from the beginning of the Mass, but when the priest elevated the host at the consecration, it became huge and Christ our Lord appeared alive in the host, looking up. From that moment on my whole life changed. I don't think I stopped crying the whole time I remained in Medjugorje.

"When I returned home to Ireland, I got into the habit of going to daily Mass. I drew all my strength and my joy from there. I never had that vision again, but Jesus became my essential food. My Hindu husband listened respectfully to my testimony, and in spite of the great change that had taken place in me, he did not seem affected. I never tried to convince him or to share my faith with him, and likewise he did not share his with me, and he allowed me to freely practice my faith. He was not ready then, but I knew the time would come, and I waited in peace. I prayed a lot for him begging God to touch his heart. Several years later, on a morning like any other morning, as I was getting ready to go to Mass, he simply said to me, 'I am coming with you!' After this he had the habit of coming with me to church. However he would say nothing to me and I would not say anything to him, knowing that the spark could only come from above. "To make a long story short, the Lord has worked mysteriously in his heart so much so that my husband is now a baptized

Catholic and we are in communion sharing the same faith. It is Jesus who did everything in His own time.

"Oh how I wish that I could start my life over again from day one, so that I could spend all my younger years with Jesus! How I regret losing time and how ashamed I am that I didn't always believe! But now, I do not let a single day go by without thanking God for revealing Himself to me and then to my husband. I pray daily for lukewarm Catholics, like I used to be! May Mary our Mother touch many, many souls and bring them to the living Jesus!"

I Can't Take it Anymore, God Doesn't Hear Me!

"Let nothing disturb you, let nothing frighten you. All things are passing away: God never changes. Patience obtains all things. Whoever has God lacks nothing; God alone suffices."

(TERESA OF AVILA)[1]

Janet gives us a precious key in helping resolve the painful situation of married couples who are deprived of spiritual communion with their spouse, especially when one of them doesn't want to pray, or to even hear about God. Many couples suffer from constant disappointment because of this.

---

[1] This is one of Teresa of Avila's best known poems found after her death, written on a piece of paper in her breviary. To some, this poem is known as her "bookmark." For more on Teresa of Avila see Pope Benedict XVI General Audience given in Paul VI Audience Hall on Wednesday, February 2, 2011: http://www.vatican.va/holy_father/benedict_xvi/audiences/2011/documents/hf_ben-xvi_aud_20110202_en.html

In fact, the lack of communion within a couple can give rise to such an interior discomfort that it can poison the whole life of the family. This burden, so heavy to carry, makes peace between them almost impossible. Imbued with frustration, they run the risk of losing hope and sinking into deep sadness. But there's hope! Our Lady is aware of such situations and recommends a simple way out.

One day a married woman named Cristina came to me, and I admit that I was a bit hard on her at first. I was hoping that by shocking her, I could help her to get out of her inner hell.

For more than fifteen years she had been tortured by the attitude of her husband. She loved him and dreamed of living a profound, spiritual communion with him even though he didn't believe in God. He, on the other hand, made her pay dearly for being so pious and active in the Church by being sarcastic and nasty to her. Sometimes he would even curse in front of her in order to provoke her to anger. Several of her children were following the way of their father, to the point that this poor woman was no longer able to sleep at night. "I'm desperate," she said to me. "The more I pray, the more I try to live my faith within my family, the worse the situation becomes. God doesn't hear me! I pray and pray and nothing changes, just the opposite happens! I have to carry this terrible weight all by myself, and now I'm exhausted, I'm falling apart!"

I looked at Cristina's face. It was a mess! She was the picture of unhappiness, even despair. Despite a certain natural beauty, her eyes, her cheeks, her mouth, everything seemed to be pulled downwards, as though drawn by a magnet into an invisible hole. She communicated an infinite sadness. The tale of the misfortunes and injustices of which she was the victim, and her ongoing failure to convert those closest to her, resulted in people avoiding contact with her. This isolation only made the frustration gnaw away at her even more. She could go on living in the illusion that she is a persecuted Christian, a martyr for the faith, and even a victim soul for many years. But true victim souls bubble over with joy. Martyrs of the faith shine like the sun!

Can you spot the dichotomy?

As Cristina started to rant again about her husband's taunting, I cut her off and said, "But do you think you're going to attract your husband and your children to God with such a miserable face?" She stared at me in disbelief! Then she examined me for a moment, checking to see if I had really said that, and that she had heard me correctly. Shocked and disconcerted, she remained speechless. 'Finally, she is listening!' I thought. I recognized that I was hard on her and, with a smile, I came close to her and whispered, "I said that on purpose, you know. Please forgive me, but it was to elicit a reaction from you!" Cristina was reassured and waited for me to explain. She knew that I only wanted to help her out of love.

"Your life is going to change, Cristina. You have good will, but until now you have done the opposite of what you needed to do to reach your goal. You have wanted to carry something that was too heavy. You tried so hard to pick up a suitcase that is God's, and it is crushing you! It's too heavy for you. Let Him do it. After all, isn't He God? He alone can touch and change the hearts of His children. Why trample over His terrain? Do only what you can, what you are given to do. Your role is to pray with all your heart and to live out your faith the best you can. In prayer, you receive a great gift from God: His peace. He gives you this peace in abundance, and He offers it to you even on the stormy seas of life. But what are you doing with this peace? Take hold of it and above all, *keep* hold of it! Safeguard it in your heart. You have probably noticed in the Gospels that the only passage where we see Jesus sleeping in blissful peace is when the apostles' boat is about to sink in a storm!

"The peace that is in your heart shouldn't depend on the attitude of others. If that were the case, we would all run the risk of never having it, because there will always be a 'Debbie Downer' somewhere! No, your peace depends on God alone, the King of Peace! And God is always there, ready to welcome you, and bless you. He knows each of your loved ones and He loves them more than you do. He sees everything so there's no need to harp on about the wrongdoings of your husband.

"If you fly off the handle because others are not what you would like them to be, you squander that peace because you are taking God's place without even knowing it! You start arguing with your loved ones in an attempt to convince them, and it's a total disaster. You get agitated, you exhaust yourself, you become bitter. You believe you are doing the right thing, but you are only disturbing God's plan and delaying it. Then, there you are, right smack dab in the middle of Satan's plan, because he is the ultimate divider, and you have allowed him to win!

"In Medjugorje, Mary said, 'Dear Children, do not get into arguments!' What a beautiful message of liberation! How comforting it is to think that the work of converting others is God's alone!"[2]

Cristina's face had already changed. There was hope again. She realized that she had placed this crushing burden on her own shoulders, and that the Lord had a plan to lift it from her.

---

[2] Message from Our Lady given to Ivan in Medjugorje in the summer of 1990.

I often say to pilgrims that if they return home and come up against family difficulties that seem impossible to overcome, above all, do not lose peace! God will give us His peace in prayer. If we encounter a major obstacle in our family, place it in Mary's heart and say to her, "Mother, now this is YOUR problem!" Then we won't be stuck anymore. We can move forward and pray for HER intentions.

This is the *swap* that she has been teaching us, "Dear children, give me your worries and your problems. In this way your heart will be free for prayer, and then, pray for my intentions!"[3] We hand over to her those situations that are not working and in exchange, we take her affairs to heart. It's a swap that works!

Words from Father Svetozar Kraljevic, OFM

In Medjugorje, we are often sought out by pilgrims to help them resolve problems that deal with relationships in their families, problems that are beyond us. One day a pilgrim asked Father Svetozar Kraljevic, one of the Franciscans who was working in Medjugorje at the time, "What would you say to a man who prays each day and who wishes to pray with his family, but his family refuses to pray with him?"

"Are you that man?" "Yes."

Then the priest said, "You are on the road to holiness!"

[3] Ibid.

11

France, You Will Not Go Under

"Dear children! Today I call you to have your life be connected with God the Creator, because only in this way will your life have meaning and you will comprehend that God is love. God sends me to you out of love, that I may help you to comprehend that without Him there is no future or joy and, above all, there is no eternal salvation. Little children, I call you to leave sin and to accept prayer at all times, that you may in prayer come to know the meaning of your life. God gives Himself to him who seeks Him. Thank you for having responded to my call."

(MESSAGE OF APRIL 25, 1997)

THERE ARE A FEW professional destroyers, including some politicians, who have taken it upon themselves to inflict major damage upon France in recent years. They ought to re-read history and realize that a country that has been chosen by God, in such a way, for so many centuries, is not going to be ruined in a few decades! If they are already digging a grave for France, they should know that it is they, poor wretches, who are going to fall into it!

It is good to call to mind here several prophets who have prayed and suffered for France and who have, to some extent, lifted the veil that conceals what is being prepared for the future.

Marthe Robin (1901–1981):
The Closest Saint to Us in Time[1]

In 1973, I went to see Marthe. I shared with her the marvels that I could see being accomplished in the early days of the charismatic renewal in Paris. I told her about everything with the enthusiasm of my own conversion, (the *beginning* of my conversion I should say because I still have a long way to go). We were living then as they did in the Acts of the Apostles: in the spirit, drunk with joy and witnesses to the power of God—not only in Paris, but also in other cities in France. After having listened to my account, stuffed with wonders

---

[1] A great article on Marthe Robin can be found on the EWTN website:
http://www.ewtn.com/library/MARY/MROBIN.HTM.
For more information see:
www.martherobin.com, or www.foyer-de-charite.com.

and miracles of God working in the lives of ordinary people, Marthe replied, "That's nothing compared to what will come!" I thought I was the one bringing good news to her, but she was the one giving it to me; and what news it was! I've never forgotten that reply.

Marthe prayed a great deal for France. It was, after all, her country. Her heart pulsed along with the heart of Christ over the state and destiny of France, and she composed several prayers for that purpose. At the beginning of the '80's, Father Van der Borgh, of the Foyer de Charite in Tressaint, who knew Marthe well, shared with me some of her words, including those that have since become famous. She said, "France will fall very low ... Lower than the other nations because of her pride, and because of the bad leaders she will choose for herself. She will have her nose rubbed in the dirt. There will be nothing left.

But in her distress, she will remember God. Then she will cry out to Him, and it will be the Blessed Mother who will come to save her. France will then find again her vocation as the *Eldest Daughter of the Church.* She will be the place of the greatest outpouring of the Holy Spirit, and she will send missionaries again into the whole world." I must point out here that these prophetic words were given in private and that one is not bound to believe what they contain. It is the simple opinion of a great mystic, and I, for my part, believe it. What follows may support Marthe's vision for France.

When Father Yannick Bonnet came to Medjugorje in 2013, I was delighted to be able to interview him, knowing that he had had an important meeting with Marthe concerning the state of France.

The eighty-year old Father Bonnet, from the diocese of Le Puy-en-Velay, was a former chemical engineer and a widower with grandchildren. He was ordained a priest in 1999. His testimony has revived hope in many hearts. In April of 1973, one year before the death of President Pompidou (who vetoed the law on abortion in France, before President Giscard passed it), Yannik went to see Marthe. As the father of a large family, he was worried about the future for his seven children. Through a providential set of circumstances he was able to meet with Marthe for fifty-five minutes.

Here are several snippets from that conversation, so pertinent for our times:

Fr. Bonnet said to Marthe, "Marthe, if I'm here to see you today it is because we just had our seventh child six months ago, and I'm worried sick about the world in which I'm going to have to raise my children. I can see everything collapsing, and I am full of anguish at the idea of raising seven children in such a world!"

Martha said in her small, bell-like voice, "Ah! But that's nothing compared to what it will be! You can't imagine just how far we will fall!" Yannik recounted to me, "Effectively, I was not imagining it at all. Then Marthe immediately added, 'But you'll see, the recovery will be extraordinary! It will be like a ball on the rebound!' Then she corrected herself, 'No! It will bounce back much higher and much more quickly than a ball!'[2]

"Then she spoke to me about this renewal, in which there would be conversions and vocations. She described to me a France in full spiritual renewal. In the same conversation we spoke about the world. What amazed me was that she could

---

[2] The postulator for the cause of beatification of Marthe Robin, Father Bernard Peyrous, declared that Marthe said, "France will rise up again, she will become once again the light of the nations!"

talk geopolitics as though she were the President of the United States! Ah, it was extraordinary!

"I appreciated all the advice she gave me, which was useful to me then as a lay person, but which is even more useful to me now that I am a priest. I believe she knew that one day I would become a priest. For example, she said to me: 'Don't complicate life! Wherever you go, wherever you are asked to go, do what you know how to do, don't make life hard for yourself! There are things you have the talent for and other things for which you don't. Do the things you have the talent for; that way you won't get yourself into trouble.' She only gave me advice like that—good common sense. We had an extraordinary dialogue as if we had known each other for years, although we had only just met."[3]

May the words of Yannik comfort us all in this time of such terrible crisis for France, for Europe, and for the world in general! May they motivate us to pray in order to hasten the day when the ball will bounce back, when the grave-diggers of Christian values will either be enlightened by God, or be put where they can't do any harm!

Filiola (1888–1976)

Let us also listen to the words of this rather unknown mystic from the French region of Alsace, who also lived in Paris for

---

[3] See the blog of Father Bonnet here: www.saintjosephduweb.com/bonnetblog. He is a graduate of the Ecole Polytechnique, was the human resources director of Rhone-Poulenc, director of an engineering school, doctor of chemistry, and a prolific and clear-sighted writer about issues concerning family and society.

a time. Jesus spoke to her and asked her to write down His words. Filiola received many words from the Lord concerning France, about the trials that await her because of her lack of faith, as well as her divine election, and her final restoration. In her very simple, sometimes clumsy French, Filiola confirms the words of Martha Robin.

On April 8, 1974, Jesus said to Filiola, "France is tearing my heart apart, because of her lack of faith in Me. I want, above all, to save France, which is dear to Me. I have chosen France to console my heart, but she has been snatched from me, she has been torn from me; that is what they are doing to me!" A little while later Filiola said, "France is going to suffer a great blow. The Sacred Heart of Jesus is so scorned, the Sacred Humanity of Jesus is so disfigured, torn apart by His own people."[4]

In May of that same year she encouraged, "Those faithful to Jesus, and to His Spirit, to His love, are minimal. But Jesus builds with them. Jesus lets me see a light that is so beautiful, a nameless power. How consoling it is! Jesus is seeking out poor souls caught in the mud, in order to clothe them with His love, to lead them, to give them life, His life. Jesus will reign through these little ones! With these little ones, Jesus will rebuild His Church that is suffering so greatly. The Spirit of Jesus will reign in His Church, which has been torn apart."[5]

The following year she said, "The enemy is gaining ground. It all could have been different! But the Church will

---

[4] Figliola, Figliola, Chemin de Lumière (Paris: *Pierre Téqui* èditeur, 1999), April 29, 1974.

[5] Ibid., May 13, 1974.

triumph despite Satan and his accomplices … I am sick at heart for France."[6]

Again, she warned, "Oh, France is going to suffer for her lack of faith in Jesus, and in His Sacred Humanity. France is going to be humiliated. Her pride will suffer. But Jesus will reign through his most Sacred Humanity. The time has come. The world no longer knows where to turn. People are looking for a place of safety. They defend their own wellbeing. And souls are being lost."

Then Jesus said to her, "France hears neither my voice, nor the voice of my Mother, who speaks, who is calling … Precious time is being lost, time that I grant so that I may be known. I have chosen France to make me known."

Saint Maryam of Bethlehem (1846–1878)

Who is the "Little Arab"? Maryam Baouardy is a daughter of Galilee and a great Carmelite mystic, who was beatified by John Paul II on November 13, 1983. She was canonized by Pope Francis on May 17, 2015. Her religious name was Sister Mary of Jesus Crucified. Her life was a succession of supernatural manifestations on par with those of St Catherine of Siena or St Teresa of Avila, ranging from the stigmata to a single combat against Satan. She lived for a time in France, which she loved very much. From the time of her infancy Jesus spoke to her, and here she reports some of His precious words: "Jesus compares France to a rose bush. The rose bush is to be pruned using three pruning shears. Only one branch will remain, and through that branch God will do great things. France will have to be greatly purified."

---

[6] Ibid., June 17, 1975.

"France, ask for forgiveness. Jesus said, ask for forgiveness! France has done too much good in the missions for God to abandon her. She will be holy, but she does not yet merit it. If the people pray and convert, the trial will be small. If not, she will fall lower and lower." Maryam said that God "will work His delights in the midst of France." But Jesus has said that first "she must be sifted, and France must be reduced to nothing, so that I may be at the head of the armies, and that all the nations may say to one another: 'Truly, it is the Most High who is leading France! All will shout it out as if with the same mouth, the same voice, in the same tone, even the ungodly."[7]

Servant of God Marcel Van
of Vietnam (1928–1959)

The cause for beatification of this young Redemptorist religious, who died a martyr in a Communist prison in Hanoi, in

[7] *Maryam of Bethlehem, the Little Arab,* by Sr Emmanuel, 2013. Buy it from: www.sisteremmanuel.org.

North Vietnam, has been opened. From the age of 7, Van was blessed with visions of Jesus, Mary, and, rarest of all, Saint Thérèse of Lisieux, who taught him her "Little Way." In the beginning, Van could not stand France, seeing in her a terrible enemy. When St. Thérèse asked him to pray for France, Van refused to do so, but she knew how to open his eyes to Jesus' love for France. Van was then no longer content just to pray for France, but later he even became Jesus' confidant when it came to France. Here are a few extracts from his Conversations with Jesus:

Jesus said, "It was in France that my love was first manifested. Alas! My child, during the outpouring of this love, while it flowed through France and the universe, France, by its sacrileges, twisted it into a love of worldly things, a love which can only diminish my love little by little. That is why France is in such a miserable state. But, my child, France is still the country I love and cherish in a special way …

I will re-establish my love there. Then, my child, my love will spread from France into the whole world. I will use France to extend the reign of my love everywhere. But in order for that to happen, a great number of prayers are needed, because there are still many who do not wish to reveal themselves as zealots for my cause. Above all, pray for the priests of France, because it is through them that I will affirm in this country the "Reign of My Love." Oh, my child, pray exceedingly! Without prayer you will encounter many difficult obstacles, and the reign of my love will be established only with great difficulty.

"My child, I am speaking this way so that France will be warned and will know to take precautions, because the enemy wants to make this country a center of discord. My child, we need many prayers."

NOVEMBER 12, 1945: Another time Jesus said, "Oh little apostle of my love, everywhere in France my love is calling for help. And what help is it asking for? The unique help of prayer, which by reviving the flame of love, will soften the hearts of the enemies of my love.

"Oh, France, country that I love in such a special way, consider these words of love I am addressing to you … French people, my children, if you push away my love, what other love can you use to re-build France? If there is no other love to re-build France, then France will see itself covered in thick smoke coming from Hell, and she will become a country opposed to my love, and she will end up destroyed. But, my child, humble child of my love, if anyone sends up to me prayers coming from trusting, simple and pure hearts, you will see me smile joyously at the country I love."

Jesus also said, "Little child of my love, listen. I am going to dictate to you a prayer, and I want the French people to recite this prayer to me. "Lord Jesus, have compassion on France. Deign to embrace her in your love and to show her every tenderness. Grant that, full of love for you, she will help make you loved by every nation on earth. Oh, love of Jesus, we hereby commit ourselves to remaining always faithful and to working with fervent hearts to spread your reign throughout the universe. Amen.[8]

"Oh, my child, tell the French that this prayer is the only one I want to hear from their mouths. It came from my heart which burns with love, and I want the French to be the only ones to recite it."

---

[8] Extracts from Marcel Van: Conversations (Herefordshire: Grace-wing Publications, 2013), §110.

Later, Jesus said to Marcel, "Little apostle of my love, write about France, the country that I love so particularly … French people, my children and you, my priests of France, I love you. Be vigilant. The enemy of my love will hurl his poison at your head before anything else. Once again, my children, be on your guard to prevent it. This society, in contrast to the Communist party, will not damage my children directly; it will not destroy in a single blow the country I love, but it will destroy it little by little. Yes, little by little it is going to propagate itself; little by little it's going to vomit its infernal fumes in order to make you die of asphyxiation; it will act in a way that will distance you little by little from my love in order to bring you little by little to the love of the world.[9]

"Oh, France, you the dearest object of my solicitude, I am enveloping you in my love, but you must take seriously the warnings that I have just given you. My children, be attentive and work with a fervent heart to bring about everywhere the reign of my love."[10]

VISION ABOUT FRANCE, NOVEMBER 15, 1945: Marcel recounted, "My Father, permit me to tell you, with my sister Thérèse, what took place last night. I was beginning to do my Stations of the Cross when I saw Jesus, sitting and looking at France while shedding abundant tears. But that vision only lasted an instant. At the hour of meditation, I saw Jesus again, sitting all alone and looking at France. He was crying and was saying in a tearful voice, 'France! France! Why have you abandoned me? … No, no … may this misfortune never happen … '

[9] Ibid., §124.

[10] Iblid., §126.

Then, without saying another word, He remained there crying.[11] A moment later, I could see my sister Thérèse, who was guiding me by the hand. This time, she had put her cloak back on, and I was very small, like the preceding time. I saw her smile, then. She leaned toward me and said: 'Let's recite together the consecration of France to Jesus.' After reciting it two or three times with me, she rested her head on Jesus' heart and cried. At that moment, Jesus was no longer crying, but he was sad."

At another time, Marcel said to Jesus, "But, little Jesus, has the spread of the reign of love already begun in the world?"

"Yes, already. But the point of departure for this expansion is inside France itself. And your sister Therese is the very person who is the universal apostle of all the apostles of my Love. Yes, it is from France that the spread of the reign of my Love has begun and is continuing now. Today, it is true, you are experiencing disgust, but it has to be that way, since it is the day when you must pray for France. And to do it right, you must pray a lot, because if there are too few prayers, what use will the promises that I made to France be to her?"[12]

AUGUST 24, 1946: Therese of Lisieux said to Van, "Little Brother, pray especially during the next month. The devil is using the power of lies and cunning to take possession of France. As for us, we will use the power of prayer to submit her to Jesus. In any case, if we pray a great deal, the devil will certainly be conquered and Jesus will be the conqueror. His spouses will triumph. However, little Brother, to get there

[11] Ibid., §138.

[12] Ibid., § 388.

you must still pray a lot … I send you a kiss." Van continued, "Then I heard my sister Thérèse give me an example which included the two categories of French people we had just spoken about. Here is what she said to me: "Even if everywhere in France there were nothing but sinners, with the exception of one just soul, the one just soul would be enough to keep Jesus from destroying France, because He would know that in the middle of that multitude of sinners, one pure soul existed."[13]

Great is Our Hope for the Future of France!

Intercessory prayer groups have been formed here and there throughout France, in order to protect the country from infamous laws which were passed without the agreement of the people, and which have been imposed to the detriment of the Constitution. Prayer chains are multiplying along with a succession of hours of adoration, rosaries, fasts, confessions, Eucharistic celebrations, novenas, and little hidden sacrifices unknown except in Heaven. These little groups are forming because of the urgency of combatting the "destroyer" with spiritual weapons. They inform people of the truth; they denounce the gross lies and deception of the government; they call again for the law of the Lord and His plans of love. Recently, when we saw the "watchmen" rise up, we understood that France had not lost its soul and that she would

[13] Extracts from Marcel Van: Conversations (Herefordshire: Gracewing Publications, 2013). See also the websites: … www.marcelvanassociation.com; marcelvan.canalblog.com & http://marcel-van.wixsite.com/amisdevan/1-association.

survive the crisis.[14] Thanks to the watchmen! We are so proud of them!

Without being formally organized, pilgrims from different countries of Europe, whom I have met in Medjugorje, have spoken to me in a surprising way. They say things like, "If France moves against the growing despotism which is descending all over Europe, then we will follow France! We are not able to initiate the resistance, but France is the *Elder Daughter of the Church.* We see her as our big sister, so we're hopeful that she will lead other countries in getting rid of despotism and its laws of death, in recovering their common sense, and in electing a government that chooses life."

---

[14] "Les veilleurs," the "watchmen" are a group of prayerful protesters in France who stand for the laws of God at the expense of their own safety. More information about them can be found on their facebook page:
www.facebook.com/LesVeilleursOfficiel, or on their website: www.les-veilleurs.fr.

12

A Temptation Brought into the Light

"Dear children! I invite you to open the door of your heart to Jesus as the flower opens itself to the sun. Jesus desires to fill your hearts with peace and joy. You cannot, little children, realize peace if you are not at peace with Jesus. Therefore, I invite you to confession so Jesus may be your truth and peace. So, little children, pray to have the strength to realize what I am telling you. I am with you and I love you. Thank you for having responded to my call."

(MESSAGE OF JANUARY 25, 1995)

CHRISTINE IS A STRIKINGLY beautiful woman. She had been happily married for twelve years to a man she loved and still loves, was the mother of three children, and was a fervent believer. She put her heart and soul into living the Medjugorje messages.

Everything was going well in her life until, one day, during dinner, she met a man. The attraction was instantaneous. It was love at first sight. Everything in her was aroused and drawn to him. She no longer recognized herself. This man took over her thoughts, her imagination, her heart, and her senses. Her whole being was captivated, awakened, and there was nothing she could do to resist it. In this troubled state, she asked God to protect her, especially since all the signs were pointing to the fact that this man felt the same attraction toward her. He certainly didn't make an attempt to hide it. For Christine, there was no question of betraying her husband, but she was afraid of giving into these temptations. So, as a precaution, she asked her husband to accompany her whenever she went out. She endured three weeks of this violent storm raging within her.

As it was time for her monthly confession, Christine sought out a priest. She was anxious to remain faithful to this practice of monthly confession that she had begun several years earlier, at the time of her conversion in Medjugorje. So on this particular day she confessed her sins. Even though she had not committed adultery, she revealed to the priest the gripping attraction she felt for this man, and expressed very simply the temptations she was undergoing, which were just about unbearable. The priest listened to her with kindness. After giving her a few pointers to combat this obsession, and win the victory of fidelity, which in this instance was an almost heroic act, he gave her absolution. The moment the words of absolution were pronounced over her, all the feelings that Christine had nurtured toward this man completely vanished! They vaporized, like a puff of smoke carried away by the wind. Christine thought she was dreaming! It was as though she was coming out of a fiction movie. She stepped back into reality, and peace had at last returned. 'But what did I see in that man?' She asked herself. 'He's nothing special!' She could not comprehend what it was that had fascinated her even just a few minutes earlier!

"I never realized until that moment the power of the Sacrament of Reconciliation," she told me later. "A simple absolution delivered me! I understood that the evil one doesn't like the light and that he needs darkness to act and to hide the ugliness of his actions. All I had to do to get him to let go of me was disclose my temptations, in all honesty, bringing them into the light before the priest, (which was quite humiliating for me!)"

Lord, thank you for this victory of the light! Thank you for this family that has avoided destruction! Thank you, dear Mother, because for Christine, your messages on the importance of monthly confession has been her salvation.

13

Step-by-Step Instructions

"When we are stressed or unable to bear the burdens of life it is often because we have misplaced our priorities."

(BLESSED MOTHER TERESA OF CALCUTTA)

A WOMAN ARRIVED IN Medjugorje very agitated and profoundly indignant. She related the details of her life to me, during which, it is true, there had been a whole series of situations and sufferings one after the other that were difficult to overcome. It was a real can of worms! Now, this woman had already come several times to Medjugorje with no apparent result. She had seen other pilgrims receive great blessings, but when it came to her, nothing! Therefore, I asked her if she was doing her best to live out the main messages given here by the Blessed Mother,

"Do you pray every day?"

"Uh, not every day, only sometimes."

"Do you practice fasting, which is so powerful in overcoming evil and preventing wars in our hearts?"

"No, I would like to do it, but when the moment comes, I give up and don't fast."

"Do you go to confession regularly?"

"I haven't gone for several months now."

"Do you read a few verses of the Bible each day?" "Yes, I read some, but not every day."

"Do you go to Mass at least every Sunday?" "Almost every Sunday."

What could I say to this woman? How could I help her in an effective way? I didn't want to let her leave with smooth but empty platitudes. The Lord would have spoken to me sooner or later about my "failure to assist a person in danger." So I called upon the Holy Spirit in my heart to come to my aid in this delicate business. Then, I answered,

"Mary is going to help you in a powerful way. She loves you infinitely and wants you to be happy. Don't be afraid. She has her plan of peace for you! But she can't make it happen without you. She doesn't act with a magic wand. We all have the temptation of wanting a magic wand, the easy way out, but that's a mirage. Mary will not be able to act in you unless you yourself use the means that she has given you. Look how simple her step-by-step instructions are! They're simple, but demanding, for sure. As Mother Teresa says, 'God loves us as we are, but He loves us too much to leave us as we are!' It is for you, personally, that Mary comes to Medjugorje. She has been searching for you for a long time, like a mother who never gives up trying to find the child she cherishes. So, apply yourself to living out what she says, and very soon you will see changes occurring in your life. Do your part and she'll do hers! Don't return again to Medjugorje before you have put these simple messages into practice! Decide this very day that you will do it! You could come here hundreds of times, but in vain because if you hear these messages without living them, things will never change!"

The lady, thanks be to God, took this exhortation to heart and even with gratitude. Let us pray for her and for all those who still hesitate to take the concrete steps to conversion!

14

Eucharistic Miracle in Buenos Aires

"Tonight also, dear children, I am grateful to you in a special
way for being here. Unceasingly adore the Most Blessed
Sacrament of the Altar. I am always present when the faithful
are adoring. Special graces are then being received."

(MESSAGE OF MARCH 15, 1984)

IN 1996, WHEN POPE FRANCIS was auxiliary bishop to
Cardinal Quarracino of Buenos Aires, a remarkable Eucharistic miracle occurred. It was the current Pope, himself, who
asked that it be photographed and who examined the matter.
The results are astounding.

At 7pm on August 18, 1996, Father Alejandro Pezet was
celebrating Mass in a church located in the commercial
center of the city. As he finished distributing Holy Communion, a woman came up to him to say that she had found a
host that someone had thrown away at the back of the
church. When Father Alejandro went to the place she had
indicated, he saw the soiled host. Since he couldn't consume
it, he placed it in a small container of water, which he put in
the tabernacle of the Blessed Sacrament chapel.

On Monday, August 26th, upon opening the tabernacle,
to his great astonishment he saw that the host had become a
bloody substance. He informed Bishop Jorge Bergoglio, who
gave instructions that the host was to be professionally
photographed. The photos, which were taken on September
6th, show clearly that the host, which had become a fragment

of bloody flesh, had greatly increased in size. The host remained in the tabernacle for several years, during which time the whole affair was kept secret. Since the host showed no visible sign of decomposition, Bishop Bergoglio decided to have a scientific analysis done.

On October 5, 1999, in the presence of representatives of Bishop Bergoglio, who had by then become an Archbishop, Dr. Castanon removed a sample of the bloody fragment and sent it to New York for analysis. Since he did not want to influence the results of the tests, he decided not to reveal the origin of the sample to the team of scientists.

One of these scientists was the acclaimed cardiologist and forensic pathologist, Dr. Frederic Zugiba. He determined that the substance being analyzed was true flesh and real blood containing human DNA. He declared, "The analyzed material is a fragment of the heart muscle found in the wall of the left ventricle close to the valves. This muscle is responsible for the contraction of the heart. It should be borne in mind that the left cardiac ventricle pumps blood to all parts of the body. The heart muscle is in an inflammatory condition and contains a large number of white blood cells. It is my contention that the heart was alive, since white blood cells require a living organism to sustain them, or they will die outside of a living organism. Thus, their presence indicates that the heart was alive when the sample was taken. What is more, these white blood cells had penetrated the tissue, which further indicates that the heart had been under severe stress, as if the owner had been beaten severely about the chest."

Two Australians, journalist Mike Willesee and legal expert Ron Tesoriero, were witnesses to these tests. Aware of the origin of the sample, they were staggered by Dr. Zugiba's declaration. Mike Willesee asked the scientist how long the white blood cells could have remained alive if they had come from human tissue that was preserved in water. Dr. Zugiba answered that they would have ceased to exist after a few minutes. The journalist then revealed to the doctor that the substance from which the sample had come had first been preserved in ordinary water for a month and, following that, had been preserved in a receptacle containing mineral water for three years. It was only after this time that a sample had been taken for analysis. Dr. Zugiba was at a loss to account for this fact. He declared that there was no way of explaining this fact scientifically.

Dr. Zugiba then asked him, "You have to explain something to me. If this sample was taken from a dead person, then how can it be that while I was examining it, the cells of the sample were in motion and pulsating? If this heart comes from someone who died in 1996, how can it still be alive?"

Only then did Mike Wallace reveal to Dr. Zugiba that the analyzed sample came from a consecrated host (white, unleavened bread), which had mysteriously been transformed into bleeding human flesh. Stunned at hearing this, Dr. Zugiba answered, "How and why a consecrated host can change its character and become human flesh and blood will remain an inexplicable mystery for science—a mystery completely beyond its competence."

After this, Dr. Ricardo Castanon Gomez arranged for the laboratory reports, written about the Buenos Aires miracle, to be compared to similar reports produced after a similar Eucharistic miracle that took place in Lanciano, Italy. Again without revealing the origin of the test samples. The experts who conducted the comparison concluded that the two laboratory reports had analyzed test samples taken from the same person. They further pointed out that the two samples revealed an "AB positive" blood type. This blood carries characteristics of a man who was born and lived in the Middle East.

Only faith in the extraordinary action of God produces a reasonable answer. God wants us to be conscious that He is truly present in the mystery of the Eucharist. The Eucharistic miracle of Buenos Aires is an extraordinary sign attested to by science. Through it Jesus desires to awaken in us a living faith in His real, not symbolic, presence in the Eucharist. Only with the eyes of faith, and not with our bodily eyes, do we see Him under the appearance of the consecrated bread and wine. In the Eucharist Jesus sees and loves us and desires to save us.

(Archbishop Bergoglio became a Cardinal in 2001 and this miracle was made known only after lengthy research). Make sure you visit the internet page where Dr. Castanon, an atheist who became Catholic, explains this miracle in Spanish (with English subtitles)! It is powerful!

Here is the link:

https://www.youtube.com/watch?v=APz1v8oz1ms.

15

The Heart of My Father

" … Merciful and gracious is the Lord, slow to anger,
abounding in kindness. God does not always rebuke, nurses
no lasting anger, has not dealt with us as our sins merit, nor
requited us as our deeds deserve … As a father has
compassion on his sons, so the Lord has compassion for he
who fears him. For he knows how we are formed, remembers
that we are dust … But the Lord's kindness is forever, for he
who fears him. He favors the sons of their sons of those who
kept his covenant, who take care to fulfill its precepts …"

(PSALM 103)

WHEN I ANNOUNCED TO my father my plan to go to
India for three months, he reacted very negatively.
Seized with fear that something terrible would happen to me,
he brought up an impressive list of catastrophes that I would
probably endure. As a medical doctor, he enumerated for me
every well-known disease and virus in India that could
destroy my health in a matter of a few days, even within 24
hours. He warned that I could get dysentery, or malaria, or
dengue fever, or worse still hepatitis; and he emphasized the
absence of reliable medical help. Quite simply, I was risking
disappearing into thin air without a trace. There was absolutely no way that he would allow me to run such a risk!

He tried every possible argument to dissuade me, all in
vain!

I was 23 years old. With my studies finished, I wanted to take a long break before exploring job offers in Paris. I just felt that I *had* to know other cultures, travel under other skies, and breathe another air than that of our society of consumerism. The desire was stronger than myself. India irresistibly tugged at me like a magnet. I had already bought my plane ticket from Paris to New Delhi, and, with that involuntary cruelty found frequently in the young, I told my father that I was going to stick with my departure plan. It didn't cross my mind that by doing so I inflicted on his heart, and his spirit, a torment that would afflict him day and night for three months.

The day of departure arrived. After kissing me, and blessing me with emotion, he took out of his pocket a rather large sum of money. He looked me right in the eyes, and with a tenderness that I will never forget, he simply said, "Here, keep this in your pocket! If anything happens to your health, this could save you."

I wasn't expecting that! Struck by such goodness on his part, I murmured a few words of resistance: "No, Papa, don't worry! I already have what I need to manage." But the money had already landed in my pocket! I was overwhelmed.

During my absence, in order to comfort his spirit and his heart, the Lord sent him a kind of consoling angel. One of his best friends told him: "Oh, you know Jean Pierre, Emmanuelle will be much safer in the streets of New Delhi than in Paris! You have nothing to be afraid of! Besides, consider yourself lucky. She isn't into drugs and she is not looking for a guru!"

My father died less than a year later in a car accident while I was on my second trip to India, exploring the state of Kashmir.

This episode remains for me the most magnificent example of the unconditional love of the Heavenly Father. That day I touched the love of the Father, and I welcomed Him in my heart better than if I had read the most sublime spiritual books. My earthly father became the living icon of that love. Later in my life, how many times I would re-live that experience! How many times have I defied God by my choices? How many times have I ignored his Word and hurt Him? Yet, He never ceased lavishing His blessings upon me, even there, where he didn't want me to go. God the Father has an obvious *weakness,* so to speak. He has a strong respect for our free will. Freedom is His sacred gift to us, for true love can only come from true freedom!

In Hebrew, the word for *mercy* is *rahamim.* According to Christian mystics, it is God's greatest attribute. Now this word signifies above all "the maternal womb," the *matrix!* But the word matrix is *rehem,* a singular word, whereas *rahamim* is plural. Not that God has many matrixes, but the plural word signifies intensity. God is intensely, infinitely merciful. When His child drifts far from Him, God the Father suffers like a mother whose womb is in turmoil, and even more than that mother: He can only renew his signs of tenderness, it is the only weapon He has.[1]

---

[1] For more on this theme see Julian of Norwich Shewings (Chapter 16). Julian articulates Christ's feminine life-sustaining power in the sixteenth chapter, "As a mother feeds her child with milk produced by her own body, Christ tenderly feeds humanity with His body in the Eucharist. Likewise, as a mother lays her child tenderly to her breast, Christ leads humanity to His breast through his open side." Julian's description of Christ's open side bears significant resemblance to the womb. It is a place where humanity is brought to new life. Christ's side is also filled with

Mother Eugenia (1907–1990)

The Heavenly Father has spoken to certain souls, expressing His immense love for His children, for mankind, but also His sorrow at being hardly known, even taken for a severe, distant and harsh God. And it's worth noting that at the present time there is no liturgical feast dedicated to Him. There are several dedicated to Jesus, Our Lady, the Saints and Angels, but none to Him. In addition there is not even a cathedral or a basilica dedicated to Him. Is there even one single parish church in existence in honor of His name?

I would like to share here intimate confidences from the Heavenly Father to an Italian woman. Her name is Mother Eugenia. Information and material is being collected about her in order to see if her cause for Beatification can be started.[2]

---

blood and water, two liquids that both sustain human life and pour from a woman's body during childbirth. Moreover, Julian contends that, as women shed their blood and water in childbirth out of love for human life, Christ sheds His blood and water out of love for humankind.

[2] Revelations given by the Eternal Father to Mother Eugenia Ravasio in Italy. Some of her writings can be found in English at http://www.fatherspeaks.net/eugenia_msg.html.

Her book, The Father Speaks to His Children has been granted an imprimatur and published in Italian by the Association "Dio e Padre—Casa Pater," distributed by Edizioni Nidi di Preghiera. The 4th Edition was printed in 1995. See also the magazine *Triumph of the Heart* of May-June 2010, no. 49.

Madre Eugenia, Italy. © "Unitas in Christo ad Patrem,"
founded by Mother Eugenia Ravasio, via del
Cinema 16, 100042, Anzio (RM), Italy.)

In one vision, Mother Eugenia saw God the Father place His crown at the foot of His throne. This gesture reveals to each of His children how close He desires to be to them. So that all unjustified fear of Him would be eradicated from their hearts. He also expressed the desire to have a feast day dedicated to Him on the Church calendar: either the first Sunday in August (a movable feast), or on August 7th.

Here is a snapshot of how the Father revealed Himself to Mother Eugenia: "In my Fatherly Goodness, I will give everything to you, provided all come to consider me to be a true Father, living in the midst of my own people, as in truth, I do."

"If anyone honors me and confides in me, I will send down a ray of Peace upon him in all his adversities, in all his troubles, his sufferings and his afflictions of every kind; especially if he invokes me and loves me as his Father."

"And all of you will know my kindness in all things, all of you will know my protection and all of you will see my power!"

"Call me by the name of Father, with confidence and love, and you will receive everything from this Father, with Love and Mercy."

"All those who call me by the name of *Father* in their heart, be it only once, will not perish, but will be assured of eternal life in the company of the elect."

We believe that everything the Father allows to happen in our life He turns to the good of those who love Him. Even those things that are painful, He allows with a view to a greater good. Like the little Maryam of Bethlehem, we would like to "be always content." Whenever we rest against the Father's heart, what could we possibly lack?

Let us take as our own the beautiful prayer of blessed Charles de Foucauld of France. This rich Parisian had been promiscuous, disfigured due to a disorderly life, bloated as a result of excesses of all kinds. But when he encountered the Father and abandoned everything into His hands, he became gentle and humble, like Jesus, beautiful and luminous, totally transparent to grace. He radiated peace!

Prayer of Charles de Foucauld

"Father, I abandon myself into your hands;
Do with me what you will.
Whatever you may do.
I thank you;
I am ready for all.
I accept all.
Let only your will be done in me,

and in all creatures.

I wish no more than this, O Lord.

Into your hands I commend my soul;

I offer it to you

With all the love of my heart,

For I love you, Lord,

And so need to give myself,

To surrender myself into your hands,

Without reserve,

And with boundless confidence,

Because you are my Father."

16

The End of Rudolf Hoss:
The Criminal of Auschwitz

"Were a soul like a decaying corpse so that from a human standpoint, there would be no [hope of] restoration and everything would already be lost, it is not so with God. The miracle of Divine Mercy restores that soul in full. Oh, how miserable are those who do not take advantage of the miracle of God's mercy! You will call out in vain, but it will be too late."

(THE DIARY OF SAINT FAUSTINA)[1]

IMPRISONED IN THE CAMP at Auschwitz, Father Maximilien Kolbe addressed these words to his friend, Father John Lipsky: "Let us pray for the Nazis, because no conversion is impossible!"

What ever happened to Rudolf Höss, that Nazi criminal who ordered one of the greatest genocides in history? Both at the trials at Nuremberg in 1945-'46, and at the national tribunal at Varsovia, he identified himself as being fully responsible for all that occurred under his command post in Auschwitz. He affirmed calmly and objectively that he sent three million people to their deaths.

In 1947, in the Krakow Prison, a little before his execution, Rudolf heard the ringing of bells at a nearby Carmelite

---

[1] Jesus to St. Faustina. Maria Faustina Kowalska, Diary, §1448.

convent. He remembered his childhood, when he used to serve Mass as an altar boy and dreamed of being a priest. Then an unimaginable thing happened, he asked to speak to a Catholic priest. When his request was ignored, he reiterated it in writing, and Father Wladyslaw Lohn was designated for the very delicate mission. This Jesuit Priest, a provincial in southern Poland, was very well informed on the camp at Auschwitz, and, in addition, he spoke fluent German. He asked for prayers from the nuns at the convent where Sister Faustina had lived and received the messages about the Divine Mercy. Sister Valerie recounted the event like this: "Father Lohn asked for the prayers of all who were in the house at that time. He told us where he had been called to, and what mission he had to fulfill. We then entrusted everything to the Merciful Jesus!"

On April 10, 1947, Father Lohn was able to meet Rudolf Höss for several hours just days before his execution. At the end of that conversation, which will remain God's secret for the most part, the former commandant of Auschwitz prayed the Credo and confessed his sins after being officially reinstated in the Catholic Church.

Father Lohn declared later that he had prepared Rudolf for confession by speaking to him about the Heart of Jesus, that same heart to which Father Kolbe also wanted to guide, "all souls through *The Immaculate.*" The next day, the new convert received Holy Communion. He remained in the middle of his cell, on his knees, and in tears. When the priest was leaving the cell, Rudolf told him, "God has pardoned me, but men will never pardon me!"

Later, as he was waiting for his execution, he wrote a poignant farewell letter to his wife and his five children, a letter in which he shared the reasons that caused him to act the way he had towards God. He acknowledged his faults but also described his sincere love for his family. In speaking about his return to God, he wrote, "It was a difficult battle, but I found faith in my God again."

On April 12, four days before his execution, Rudolf Höss drafted a declaration in which he officially asked pardon from the Polish people.

"During the time of my detention," he wrote. "I recognized bitterly, and profoundly the terrible crime I committed against humanity. Oh, may God pardon me for all my actions! And from you, people of Poland, I ask forgiveness! It is only now in a Polish prison that I have understood what human kindness really is. In spite of all that happened, I have been treated well here. I didn't expect that, and I am ashamed."

Rudolf was hanged on April 16, 1947, next to the crematorium of the former Auschwitz concentration camp. In the statement of the prosecutor of the Republic, one reads, "Rudolf Höss remained until the last moment completely calm and expressed no last wishes." Like the Good Thief, Pranzini, and all last-minute converts, Divine peace had finally conquered this heart which had forgotten for all too long that it was created for love. Happily for all of us, God always has with Him an inexhaustible dose of mercy ready to be applied to whoever decides to reconcile with Him. It's the "last chance dose"! It surpasses all imagination, because the Heavenly Father is infinitely happy to bring back to righteousness a soul that He almost lost forever.

How can we not think of the millions of victims who saw their former executioner arrive in the next world vested with the pardon of God? We know that the elected in Heaven love us with the very same love that God has for us. We know also "that there will be more joy in Heaven over one sinner who repents than for 99 righteous souls who have no need of repentance," (Luke 15:7). If the angels rejoice so much over this conversion, what will the ones condemned to death say when they see their former executioner transformed, turned into their brother, restored in the grace of forgiveness, and clothed with the mantle of mercy! Only God could invent situations like this. May He be blessed and glorified!

17

Ivona Has Chosen to Love

"Dear children, may your only way be always love."

(MESSAGE OF JULY 31, 1986)

A GREAT FRIEND OF GOD visited us in November of 2013. Beautiful, simple, smiling, Ivona, a 49 year old widow, with two adult children. She worked as a florist, and was coming to Medjugorje for the third time. Her extreme fervor took us aback! Everyday, despite the cold, wind, rain, and mud, she climbed and descended down Mount Krizevac barefooted. Ivona didn't want to tell me her story. It was too personal to be made public, she said, but she gave in when I told her that it would help other women regain their courage.

In 1984 she married in the Ukraine and lived in a two-room apartment there. Igor, her spouse, quickly revealed himself to be loathsome; he drank, treated her with disrespect, and sometimes he beat her. She eventually learned that he had a mistress, a married woman who was the mother of three children. Although he was Catholic, Igor spoke badly of priests and refused to go to church, except on feast days. But Ivona sincerely loved her husband and prayed a lot for him. One day he fell gravely ill and had to quit work. He needed constant care, and his mistress abandoned him.

Realizing that he was going to die, Ivona worried about his Eternal fate. Out of love for him, she didn't stop at praying for him, she also offered fasts to God. In August of 2009, she came to Medjugorje to obtain his reconciliation with

God. Everyday in the torrid heat, she made the ascent of Krizevac in bare feet over burning stones. She pleaded with God, "Don't let him die without going to confession!" Because Igor was vicious to their children, she prayed for the unity of their whole family. "Even if Igor has to hate me," she said to the Lord. "Give me the strength to put up with him!" In spite of her good care of him, day and night, Igor still insulted her. Nevertheless, Ivona had peace in her heart, because her prayers kept her in union with God.

One day, Igor was hospitalized. Ivona didn't let up, and spent hours at his bedside. She continued her fasts and prayed with faith, certain that God would listen to her. With great hostility, Igor rejected the chaplain, who proposed that he make a confession. Ivona kept quiet and did not give in to discouragement. Glued to his bedside she interceded with all her heart on behalf of her husband, and renewed her trust after each of his refusals. Recitations of the rosary and the divine mercy chaplet continued amidst all of the medical care.

On January 6, 2010, the morning of his death, a miracle happened. Igor caressed the hair of his wife saying, "Even when I am mean to you, you continue to love me and take care of me!" Finally, a little balm for Ivona's wounded heart. Igor's legs had turned black, but he was still conscious. That day, Ivona had to leave the hospital for several hours for the first Communion of her daughter. When she returned, she bumped into the priest and suggested that he make a new attempt at a confession for Igor. It was a matter of hours before he died. The second miracle then occurred–the priest answered that he had just come from Igor's room, and that Igor had made a good confession after twenty years without the sacraments. Ivona learned the news in the hallway of the hospital! She nearly tumbled over with joy!

When she returned to the room, she put an image of the Merciful Christ in Igor's hands, and, to her great surprise, Igor put it between his fingers, lifted it up, and contemplated it with serenity. Then he asked his wife, "How will I get up there?" "You're going home, don't be afraid," she answered! "Jesus will light the way to Him, and you'll have the three Kings to escort you!" (It was the feast of the three Kings, January 6th). Seeing that he was suffering, she said, "Remember that Jesus also suffered before going to His Father." She asked forgiveness for all the times that she made him suffer and explained that on her part, she forgave him for everything he had done. Already, Igor was no longer speaking, but only shed tears in response to her. His heart was finally touched. Ivona thanked him for all the years they spent together. Then, with a big smile, she said, "Now you can go peacefully into the house of the Lord!" At those words, Igor's eyes became fixed ahead. He was gone.

Ivona had persevered in prayer and fasting, and all that she asked of the Lord was given to her. Igor confessed at the point of death, six hours before his passing, right before his loss of speech. During the Lent following Igor's death, Ivona fasted 40 days on bread and water to thank God for having converted her husband.

Ivona has not ceased working since Igor's death. Her son, Boris, is very ill. Returning to Medjugorje for him, she hoped to soften God's heart for his healing and especially for his conversion, because he too left the Church, and had taken up with a person who was involved in the occult and practiced other dangerous things. So, Ivona made a deal with God, "You, Lord, dedicate yourself to my son Boris, and I will dedicate myself to Your sons, Your priests!" Last November 25th, after climbing the hills of Krizevac and Podbrdo in bare feet, she spent the entire night in the church, praying for priests in front of the exposed Blessed Sacrament!

If anyone crosses paths with Ivona in the street, he will not realize whose path he has had the honor of crossing. She will pass unnoticed. However, thanks to her and those like her, without making themselves noticed, the world continues to turn as they continue to live the commandment to love, even to the point of heroism. God hides his saints well! He has many of them, although still not enough. Oh, the surprises that awaits us on the last day, when every truth will appear in the light of God!"

The Virgin Mary tells us, "I invite you to pray without ceasing for the gift of love, to love the Heavenly Father above all. When you love Him you will love yourself and you will love your neighbor. These two cannot be separated. The Heavenly Father is in each man, He loves each man and He calls each man by name," (November 2, 2013). She also said, "May love prevail in your hearts dear children, not human love, rather Divine Love." Ivona is among those strong souls who have chosen to take hold of heaven, whatever it costs. She will not be disappointed!

Jewish Wisdom

A rabbi expressed the same idea in his own magnificent story! "Rabbi Yoël Toteilbaum Zatsal was known to practice 'justice.'

His door was open to those who wanted to have a discussion or take advice from him. One day, a man arrived on crutches at the rabbi's house and recounted all his sufferings: 'Rabbi, I have been a widower for some time, and the care of my children falls entirely on me. As if that were not enough, I broke my foot and the doctors think it's impossible for me to heal. I don't know what to do, Rabbi. I'm lost.' The rabbi comforted this unfortunate man, as he always did when encountering the poor, and he gave him a large sum of money. The man left the room, followed by the rabbi's secretary, who called the next person.

"Suddenly, the secretary reappeared and exclaimed: 'Rabbi, the man who just left threw away his crutches and continued serenely on his way! He didn't have a broken foot! It's a scam!' The rabbi flinched, and murmured a prayer. Seeing the rabbi's reaction, the secretary left again to see if the man was still around, she abruptly returned, 'Rabbi!' she exclaimed. 'That man lied to you twice over! He isn't a widower. He just rejoined his wife who was waiting for him outside. He wanted to steal money from you!'

"The rabbi exclaimed, 'Baroukh Hachem! (*Blessed be His name!*) Thank Hachem, I am so happy that this man didn't have a broken foot! I'm very happy that this man isn't a widower. Thank you, my God, for having permitted me to hear this good news. Thank Hachem, I am very joyful.'"

18

Do Not Abandon Fasting!

"The one who prays is not afraid of the future and the one
who fasts is not afraid of Evil."

(MESSAGE OF JANUARY 25, 2001)

AN ANCIENT GREEK PROVERB SAYS: "Choose the lesser of
two evils." Many people have eliminated from their lives,
for various reasons, the message of Mary on fasting. Quite
often I hear people say, "It's too hard for me. I'm very attached to food. I don't want to put this stress on myself."

Fasting is one point of the Medjugorje messages that is
very often rejected. Don't be mistaken, it's not by accident! If
one of the numerous benefits of fasting is to keep away
demons, then it makes sense that those demons are doing
everything possible to turn us away from the practice of
fasting. They convince us that fasting is reserved for a few
people who are already holy, in whose company we of course
don't belong. [1]

Jesus Himself responded to this dilemma in Scripture in a
luminous way. Remember that Jesus sent his apostles ahead
of him to preach, to chase away demons, to heal the sick, to
raise the dead, and to announce the Good News? One day

---

[1] For a satirical, but poignant example of other strategies employed
by the "other one," see C.S. Lewis, Screwtape Letters, (New York:
HarperOne, 1942).

the apostles came back quite happy, even excited (as you can imagine) and told Jesus, "Even the demons have submitted to us in Your name," (Luke 10:17). You can easily understand their satisfaction at having seen the defeat of the enemy in the hearts of numerous afflicted people who had come to them for relief from the devil's torments.

Another time, the apostles gathered around Jesus after he had returned from the mountain of transfiguration with Peter, John and James. But He kept silent, undoubtedly a little troubled by their failure. It was the father of a child who addressed Jesus then, directing him to notice that his disciples had not succeeded in chasing the demon from his son. He asked Jesus, "Why?" Jesus responded, "That type can only be cast out by fasting and prayer," (Mark 9:28–29). The answer jumped out, it was crystal clear, transparent, indisputable![2] When Jesus mentioned that type of demon, one had every reason to believe that he was speaking of demons that were a great deal more evil and cruel than the first demons chased out by the disciples in prayer, simply at the name of Jesus. But, as a matter of fact, just as it is for angels and saints, there exists a hierarchy among demons, which explains their different capacities to do evil. For that type, which resisted the apostles so well, you need a strong and powerful remedy associated with prayer: fasting. But the apostles had omitted it. They had only done half of their work. That's why they did not succeed in freeing the poor child from his demon.

What does that tell us? That we have a choice to make. If I choose only to pray, even if I choose to pray a lot, the

---

[2] The message on fasting is not addressed to those who suffer from serious illnesses or certain weaknesses, physical or psychological, or to those who are on heavy medication.

temptation is to think that because I have conserved the effort I would have put into fasting, I can enjoy life and its good things all the more. I can sit back and relax knowing that I have put all of my energy into prayer. Then I can eat what I like. But what about dealing with the type of demon that comes from the most difficult category? Noticing that I have not fasted, these demons will find the door to my heart ajar, and I take the risk of allowing them in: they could truly take hold of me and submerge themselves in my heart in order to do the kind of damage that delights them. In particular, they could destroy my inner peace, my family, my health ... When I don't fast, I don't guarantee that my door is closed.[3]

If, on the other hand, I choose to pray *and* fast, then the door to my heart will be closed to every kind of demon. For some of us it may require a certain amount of sacrifice, and that it may be a bit difficult at the beginning when I have to break old, well-entrenched eating habits. But noticing that I am fasting, that most difficult type of demon will see that he is prevented from causing me harm, because, with the grace of God, I have shut the door to him. These demons are disarmed. They can't come to attack me, so I am able to enjoy a great peace. I avoid trouble and diffuse the deadly plots they were hatching against me, against my family, and my health. That way, I do all that is in my power to do

---

[3] Those who are not able to fast on bread and water because of their health, don't leave the door open to demons! The Virgin has pointed to other forms of sacrifice. See the book Freed and Healed Through Fasting, by Sister Emmanuel, or the CD Fasting: The Door to God's Power both can be found at: www.sisteremmanuel.org or www.childrenofmedjugorje.com.

nothing less, of course with all my heart, and I leave God to care for the rest.

So I ask the question: do we prefer to endure the sacrifice of fasting, or to be the target of greater sufferings, the kind generated by these invisible, but no less harmful enemies who are demons? For my part, the choice has been made. In the past, I've had the experience of suffering from demons on several occasions, in particular following the occult practices of my youth. Their torture was intolerable. Everyone afflicted by evil spirits knows all too well, that compared with the torments of demons, the effort of fasting seems like a gentle caress![4]

A Battlefield

Why does the Blessed Mother invite us repeatedly to fast two days a week? It's because she's a mother, and her maternal love surpasses, in intensity, all we can possibly imagine. She knows that today her children are on a battlefield, temporal as well as spiritual, and she doesn't hide that fact from them. "Today as never before," she says. "Satan wants to destroy all that is holy in you. He wants to destroy your families. He wants to destroy nature and even the planet on which you live. Satan wants war." Now, finding yourself on a battlefield knowing neither the identity of the enemy, nor his methods of destruction, then marching ahead without bringing adequate weapons, is like walking onto a minefield totally unconscious of the risk involved, and condemning yourself to defeat. If, on the contrary, we listen to the voice of Jesus in the Gospel, reiterated by His Mother in Medjugorje, then we

---

[4] You will find recipes for the fasting bread at Appendix X.

will bring the proper weaponry. We will put on the impene-
trable armor of fasting, and the enemy will be defeated.

Some people say to me, 'This instruction is difficult to
accept.' "But," I counter. "Is it the instruction that is difficult, or is it the current evolution of our society?" Of course,
nothing is automatic with God, because He can protect one
of his children who never fasts. But let's look around us.
Where is the world heading? Aren't we already in trouble?
Mary herself always chooses her words carefully to make
them positive and encouraging. Nevertheless she told us on
September 2, 2011, that "everything is falling apart!" In an
emergency situation an urgent plan is required.

To save a person who has been injured in a car accident,
emergency routes developed to save them are always accepted
without contest. But how does it work for injuries to the
soul? Father Slavko Barbaric, a holy priest of Medugorje and
champion of fasting, made this point to us: "Suppose you are
invited to the house of some friends and you are on a strict
diet because of your high blood sugar. Those friends will
easily accept the fact that you have to abstain from sweets or
other delicious foods in order to prevent a crisis, which could
harm you. They will not oppose this basic medical wisdom.
Likewise, you yourself have to abstain from those foods that
you used to like, but which now threaten the health of your
body and soul."

What about the health of our souls, which are called to
live for all eternity? Isn't it necessary to protect them with
infinite delicacy? And the health of millions of other souls
who do not yet know the love of God, those who wander
around aimlessly, isn't it worth the trouble to fast so that they
can find the light?

Noticing that Saint Macarius of Egypt, fourth century
hermit, was tirelessly working and fasting a great deal, some

of his close friends proposed that he slow down. He responded, "Leave me alone! This is how I torment the one who is tormenting me!"

Shall We Take or Shall we Give?

Our decision of whether to fast or not depends on the depth of our commitment to follow Jesus and to serve our neighbor. For example, people who work in private companies may have different degrees of commitment. Some will choose to give themselves completely—even to *over-achieve* in the good sense of the word, and to do excellent work. Others seem to be active, but less motivated. Still others only work to meet their own basic necessities, and don't have within their heart the future of the company.

It's the same with our spiritual life. There are those who sincerely care about the fate of the Church as a whole. They invest themselves deeply in making Christ known and loved, whatever their status among Christian people. They don't spare themselves any pains. These people give without counting; these are the saints, hidden and unknown, without whom God knows what might happen to the Church. Then there are others who commit themselves in a less radical way, up to and including those who participate in the church for a few hours from time to time in order to fulfill a duty out of obligation, without putting their souls into it.

Of course, the quality of the commitment does not depend primarily on *what* we do, but on the *way* we do it. As Mother Teresa of Calcutta famously says, "We do small things with great love!"

In the practice of fasting, there is the same range of motivations. Certainly, it is possible to go to Heaven without ever having fasted. You can even lead an authentic Christian life without fasting. But if those who don't fast are sometimes still protected (yes, sometimes), let them ask themselves this question: who has fasted for them? Who has had enough love to carry them in His heart to the point of sacrificing Himself for them and for their health? For how many thousands of sinners did the Curé of Ars fast? And when Sister Faustina Kowalska, the little sister without education, fasted as much as obedience allowed her (she changed cells, so that no one would know), little did she know that millions of Christians and non-Christians were going to benefit from her sacrifices and from her holiness. Did she know that through her writing, inspired by the divine mercy of God, millions of sinners were going to return to God's embrace?[5]

With this extraordinary freedom that God has given us, we choose what level of commitment we want to make for the coming of the Kingdom here on earth. We can be consumers or generous donors. Can you guess which ones are infinitely happier here on earth, and in the other world?

Faced with Disastrous Pathways, a Remedy?

I often encounter parents who complain about the disastrous path taken by one of their children: to name just one, the use of drugs. These parents pray with fervor, make pilgrimages, and pray novena upon novena, but they get discouraged when they see that the problem is not going away. They ask me, then, to pray and to ask the visionaries of Medjugorje to pray for them. I reassure them by telling them that their own prayers are of great value in the eyes of God. I then ask them this crucial question: "Are you also fasting for your child?"

[5] Maria Faustina Kowalska, *Diary.*

"Uh, no, Sister, but we pray a lot!"

"That's very good, but why aren't you fasting?" "Uh, well, it's because we love food, Sister!"

"I understand, but are you prepared to add fasting to your prayers for the health of your child?" They remain quiet for a time, then often finish by saying, "Okay, we'll fast for him." And it is then, in most cases, that the miracle finally occurs.

We never give enough consideration to the other benefits of fasting. The list is impressive! While disarming demons, and thereby protecting us from harm, is important, it is actually only one of the numerous fruits of fasting. I would like to cite—in no particular order—the most obvious among them: We fast to obtain healing—physical, psychological, or spiritual; to liberate souls who still suffer in Purgatory; to create in our hearts additional space for the Holy Spirit and to be, therefore, more inspired by Him; to have a clear mind; to prevent and stop wars (in and of themselves, in families, and in the world); to suspend natural laws (such as tsunamis, avalanches, earthquakes, floods, and other natural catastrophes); to understand better the plan God has for us and to permit Him to carry it out more effectively; to acquire greater inner peace; to feel more free; to diminish or cancel our own time of purification in Purgatory; to reveal our hidden dependencies, as a brain scan might do, and to be able to conquer them; to improve our health, because many premature deaths or chronic, serious illnesses are due to the fact that we eat too much (30% too much in the West); to be able to achieve inspired work, such as a song, a house plan, an icon (Painters of icons fast before beginning their work; that's a rule!); to gain the blessing of God on a plan for marriage; and to obtain a favor from God for oneself or for a dear one—for example, a conversion, a reconciliation, the return of a spouse, or of a prodigal child. The list goes on.

All these graces do not come from dreams. We often experience them in Medjugorje!

Be assured, we are not the only ones to fast! People of all religions fast: Jews fast, Muslims fast, Hindus fast, even Buddhists fast, as do a variety of Christian denominations: the Orthodox Churches, Melchites, Marionites, Protestants, Pentecostals. Jesus fasted. Mary and the apostles fasted two days a week. All the saints fasted. Why did they hold on so tightly to the practice of fasting? They fasted not only out of obedience to the Word of God, but also, having experienced the power of fasting, they drew their own conclusions as to how fasting increased their peace and happiness. They are wise because they simply judged fasting by its fruits!

Why then have the majority of Latin rite Catholics abandoned fasting? Replacing meat with fish or eggs on Ash Wednesday and Good Friday has not proven to be sufficient to block the evil that has been unleashed on the Church today. Are we going to allow this evil, this destruction on the part of certain groups, to torture us, and our children?

The Visionary, Ivan Dragicevic, Speaks About the Future of the Church and of the World

On August 14, 2012, Father Livio Fanzaga interviewed Ivan on Radio-Maria in Italy. Here is an extract from his speech, which would be good to contemplate:

"When the prophetic secrets of the Gospa are revealed in Medjugorje, the Catholic Church will find itself undergoing a great trial, both for the world and for the faithful, and a little of this suffering has already begun … Satan is stronger than ever today, and he particularly wants to destroy the family and its young, because they are the foundation of a new world …

" … Presidents and leaders derive their power from God; but too many of them exploit it for their own interests. The result is a disordered society. Without God, the world has no future. That's why the Gospa invites us to come back to God and to re-direct ourselves towards a future with God, so that peace and harmony may be ensured. A government without God is anarchy. It's a deceptive government. So it's important for God to be present in the government and in the first position. Since that understanding is absent in many places, peace is unceasingly threatened. The most terrible war is the one that is being waged in the human heart. THE ABSENCE OF GOD HAS LEFT A VOID, WHICH GIVES SATAN MORE SPACE THAN EVER." Ivan asked his listeners to pray that Mary's plan may be fulfilled.

During an encounter with some pilgrims in Medjugorje, Ivan declared, "The first objective of Satan is the destruction of the family and the young people, and his second goal is to destroy the Church. He wants to prevent the flowering of priestly vocations."[6]

The trials that we endure today could have been avoided! Those of the near future can still be avoided! Our Lady also tells us, *"Dear Children, by fasting and prayer you can obtain everything,"* (Message given to Jelena Vasilj in October 1983).

---

[6] Ivan received from Our Lady the mission to pray for Priests and families. On Thursdays, in Medjugorje, he opens his chapel to priests who wish to pray with him during the hour of the apparition.

19

The Gospa's Warning Signs

"Dear children, prayer is the only path which leads to peace.
If you pray and fast, you will obtain all that you want."

(MESSAGE GIVEN TO THE PRAYER GROUP IN THE 1980S)

MATTHEW, A VERY DEAR friend, has been a faithful pilgrim in Medjugorje since 1996. That year, after receiving a particular grace on Mount Krizevac, he experienced a conversion so deep that his life radically changed. Much to the great joy of his wife, who had been praying, praying, praying for a very long time, he wholeheartedly embraced the key messages of the Queen of Peace, called the five "stones," and began his "education" by doing his best to live out the messages in order to grow in the faith. [1]

Maintaining his commitment to Our Lady's formula was something he couldn't guarantee after only five days in Medjugorje, but little by little, he succeeded in climbing on the way of the faith. Two years later, he no longer had any difficulty with monthly confession, the Eucharist, the daily reading of the Word of God, and the praying of the rosary.

But fasting, that preeminent endeavor among the five stones seemed impossible! There was nothing he could do.

---

[1] The five "stones" of Our Lady's messages in Medjugorje are: prayer of the Rosary, fasting, reading the Bible, going to confession once a month, and frequent reception of the Eucharist.

Every attempt on his part proved to be in vain. He was a connoisseur of the best wines in France, he enjoyed gourmet food, and in general, he was a health nut! Mealtime remained for Matthew a sacred and incontrovertible necessity. He and his wife were excellent cooks, and their sense of hospitality often meant, to them, a bountiful table. In fact, when Matthew came to Medjugorje he used to jokingly tell his friends, "When you go to Sister Emmanuel's house, if you want to eat well, don't go there on Wednesdays or Fridays!"

One day, Matthew asked me for advice: How could he finally succeed at fasting? Was he expecting me to reveal a quasi-magic remedy? Not really, because he had no actual hope of putting his problem to rest. He admitted to me that each time he took one step forward in his attempt at fasting, he had to take two steps back when it became obvious that it wasn't working for him. All the warning lights from the Gospa in her messages on the necessity of fasting had become for him points of discomfort, of suffering, even of guilt. He enumerated for me a number of disastrous symptoms that attacked him when he began to fast.

"I tried forcing myself," he told me. "But to no avail. I ate bread, but then I'd have a bad day. I'd be in a bad mood, and at 2 o'clock in the morning, when I couldn't sleep, I'd get up and go into the kitchen to have an omelet or something like that, so I could get back to sleep. Eventually, I gave up. Since I retired from work, my wife and I organize our daily schedule, always putting Jesus first. Since I don't have anymore professional or family obligations (my children have started their own families) each day we attend morning Mass, meditate on the rosary, and sometimes adore Jesus in the Blessed Sacrament in the early afternoon. But there's still the problem of fasting on Wednesdays and Fridays. I want bread to become my only nourishment two times a week, the way it is for the other disciples of the Gospa!"

"You ought to try bread made with spelt," I told him. "That flour is really rich and contains all you need. It will fill you up.[2] You can also use it in a bread machine.[3] And don't forget to give your struggle over to Jesus, from morning to night; you'll see. He'll help you!"

[2] Spelt originated in Persia, around 5,000 to 6,000 years before Christ. It has been grown in Europe for more than 1,000 years, and for only 100 years in North America. Spelt is an unprocessed grain that is well known in Germany, Austria and Switzerland today. It is both a tonic, and a food that stimulates all of the organs. It has a regenerative function at the cellular level, and its specific effect is most clearly seen in the revitalization of cell and sensory organ activity. It is known to improve blood circulation, and contains many necessary nutritional and dietetic qualities, which come from eight essential amino acids. It is an exceptionally complete and very digestible food, ideal for fasting! The Bible mentions its use in Exodus 9:32, Ezekiel 4:9, and Isaiah 28:25. The success of spelt in Germany is mainly due to the influence of St. Hildegard von Bingen (1098–1179), Doctor of the Church. She said the following about spelt, "Spelt is the best of grains; it contains sufficient fats, provides strength and is easier digestible than any other grain. It makes man's spirit cheerful and serene. No matter how it is prepared, be it as bread or otherwise, it always tastes good and sweet." Saint Hildegard von Bingen was a Benedictine abbess, and a mystic. Her work continues to be studied by theologians and philosophers. Her work is also active in classical Gregorian music, botany and cosmology. See the spelt recipe in its entirety in the Appendix at the back of the book.

[3] Bread machines allow you to make bread in 2 or 3 hours, depending on the machine. Those who fast can choose their flour and produce "homemade bread" without spending too much time on it. Plus, you cover the cost of the machine by saving your health, keeping in good spirits and longevity!

Matthew accepted the challenge. "I followed your advice," he wrote to me later. "The other day, after I decided to buy a bread machine and spelt, I went to my local bakery to get some information on it and saw some loaves of spelt bread on the display shelf. It was a Tuesday, so I bought enough for the next day, Wednesday, but with no conviction that it would work. Wednesday morning I cut into my new spelt bread with the firm resolution to eat only bread until the next morning. At morning Mass, I entrusted my fasting to Jesus, so that He would help me. It was miraculous! The bread alone was enough. I fueled up all day on it. What a marvel! I was amazed to pass morning, noon, and night on spelt bread with a little honey and water.

"The fasting wasn't difficult. On the contrary, it was astonishing because I hadn't suffered my usual upset stomach. I had a very good night, as though I had eaten normally at dinner, and woke up at 7 in the morning with no heaviness in my stomach. What's more, the entire day, Thursday, was spent in joy. I then committed myself to fasting on Wednesdays and Fridays for the intentions of our heavenly Mother. And to think it took me 17 years to find this recipe! Maybe it was a gift from St. Therese as well, because I had to live in Lisieux to find a bakery that made this kind of bread. Fasting is no longer servitude but a source of joy that my wife shares with me."

Matthew was not afraid to leap into the water. All too often we want to understand a message from Mary, or a verse from the Bible, before putting it into practice. What a mistake! We miss so many graces that way. If Heaven asks us to do something, what do we have to fear? Certainly, we have to organize ourselves in a way that allows us to live peacefully, looking for methods that are best adapted to our health, our families, etc., but it is only in living out the message that we discover the new horizons that are hidden within it. There are secrets that don't reveal themselves until we act with confidence.

Fasting without love means you are just on a diet!

20

Saint Joseph, Please Give
Us a Sign of Your Goodness!

*Statue of Saint Joseph in the author's
oratory in Medjugorje. © EDM 2009)*

4,000 DOLLARS? BUT THAT'S a huge amount of money! Our account in America is already in the red. It's a catastrophe!

It was March 19, 2003, and our little fraternity had just finished a novena to our dear Saint Joseph, not a nine-day novena, but a thirty-day novena! For a whole month we had been passing on to him some very serious prayer intentions (and there's no lack of them in Medjugorje), since he excels in intercession before God. That's no secret to anyone. He so loves to help those who put their trust in him! Also, knowing his great natural tenderness, we didn't shy away from asking him, during those thirty days to "Please, give us a sign of your goodness!" The bad news, therefore, hit hard, on the very day we were celebrating his Solemnity! And I took him to task over it: "Saint Joseph, is this how you give us a sign of your goodness? I don't understand what you're trying to tell us!"

The fact is that we had just received a message from a person who had worked as a volunteer for us for a year in the States, but who later turned against us. (These things happen sometimes and it's always hurtful.) The message from this person was very clear: she was asking us to pay her for her hours of work, her travel expenses, mileage, etc. and to send her a bank transfer of $4000.00. At this news, there was an outcry in the house: "But that's impossible! It's not fair! How can she ask for that?"

I have to admit that, shocked as I was myself by this announcement, I had to struggle against the sadness that invaded me, because it was out of the question that this beautiful feast day should be marred in any way! But one question kept bothering me, because never in the past had Saint Joseph left us at such an impasse: "What is he cooking up for us? I can't believe this is his last word. No doubt he's hiding something from us, but what?"

A passage from the Gospels worked its way, little by little into my mind, a very short verse, but one of the most clear ... too clear! At first, I tried to ignore it completely. 'Those words of Jesus have nothing to do with this situation,' I told myself. However, like waves that unceasingly lap calmly against the shore every ten seconds, Jesus' words constantly returned to my mind. Like a leitmotif, they quietly insinuated themselves, despite all my efforts to chase them away. I had no choice but to take them seriously!

"Give to whoever is asking of you." Jesus said these words in his discourse on loving your enemies in Luke 6:30. The decision, therefore, was obvious to me. It was inescapable. I gathered the household together and took a deep breath …

"So, there it is, we're going to give her the $4000 dollars! If we are in Medjugorje to live out the messages and we don't live out the Word of God when it becomes demanding, we are hypocrites. What's more, if this bomb has exploded on the Feast of St. Joseph, for sure he will get us out of this. The ball is in his court."

I'll skip the reactions that this little speech provoked, since the reality was, we just didn't have the money in our American account. But we knew that the Lord is and always will be a banker outside of the norm, who invites one to give even what one does not have, and who also knows how to multiply things when required.

The next day I had to leave for Rome for several days, and the question that occupied my mind had evolved, "Saint Joseph, how are we going to get out of this? Now your honor is at stake, don't abandon us!"

As soon as I arrived in Rome, I hurried to a chapel, hoping to attend evening Mass. Having arrived five minutes late, I sat down to listen to the first reading when I noticed a person gesturing to me from a distance with friendly motions. She seemed to be a foreigner. When Mass was over, she ran towards me and spoke to me with extreme kindness. This lady was from the United States. "I'm only paying a flying visit to Rome," she said. "And here I find you in this little chapel! I can't believe my eyes! I have all of your CD's, and for years I've been nurtured with what you have produced in America!" We then had a very pleasant conversation after which she asked me how things were going with our apostolate in the United States. I let her know that we had brought out a new book in English, but that all was not rosy over there, as one of the volunteers was giving us trouble. Without any other explanation on my part, and like a ball on the rebound, she replied, "How much is she asking for?" "Oh, an extravagant amount!" I said.

"How much?" she insisted. "$4000.00!"

At that moment, physically touching Saint Joseph would not have had a greater effect! Was I dreaming? I watched as this woman opened her purse, took out her checkbook, and signed a check, after filling in the sum in question. I stood there, flabbergasted, embarrassed, dumbfounded, not knowing what to say. The whole thing was taken care of in the space of three minutes.

Saint Joseph, thank you for this sign of your goodness! To bestow it, it barely took you twenty-four hours. You were waiting, no doubt, that we ourselves first showed a sign of goodness towards your son Jesus by accepting His word? My guess is that you also wanted to please Him, while you were at it, by helping us to grow in our trust of Him! You simply added the gift of a spiritual grace to the material gift of dollars. Once more, you have surprised and delighted us. I can easily imagine you at Nazareth, while you were teaching your little Yeshoua the Torah, might you not already have told him, "Give to whoever asks of you?" That's what you practiced yourself, right?

Now I know you a little better, and I know that you never fail to come to the aid of those who pray to you with sincerity. And when one of those in your care finds themselves in need, if you seem late in responding, they should never believe that you are there with your arms crossed doing nothing. No, it's because you are concocting some surprise that is going to surpass their hopes!

In the Heart of China

During my trips to China, I've noticed how avidly some Chinese people devour everything that has to do with Christ and his evangelical message. From the time of Matteo Ricci until today, the Christian faith has never been extinguished there, and it has given the Church some magnificent figures, both confessors and martyrs.[1] I can't wait to get to Heaven to hear from their own mouths the astonishing stories of their lives of faith. They are a hard-working, jovial, and extremely courageous people.

Among the hundreds and hundreds of millions of Chinese "who do not yet know the love of God" (to use the Blessed Mother's own expression when referring to unbelievers), there are some who have had the grace of encountering God, living and true. This God then becomes for them an inestimable treasure. In the midst of the dense darkness that crushes this country in so many ways, they know that yes, truly, there exists a Creator of the universe who loves mankind! There exists a Heaven where eternal happiness reigns! There exists a Spirit that is holy and that can live within us and guide us! Each person has a soul that is made to love, and this soul is immortal! There exists a God who became man on our earth to save us and to take us with Him, a God who has come among us, who has spoken to us, and who shows us the path to follow in order to be with Him, a God who was able to raise the dead! There exists a God who is the

---

[1] The Servant of God, Matteo Ricci, was a Jesuit priest who was among the first to introduce Christianity to China. The cause for his beatification opened in 1984.

true King of the universe and before whom every knee will bend! Our time on earth is only a brief passage where even suffering has an eternal meaning and value! Yes, truly, all this exists![2]

For them, compared to the dreariness of an existence at the bottom rung of an earthly life with no future, this life of faith is pure gold! What extraordinary perspectives they acquire by discovering faith in the true God! These people have suffered so much that they know the difference between real gold and fake. How could they give up their precious Christian faith for values that are deceptive and transient?

Saint Joseph is loved so much in China, that, among the boys born into Christian families, a great number of them receive the name Joseph. If you don't happen to know the name of a priest, call him Father Joseph, and fifty percent of the time you'll be right! In return, St. Joseph is not stingy with them.

Among the many Jesuit Priests over the centuries who travelled across China inspiring the people there, one Austrian brother stands out, Brother Gervasius. In 1976 he gave an account that could be found in the stories from the lives of the saints.[3]

In Southern China, Brother Gervasius had accompanied Father Gotsch, another Jesuit Priest, who was going to the home of a dying man in Kaotai. They needed to cross 200 kilometers of mountains and hills on horseback to arrive at the house. But when they presented themselves, they were

---

[2] When she first came to Medjugorje, in the midst of the Communist regime, Our Lady declared, "I have come to tell the world that God exists, and that He is Life!" (June, 1981).

[3] Adapted from the German magazine Weite Welt, January 1976.

too late. The man had already died. They stayed to bury him, and after the burial they took to the road again. Halfway home they encountered a young man who seemed to be waiting for them on the side of the road. The man asked them to follow him to his sick mother's house. They followed him for nearly 15 kilometers to a little village. There, in a ramshackle dwelling, a woman was dying. Seeing the priest, she asked him,

"Stranger, will you tell me the truth, if I ask you a question?" "Certainly, Mother."

"Does there exist a God in which there are three persons? Does there exist another life, with a place of happiness for good, and a place of terror for the bad? Is it true that God came to this earth to die for mankind and open for them this place of happiness? Stranger, is it true, all of that?" Stupefied, the priest answered, "Yes!" But he wondered from whom this woman could have learned all of that?

The sick woman continued, "You have the water with you. Wash me so I can go into the place of happiness!"

Brother Gervasius couldn't understand how she knew that the priest had holy water, to use for baptisms, with him. Her determined attitude had something childish, but convincing about it. The priest briefly explained the liturgy to her and the meaning of the sacrament, then he baptized her.

The sick woman, continued full of joy, "You also have the bread with you. It's special bread, because God is inside it. Give me some of this bread!" The priest took from his bag the consecrated host that he carried with him. The sick woman knew that he had "the Bread"! The priest explained the meaning of the sacrament of the Eucharist to her, and gave her holy communion. He also gave her the last rites (the confession of sins and the anointing of the sick). Then he said to her, "Up until now you have been asking all the questions. Now it's my turn to ask you some! From whom did you learn the truths of the faith? Did you meet some Catholic believers?"

"No, Stranger."

"So, you have read Christian books?"

"I don't know how to read, stranger, and I didn't even know books like that existed."

"So, from where, and from whom did you acquire this knowledge of the faith?"

"I have always thought that that is the way it should be, and for the past ten years I have lived that way. I have also instructed my sons in this way, and you can wash all of them," (she meant baptize them).

"But you knew that we would be passing near here to-day?"

"Of course! I saw a man in a dream, and it was he who told me to send my youngest son out to the road, and to call to the two strangers who would pass by. He told me that they were going to "wash" me so that I could go to the place of happiness after death."

The missionaries were profoundly touched. The attitude of this woman facing death was so peaceful that there was no room for doubt. Before leaving, the missionaries offered her a picture of Saint Joseph, patron saint of the dying. Filled with joy, she cried out, "But this is him! I know him! He has often come to visit me. He was the one who told me to send my son to the road to call you!"

She didn't know if it had been a dream, or if St. Joseph really came to visit her in person. In any case, that wasn't the important thing. The important thing was what St. Joseph had taught the sick woman. The missionaries learned later that the woman died that very night.

The Young and Healthy
Saint Joseph in the Limelight

A very ancient Jewish law prohibited men from marrying women who were a lot younger than they were. In general, the age gap couldn't be more than five, six, or seven years. It is obvious then that St. Joseph could not have been the old man so often represented by painters. He had to have been healthy and fit enough to flee to Egypt in the night with a very young spouse and a newborn; but also, once in Egypt, he had to ensure at least a meager subsistence for his family. Local traditions in Egypt depict St. Joseph as a responsible man who was forced to constantly evade Herod's spies. Herod, knowing that he had missed his target despite the massacre of the innocents in Bethlehem, never stopped searching for the little King of the Jews that he feared so much! The Holy Family had to travel thousands of kilometers in the space of four years before the death of Herod. Later, in Nazareth, Saint Joseph had to start again from zero, rebuilding a life for his family, taking up again his beautiful trade of builder and carpenter. Every day in his workshop he had to lift heavy loads, beams, paneling, carts, furniture and other objects he had built, as well as delivering them to his customers. Was it not he who taught Jesus to carry heavy beams on his shoulders, thus preparing him for his sorrowful walk towards Golgotha?

21

You Were the Only Ones on the Set

THIS AMAZING STORY BEGAN with a telephone call I received in Normandy, France, in the fall of 1989.

The national television channel *Antenne 2* made a proposal to several members of my Community that we participate in their program on homosexuality, which was to take place several weeks later. During this call, I received an inner conviction that we should respond, and that certitude remained strong in me. Of course, I was aware that if we had been invited as a Catholic community, it was probably in order to use us to ridicule the Church. My Superior himself put me on guard, but seeing my conviction, he accepted the deal, and we made our way over to the show *Stars à la Barre*. There were three of us, one of whom was a doctor.

The studios were located on the top floor of a very high tower in Paris. My heart was pounding because I was not familiar with the question of homosexuality and its ramifications, and I felt like a fish out of water in this arena. For several days I had been devouring some documents on the topic, but I wasn't that much more knowledgeable having done so.

Several key people were in the studio, on the set with us, who had a lot to do with our topic, including a Catholic priest practicing homosexuality, and a Protestant pastor in charge of a congregation where he blessed homosexual unions. The pastor brought along with him a short video that illustrated his views. (This man was murdered two years later over sex offences.) There was also a writer, a lawyer, and the famous David Girard, (the "emperor" of gay culture in the '80s who founded a corporate chain that included gay restaurants, bars, saunas, massage parlors, and a newspaper.) He was the most virulent against the Catholic Church, and against us, letting loose several violent and carefully poisoned diatribes during the show.

As we expected, the microphones that had been assigned to us were often cut when we wanted to talk. The entire program went in the direction of a glorification of homosexual practices, justifying the situation of gay people with the intention of passing new laws in their favor. Even so, we were able to fit into the discussion several important points. Eventually, the studio lights went down, and it was time to head home. We began down the stairs to the basement to put on our coats and leave.

It was then that an event of the most unexpected kind took place. David Girard came towards me to shake my hand very warmly. He looked me straight in the eye and said to me in a tone which left no doubt of its sincerity: "I congratulate you, because you three were the only ones on the set speaking the truth!" I stood there mute, stupefied! In his look, I had seen a window of real purity. Then he disappeared very quickly into the night, and I left the place with my two brothers without saying another word.

Upon my return to Medjugorje, this memory haunted me, and I never stopped praying for David. That prayer kept coming back to me without any provocation. It was stronger than me. I was pleading with the Lord constantly on behalf of David, especially because of that moment of light captured in his look. That spontaneous intercession was so firmly entrenched in me that I ended up asking myself a question: "Does the Lord want me to meet with David?" I decided to try. I obtained his contact details from the office of *Antenne*

2, and I wrote him a simple letter saying that I wanted to know him better, and proposed that I share something of my life with him. He answered by return mail with a kind note in which he invited me to meet him at the most fashionable tea salon on the *Rue de Rivoli,* at the *Angelina* the next time I was in Paris.

What a memorable encounter! David took me into his confidence and opened up his heart. I learned details about his childhood and his adolescence that he had never made public, and I understood also, that in the area of religion, he knew nothing. I mean absolutely nothing. The most fundamental ideas had escaped him completely, so he bombarded me with questions about God.

Seeing the excellent turn that our conversation was taking, I finally asked him the question that had been burning on my lips for a long time, "After the show, when you said goodbye, you added, 'I congratulate you because you were the only ones on the set speaking the truth!' Why, then, did you attack us with so much virulence during the show?" "But ... because so many of my fans were there, watching! I really had to do my job! I made up the whole show for them, but deep inside I knew well that you were the ones telling the truth!"

I don't think he took into account the enormity of what he had just thrown at me. An enormity that we should keep in mind today and spread widely! During our conversation, every five minutes he would say, "You should make movies. You would come across very well on the big screen." (At the time I was only doing audio cassettes, happily hidden in our tiny studio, without the least desire to be filmed!) David's curiosity and his somewhat innocent opening up to the things of God impressed me. He said to me, "This world is disgusting! I've had it with all this filth! I love purity! But since that doesn't exist on this earth, I can't wait to leave it! It wouldn't bother me at all to die. In you, I see purity. You really ought to put yourself on the big screen, people need people like you!"

Our conversation became so intense that we didn't even realize that everyone else had left, and the tea room was closing. We had to leave too, but we didn't even consider shortening our exchange! We were so avid to follow up on our discoveries that we walked around the block several times. I said to myself: 'if his fans could see him conversing like this with a nun, they would really be taken aback.'

I invited him to spend a weekend with us in my community in Normandy, so he could see with his own eyes the life we had there as brothers and sisters. He accepted with joy. But eventually he couldn't come on the weekend we planned, because the doctors had put him on morphine for an extremely painful throat malady. I understood on the telephone that he had probably contracted AIDS. Since I had to return to Medjugorje, I promised I would visit him on my next trip to Paris.

A date was set for three months later, and when the day came, I told David that I would not be coming alone to meet him this time, but that I would be with a good friend of mine, a priest, because this friend could tell him more about life with God. So, the dialogue promised to be very interesting. At the last minute David let me know that he would not be receiving us at his business office, but in his private residence because he was still unwell. When the priest and I arrived at his home, we discovered an immense triplex, the height of Parisian chic. David welcomed us warmly, but I noticed with sadness that he had shrunk by half, and I had to face the evidence: this would be my last meeting with him on earth. In other words, the priest and I had only one hour to prepare him to meet face to face with his Creator and to brief him on the ultimate purpose of man.

Since I had just returned from a meeting in Austria with Maria Simma, a peasant who was receiving visits from the souls in purgatory, I used the excuse of my interview with her to share with him a few of the realities about heaven, purgatory, and hell.[1] With the help of concrete examples, this was a highly condensed version of the basic catechism on the immortality of the soul, the immense mercy of God the Father, and the tremendous desire of Jesus to welcome him, David, into His heart, which burned with love. David listened attentively. I spoke to him also about the power of the Mass, of pardon for sins, and of the free choice each person makes at the moment of his death, for his eternity.

The priest who accompanied me launched into a very realistic description of his work with young people who gather each year at a school for Evangelization. I witnessed then a most unexpected scene, worthy of the best hours of evangelization: a fraternal dialogue between the idol of the gay community and this priest, who presented with serene calmness the benefits of chastity among the young. Those who say that life with God is boring should revise their opinion! A great friendship was born between these two men, who hadn't had the same life journey, to say the least! God's sense of humor is so touching!

Despite his physical exhaustion, David listened to each of our words like an earnest little schoolboy discovering the world with his teacher, and didn't even notice time passing. At the end, he got up, went to the white wall near his chair, pointed it out to us with his finger and said, "Well, I am like

---

[1] See The Amazing Secret of the Souls in Purgatory, about my interview with Maria Simma. It can be purchased on our website: www.sisteremmanuel.org. See works from the same author page 397.

a white canvas. God, if you want to write something on it, do so, I am ready!" Then we had to leave to allow David to stick with his schedule of rest. But stepping out of the door, the priest turned around and shouted out to him, "My brother! You are not far from the Kingdom of God!"

When I returned to Medjugorje, I continued to keep David in my prayers. During my next trip to Paris several months later I called his office. One of his close collaborators, whom I had met previously, told me, "Oh, Sister! David died four days ago (August 23, 1990), and we buried him yesterday. It's a pity that you missed him by such a short time. But I have to tell you, Sister, that we, his friends, were struck by everything he told us about you and your friend who came to see him. On his deathbed he repeated that he had never met people like you, and that you were pure, and that you knew the real things about life. He said that you had something that he wanted. He spoke of you two with great admiration. What's more, he surprised us! He said that when he died, he wanted a funeral Mass said for him. So a lot of his friends retaliated asking him, 'A Mass! But that just doesn't make sense! Have you become a Catholic?' To which he forcefully replied, 'I'm not asking your advice. I'm asking you for a Mass, and you'll have to do it!'

"Sister, you should have seen him! He persisted in spite of the criticism of his friends! We didn't understand what was happening to him, but that was it. He wanted a Mass! We wanted to honor his last wishes, and so we looked for a church to have his funeral Mass. Since he was going to be buried in his grandmother's cemetery, we asked at that Parish. After asking a number of questions about his life, the priest accepted. He also wanted to read the biography of his life that David himself had written. He celebrated the Mass, and afterwards we all went to the cemetery. Give me your address, Sister, I'll send you his death announcement."

When I received the announcement, I decided to call the pastor of that parish to ask him how he had managed the burial and how the Mass had gone. He answered me, "The Mass? But there was no Mass! When I read David's biography and found out about his lifestyle … there was no question of saying a Mass!" I swallowed hard and asked him in a livid voice, "So what did you do?"

"I said a simple blessing, that's all." "And who participated in this prayer?

"Ah, well Sister, they were all there, all his friends, the church was full. There were at least 200 of them, all with their pierced ears …"

In shock, I murmured a vague thank you before hanging up. I could hardly believe what I had just heard. 200 sheep who had never set foot in a church, and there they were gathered in a church, and no Mass! Right away I picked up the telephone and dialed the number of my priest friend who had met David. We couldn't steal David's Mass from him, not after he had acknowledged himself to Jesus in front of his friends, right up until his death!

"Listen, Father," I said. "David asked for a Mass, and he will have a Mass! Do you realize that he had turned his heart towards Jesus, and that he had understood the importance of the Mass? Could you offer a Mass for him? Please!"

"Certainly! We'll get all his friends together again and say a great Mass for them in Paris, you'll see."

I don't know how the priest managed to sound the alarm for all of David's friends. I only know that several months later, he celebrated the Mass in one of the raciest areas of Paris, in the little church of Saint Leu, surrounded by David's biggest supporters. He asked me to say a word of introduction. Then, before praying the *Our Father,* he prostrated himself on the floor in front of the altar and asked pardon from those assembled, in the name of the Church, for all those times when priests had expressed contempt for homosexuals or had rejected them. Many of those present wept, and the homily that followed brought out even more handkerchiefs.

The priest managed to stay in contact with a number of David's friends, and in the following years he accompanied several of them spiritually as they were dying from AIDS. He visited them when they were in the hospital and helped them to turn towards God. One of them was the director of a gay theatre near that church. After meeting the priest, he left that job, and changed his life.

I understood why the Lord had invited us to participate in the TV show *Stars à la barre*. We were not stars, far from it, and the bar was too high for us. But we were carrying inside of us Him who is the "Sun" of Justice. And, this "Sun" knew that, on the set, one of His beloved sons was hungry for His rays! One of His children was longing for Him in the world of the night, without knowing it.

22

The Jack Attack

"Dear children, Satan wants to work still more fiercely to take away your joy from each one of you. By prayer you can completely disarm him and ensure your happiness."

(MESSAGE OF JANUARY 24, 1985)

THIS PARABLE IS SET in Limousin, in the heart of France, in the '90s. A man was in a hurry. He needed to get to his sister's house as quickly as possible, and he had a good four-hour journey to get to her village. Very little traffic on the narrow roads in this part of France, which was nested deep in the hills of the countryside, made it the perfect time to leave!

The man checked the entire car over: the oil, the water, the brakes, etc. Then he asked his son to put the spare tire that was lying around in the garage, back into the trunk of the car. After a nice strong coffee prepared by his wife, the man took off. He had only traveled a few miles when his mind took him to the evening he was about to spend with his sister, and his heart filled with joy at the thought of a 24-hour break from his daily routine.

Two hours later … the front left wheel punctured. 'Oh, of course this had to happen to me today!' He thought. 'Fortunately, my son put the spare tire in the trunk!' The man opened the trunk, took out the spare and, in vain, looked for the jack. After checking every single nook and cranny in the car, he had to face the obvious: his son had forgotten the jack. So it was impossible for him to change the tire!

What was he supposed to do? The place was deserted. There was no hope of finding a garage for miles. The man didn't waste time over negative thoughts about his absent-minded son, but set about finding a solution as quickly as possible. Should he hitchhike? But there was no-one around to pass by, except a few cows and lots of sheep.

As a natural doer, the man decided to walk all the way to SaintSulpice-les-Champs because he remembered that there was a garage at the beginning of that village. Walking at a good pace, he remained quite calm until a thought struck him. 'A jack, how much will that cost? Oh well, it shouldn't be too bad. I can probably get one for 20 or 30 dollars.'

He started walking faster and had covered close to a mile, when suddenly a second thought seized him: 'Oh, I am completely crazy. There is no way I will find a decent jack for 25 or 30 dollars. The guy is going to see me coming in, completely out of breath and desperate, and he'll probably charge me 40. That's the way businesses work these days. You can never fully trust them; money is all that matters now!'

The man was starting to get nervous and tired. After all, he's no spring chicken! Just then, another thought came to him: 'Here I am, thinking about 40 dollars, but who's to say that this guy will be satisfied with that? What if he wants 60? What nerve he has to charge me 60 bucks! Seriously, that kind of guy should just disappear from the face of the earth! Making money like that, taking advantage of other people's misfortunes.'

Now the man was clipping along at a double march speed. He was freaking out. His face was sweating and distorted, it looked like he was ready to bite someone's head off. Imagining the whole scene, his blood was boiling with anger;

he was choking on it, frothing at the mouth. Now he was so obsessed that he started talking out loud in a sharp, harsh tone. The animals in the fields watched him with placid expressions. The jack certainly was not *their* problem! "You know what," the man said to himself (and the animals), "I bet he won't sell it to me for $60, he's going to want $90 for that jack, and for sure, he'll refuse to take any less! Let me tell you—I've had it. I'm going to give it to him good and proper! Does he really think I'm just going to cave in? No way my man, just you wait! A punch in the nose is what you'll get! Just great, this is what France has come to! Always the same people raking in the dough! And always the same stupid ones to be paying, paying, paying!"

Suddenly the man spotted the garage, right there on the edge of the village. Boiling with rage and forgetting how exhausted he was, he started running very fast. Getting to the garage door, he flung it open and started yelling at the young girl of 18 employed there, "You know what?! At that price, your damn jack, you can keep it for yourself!"

The poor girl understood that there was a problem with a jack, so she walked over to the display very calmly and took out a brand-new jack, where the man saw a little fluorescent yellow label showing the price: *On Sale $15.00 reduced from $23.99!*

Much of our suffering is due to our imagination, which we call, in French, the "crazy lady upstairs," or the chattering of the mind. Starting with an event, we create a whole film in our mind of the worst possible scenario, which would actually be painful if it happened, and then we start anticipating the pain. A pain that is completely self-manufactured!

This is what we call *the Jack attack:* a great parable that warns us of who we can become when we face a difficult challenge. When the evil one, with the help of our restless imagination, injects doses, drop-by-drop, of his own storage of poisons—anger, hate, bitterness, and even despair—into our minds, we often do not realize, as it is happening, that this whole messy process is going on inside of us. This slow and subtle accumulation of poison ends up completely disconnecting us from reality and we get locked up in our own bubble.

In my community, when a brother starts getting agitated and worried about an imaginary misfortune that will probably not play out, we tell him, "stop it with your Jack attack!" That simple phrase opens his eyes to the trap he is falling into, and so, surrounded by all our smiling faces, he immediately jumps back into reality.

23

A Tree That Falls

"A tree that falls makes more noise than 1000 trees that grow."

(CHINESE PROVERB)

LET'S SUPPOSE THAT A prayer group, a community, or an association consists of 100 members, and one of them brings scandal into the community because he or she is a pedophile. Very soon you will hear whispered, "We have to avoid that group. It's made up of a bunch of pedophiles!" The harm unleashed by those whispered rumors is immeasurable!

Several years ago the Lord gave me a lesson, which remains forever engraved in my memory. One morning, in Medjugorje, I went to the 10 o'clock English Mass. I noticed that the priest celebrated the Mass with enthusiasm and with a strong anointing of the Holy Spirit. It brought great joy to my heart. But in the afternoon, I saw him near the church in a tender embrace with a very beautiful woman, with whom he was obviously in love. My eyes popped … It really was him! I was perplexed but prayed for him and said nothing. The next day I went to the Mass in English again. And it was again he who celebrated it, with the same fervor. And again I saw him later seated on one of the exterior benches of the church, looking tenderly into the eyes of this same beautiful girl. My prayer for him became more intense. Despite my desire to speak about it in my community, so that everyone could pray for this priest during this bad time I decided not to say anything to anyone. (Here I would like to take a moment to share a general rule. Basically it is this: sometimes a subtle temptation may come over us to invite someone close to us to pray for another person. Of course, the intention is under the pretext of doing good, for that person. Then, slowly, slowly, we start to list a number of sins that we *think* this person has committed. It goes like this: "You know, we have to pray for such and such, because if you knew …" And then the deadly gossip begins!)[1]

I was worried for this priest. I couldn't understand how he could live this double life so easily. He never even tried to hide himself!

Several days later, I saw both the priest and the "lover" in fraternal conversation near the church. Oh my!! To my great surprise they were actually twins and looked almost identical! I immediately began re-thinking all I could have said about this bizarre priest, and with what ease I could have destroyed his reputation, or at least dealt it a terrible blow. The fear of God came over me when I understood the rapidity with which our tongues can destroy, in several seconds, a beautiful work of God.

A story from the life of Saint Philip Neri, a master of self-denial, who is often cited by Mother Teresa, casts an interesting light on our use of language. There was a woman in Rome who hated a certain community and its founder (Philip Neri), because her daughter had entered that community against her advice. In fact, this woman had contrived wonderful marriage plans for her daughter, and schemed to have her leave religious life, alleging all sorts of misdeeds by

---

[1] In precise cases where it is a question of preventing danger, one must speak; but always with the aim of protecting a third party, never of spreading a tale of evil committed by a brother. This gossip is profoundly displeasing to God.

this community. But one day, she had a pang of conscience and went to confess her sins to Father Philip. She admitted her deceptions and her calumnies.

Then Father said to her, "Before I give you absolution, go to the marketplace and buy a hen. Pluck its feathers carefully and bring it back to me." The woman did as he said and brought the plucked hen to the priest, who said to her, "Now return to the marketplace and gather up all the feathers of this hen!"

"But," answered the woman. "That's impossible! The wind has carried them all away!"

"Exactly, " answered Philip. "You understand now what calumny brings about: it spreads everywhere, like feathers in the wind! Its consequences are beyond repair! "

Gloria Polo

At a Marian Conference I met Gloria Polo, a dentist from Bogota, Columbia, who has a striking story. She had developed a certain egotism, and a fierce pride because of her great beauty, her wealth, and her superior intelligence. She was contemptuous of others, detested priests, and mocked God. She had trampled on all the commandments of God, one after the other, and she had taught others to do the same.

In the midst of a terrible storm one day, she was fatally struck by lightning and found herself in a state beyond this life. When she arrived in the other world, she saw herself sinking down into a bottomless well of darkness. She knew that she was headed for Hell. But just before the threshold, through some unique grace, she remembered a few words that one of her patients told her, "Gloria, you are very materialistic. Someday, you'll have problems with God! Always remember: God is merciful, so cry out to Him to obtain His forgiveness!" Gloria began to cry out, "Lord, forgive me! Please give me a second chance!"

At that exact moment she was pulled upward by an invisible force, and she felt herself moving up towards the light. Then she saw Jesus. He spoke to her and entrusted to her a mission to be completed on earth. She began to revive, and her body that had been so torn apart in the accident, was miraculously restored.[2] The Lord revealed to her what she needed to know to accomplish a great mission in the Church. She then became the opposite of what she had been before. Her testimony is so authentic, powerful, and convincing that—I have seen it with my own eyes—hundreds of people go to confession after hearing her!

Ever since that overpowering experience, Gloria has lived as a saint. She got the message! Her story is rich, only an entire book would do it justice. Here, I will stick to one striking example of her current behavior. It occasionally happens that she finds herself at a meal or a meeting with people who, little by little, let their tongues loosen, and divert the conversation into criticism. Hearing that, and without saying anything to anyone, Gloria suddenly leaves the table and goes into another room where she prays fervently. Upon being questioned about this action, which is surprising and somewhat impolite, she admits simply that such conversations make her blood boil, and she feels obligated to run away from them! She explains to anyone who will listen that slander—and even worse, calumny—is a horror before God, and she describes what terrible suffering

---

[2] Gloria's medical records substantiate the terrible impact of the lightning strike on her body, and that she was officially dead and came back to life.

souls (whom she saw during her passage in the world beyond) have to endure to be purified of this sin.[3]

Saint Faustina Kowalska reveals to us several virtues of silence that are often hidden. She writes, "Silence is a sword in spiritual combat: a talkative soul will never reach sainthood. The sword of silence will cut away all that wants to attach itself to the soul. We are sensitive to what is spoken, and, being sensitive, we want to respond immediately, without asking ourselves if it is the will of God for us to speak. The silent soul is strong: if it perseveres in silence, no vexation will touch it. The silent soul is capable of uniting itself to God in the most profound way. It almost always lives under the inspiration of the Holy Spirit. In the silent soul, God acts without encountering any obstacle."[4]

But What Are We Going to Talk About?

During a mission in Italy, surrounded by a dozen friends at a meal, I suggested that we should not talk about food but try to bring up topics, which could enlighten our souls and therefore help us grow. Of course, we all had in our hearts the desire to talk about Jesus, about what He had helped us understand through the Gospel, or through an event in our lives, so the result of my proposal came more quickly than I thought! At the end of the meal, it was difficult to leave each other because everyone wanted to go deeper into these topics; our hearts were so on fire! A little like the pilgrims at Em-

---

[3] For more information on Gloria Polo, see her website: www.gloriapolo.com.

[4] Maria Faustina Kowalska, Diary, § 477.

maus, the presence of Jesus in the midst of us was tangible, and we wanted to say to Him, "More! Stay with us longer!"

It works well to decide this just before the meal. We have fallen into the habit of sitting down at the table without reflecting on the greatness of the special time for meals planned by God. We blurt out every little thought that crosses our minds, and so we talk about petty things, or, even worse, we talk unkindly about our neighbors! However, that time together can be a marvelous moment of sharing, in which each person helps to build up the Kingdom of God in his neighbor at the table. If we decide to do this during the blessing, which precedes the meal, we notice very quickly that God comes to the gathering (all too happy to be invited, for once) and that the meal takes a whole new turn!

A Croatian grandmother had the custom of going to Mass every day. When she returned home she would share with her family what the priest had said during the homily. At the beginning of the apparitions in Medjugorje, she couldn't get to church for health reasons, but her family went. When they got back, the grandmother asked them what Father Jozo Zovko (the pastor at the time) had said. Now on that day, Father had asked all the parishioners to commit to not saying a single negative word against another person for the entire rest of the evening. When she heard this, the grandmother cried out spontaneously, "But, then what are we going to talk about?"

When Jesus was on earth He Himself loved mealtimes. What a beautiful opportunity for us, also, to make it a time of blessing instead of a time to fill the vacuum with idle words, or talk that is offensive to God. I often notice that Jesus honors the desire of anyone who asks, "Lord, make use of me during this meal so that it may all be for your glory!"

Pope Francis is very clear when it comes to slander. He exhorts everyone around him to ban it because it destroys unity.[5] He used the occasion of the Feast of Saint Michael to address clearly the problem of gossip. This Archangel is, of course, the patron saint of the Swiss Guards, charged with security at the Vatican.

That day, the pope invited the guardsmen to add another battle to their current responsibility of protection: the battle against gossip and slander, two spiritual maladies which sow discord and destroy the unity so dear to Christ. "I ask you not only to defend these doors, these windows of the Vatican, but also, like your patron Saint Michael, the doors to the hearts of those who work at the Vatican, where temptation can enter. I would like to say to you—I say it for everyone, for myself, for all—it's a temptation, which greatly pleases the devil: the temptation against unity; the unity of those who live and work at the Vatican. The devil seeks to create internal war, a sort of civil and spiritual war. That war isn't waged with the weapons we are familiar with, but with tongues. I ask you to defend us mutually against gossip. In concrete terms, this defense consists in not speaking ill against one another and never listening to slander. And if I hear that someone is maligning people, I will stop him! This is not accepted here; go to Saint Anne's gate, leave and do your gossiping over there! Here, no!"

---

[5] Pope Francis, Homily, November 29, 2013. See the homily and hear a snippet from it translated in English: https://www.youtube.com/embed/AwUhXzokGmM?version=3& f=user_uploads&app=youtube_gdata&wmode=transparent& rel=0

24

To See or Not to See the Child

"Whatever you did for one of these least brothers of mine,
you did for me."

(MATT 25: 40)

To SEE OR NOT to see the Child! Among the Gospa's
faithful apostles, physicians and all kinds of specialists,
one of them, a famous cardiologist and defender of life, told
us this unusual story:

A woman 6 months pregnant was sent to him for cardiac
advice because a fetal ultrasound suggested that there was a
problem with the baby. After expert collaboration, the Doctor confirmed the presence of a cardiac malformation in the
fetus. But he reassured the family saying that the malfor-

mation is something quite operable, with a very good chance of success. He added that this type of heart malformation is associated with Down syndrome in 30% of cases. The couple decided to have an amniocentesis done (biopsy of the amniotic fluid surrounding the baby), to see whether their child had Down syndrome, and to give some thought as to whether or not they should keep the baby.

The "verdict" of the amniocentesis came: the baby was unquestionably a Down syndrome child. Dr. Sharbel tried to convince the parents to keep the baby because he knew all too well how much pressure physicians, and the majority of medical professionals, put on parents by presenting abortion as the unique option for parents who have children with genetic malformations.

Despite Dr. Sharbel's insistence that the couple keep the baby, the couple decided to interrupt the pregnancy at 35 weeks, about 8 months. This meant that labor would be induced, and the child would likely be killed before exiting the maternal womb. Nowadays, the vocabulary is significant in the will to water down the terrible reality. One cannot say that "the life of a human being is condemned to die." Instead, one must refer to a "bad pregnancy" and affirm that the best solution for everyone is "to stop it and have another baby."

The prayer group of Dr. Sharbal and his wife made a dramatic plea to Heaven: that the couple would renounce their intention to abort the pregnancy, and that the child, a creature of God, may see the light of the sun. "D-Day" came for the mother to have the abortion. The day before, our friends had called her to ask how she was doing. There was no changing the couple's mind, they were determined to interrupt the pregnancy, and the mother was to be admitted to the hospital at 7 am the next day. Our friends, brokenhearted by the decision, increased their prayers.

Indeed, their prayers were not said in vain. The next day, at around 3:00 A.M., the mother suddenly had contractions very close to one another and in less than one hour she gave birth at home before being transported to the hospital! The little one had the good idea of being born, spontaneously, a few hours before his execution!

The ambulance took the mother and child to the hospital. The father followed separately. Dr Sharbel arrived at the hospital where he found the parents in the maternity ward in a state of shock. They were overwhelmed holding their baby in their arms and tapping their foreheads saying, "Yesterday we signed his execution ourselves. We were going to kill this little being! We are criminals! We are unworthy of being his parents! Doctor, please, do whatever it takes to save him!" The mother with deep tenderness embraced and kissed the child who was peacefully sleeping against her heart.

Parents, isn't your baby the same person within the womb as he is out of the womb? Why was the sick little baby rejected and condemned to die while he remained hidden in the womb, then when he was born, when he was visible, he had to be kept and protected at any cost? Do we need to wait until we see our baby with our own eyes and hug him with our own arms, to realize that he is a treasure, a creature of God who deserves to live?

Soon after the child, who was able to trick the trap set for him, was born, he was operated on and is now in good health. Even with Down syndrome, he belongs to those saints among us who are a flickering light in the midst of our agitated and materialistic world. Let us not reject them! These children have become rare because we get rid of them before they see the sun, and we believe that to do so will improve our own wellbeing. What a wrong calculation! Can we protect our own wellbeing over the blood of an innocent child? They remind us that the human heart and its huge capacity for love is more important than anything, and that on the last day, it is the innocence of the children that will win over all the destructive Goliaths who spread our sad culture of death. True greatness is on their side, and on the side of those who welcome them!

Hasn't Jesus, the Son of God himself, told us: "Whoever receives this little one in my name, receives Me?" (Luke 9:48)

Prayer to the Infant Jesus

"Infant Jesus, God Child, you came, so small, so vulnerable, so poor, so weak for us. I offer you the fears of my weakness, of my vulnerability, of my smallness, of my poverty. I put down all I am to your Innocent and pure Heart. Yes, I consecrate myself to You child Jesus. King of love I consecrate myself to Your innocence, Your purity. Yes, You are true Love, true beauty, You are The One who does not suspect anything. The innocence of Your gaze will save us! Infant Jesus, save me by your innocence!" [1]

---

[1] Jean-Marc Hammel, a brother of my community who composed this prayer.

25

What Is Your Secret Valentina?

"Dear children, today I invite you all to rejoice in the life which God gives you. Little children, rejoice in God the Creator because He has created you so wonderfully. Pray that your life be a joyful thanksgiving, which flows out of your heart like a river of joy. Little children, give thanks unceasingly for all that you possess, for each little gift which God has given you, so that a joyful blessing always comes down from God upon your life."

(Message of August 25, 1988)

Valentina, 29, comes from the Ukraine. Upon seeing her, you'd believe her to be a "normal," young, girl. However her story is far from ordinary! From an atheist background and marked by the hardcore communism of those regions, she grew up in material poverty and spiritual emptiness. One day, she "won" a green card for admission into the United States![1] She was only 18 years old, and worked as a hairdresser in the Ukraine. So she left, considering the horrible conditions of her life, and not seeing any future in her country. In the beginning it was very hard—she didn't speak a word of English. Her work did not fulfill her,

---

[1] When immigrants enter the United States, they are awarded a green card based on a lottery system where the "winner" is chosen at random.

and a terrible feeling of emptiness overcame her. She asked herself the questions that the Queen of Peace asked all of us on July 2ⁿᵈ 2012, "*In a maternal way I invite you to stop for a moment and reflect on yourselves and on the transience of this, your earthly life. Then reflect on eternity and the eternal beatitude. What do you want? Which way do you want to set out on?*"

In the darkness of her soul, she couldn't help thinking that there was, perhaps, another dimension to life. So she tried saying a few tentative words to a celestial Father, to whom her Ukrainian grandmother used to pray, but who was totally unknown to her, "If you exist, if you are a father, show me!" Through this prayer she received rivers of peace in her heart! Her faith was born! Day after day it increased, and Valentina became a fervent Catholic.

One day she met some pilgrims returning from Medjugorje. Their testimonies inspired in her a deep desire to go there, and in 2007 she undertook the trip. There, her heart was so taken by the presence of Our Lady that she felt strongly moved to make a deal with Her. While praying the rosary at the Statue of the Risen Christ, she consecrated her life to a great mission: to pray for the young people of Ukraine, and to bring them to Medjugorje. This call was crystal clear in her heart. She trusted that on each side Divine Providence would open the hearts and doors for her.

She had found her vocation! She made her way back to her accommodation, full of happiness, and on the path she encountered a man, a stranger, who said to her point blank, "Please excuse me if what I'm going to say to you seems stupid, but I have to say it to you. I sense that you are called to bring the young people of your homeland here to the Gospa. Also, I have been looking for you to tell you I would like to sponsor this mission!" Valentina could not believe her ears! She had committed herself to the mission only moments ago at the Risen Christ! Valentina went back to her homeland to begin her work.

She organized her first pilgrimage in 2008, and all the young people of her parish responded to the call! People's hearts were opened to her purity of heart, her youth, her determination, and especially the anointing of the Holy Spirit, which rested upon her. She dedicated a great deal of time to prayer. Very quickly she was drawn to the poorest of the poor, and God led her into the medical field, where she found enormous moral poverty. The sick were abandoned. With the aid of Divine Providence (she herself had no money), and inspired by Mother Teresa, she undertook the creation of hospices where the sick at the end of their life could regain their dignity. She also proposed to some atheist doctors that they go with her to Medjugorje, and that is how she turned up one day in June of 2011 with 50 pilgrims from a medical organization made up of almost all atheists. The doctors who came were professional abortionists! Valentina clung to the Gospa, who wants to invite all her children, without exception, to come under her maternal mantle.

Among them was a gynecologist in her sixties. She climbed Apparition Hill along with her whole group from the Ukraine. Little did she know that Valentina had prepared a contingency plan inspired by the Gospa for all her pilgrimages—atheist or not. When they arrived at the top, everyone consecrated himself or herself to the Immaculate Heart of Mary! Like everyone else, the gynecologist also consecrated herself. In the evening, back at the hotel, the gynecologist gathered the group together because she wanted to share something very important. Her throat tightened. She had difficulty speaking. She, this VIP who oversaw all the services of her hospital said, "I had scarcely put my foot down on the hill when everything changed before my eyes. The rocks disappeared. The hill was suddenly covered with the bones

and skulls of all the babies I had aborted over forty years.
Look at these hands!" (Here, she stretched out her hands
before the group). "Here are the hands that killed an entire
city!" She was crying and in the room, handkerchiefs came
out, one after another. All the abortionists who were present
retreated into themselves. For the most part, they would leave
changed, converted, intent on stopping abortions, and
walking with God.

Valentina is continuing her beautiful mission. As of today,
400 abortionist doctors have come to Medjugorje at her
beckoning. She doesn't ask for any payment to cover the cost
of the travel, or accommodation, because she doesn't want
the money from innocent blood to be mixed with the grace
the doctors will receive. How does she manage it? Each time
there are new challenges. The money comes at the very
moment it is needed to finance the pilgrimage of these rich
doctors. Since she brought her first pilgrims to Medjugorje,
several hospitals have stopped performing abortions and the
practice of euthanasia. Valentina, and all those who now
support her, have one goal: to cleanse all the hospitals of the
Ukraine from these deadly practices, and to bring down
upon them the blessing of God. She wants to give back to
the doctors of the medical organizations the dignity of their
profession. Today, so many of those hands, which killed
innocent ones, are transformed and Heaven uses them to
protect and promote life![2]

I have never seen the sun spinning in Medjugorje, but this
miracle, the whole world can see it! Valentina is convinced
that this river of grace will not be limited to the Ukraine. Let
us pray for her and her friends, that they may be protected!

---

[2] For more information about these pilgrimages see:
    www.chaliceofmercy.org.

And let us ask on behalf of all nations for the grace of this burning zeal and living faith, which has moved and will move many more mountains!

A Deal with Mary

In 1990, a little before the Balkan War of 1992–1995, which caused so much destruction to our area, I was climbing the hill of Krizevac in order to pray the Stations of the Cross. I came across an engaged couple, Karlo and Daniela, who were to be married the next day in the church at Medjugorje. Karlo's family lived in the hamlet of Sivric, which a lot of French pilgrims know. Daniela is Irish, very devoted, and she chose to become an ex-patriot in order to begin a family with Karlo. But after their marriage, Daniela stayed many hours in the church to pray and to plead, devastated by the fact she did not have children. The years passed, and nothing!

One day, after 5 years without a baby, she was present at an apparition at the home of the visionary, Marija Pavlovic. At that time Marija's apparitions still took place in a little room in her private home. It was then that Daniela, one more time with all her heart, entrusted to Our Lady her desire to be a mother. Suddenly, she felt moved to make a rather audacious deal with her. She said to Our Lady in her heart, "I beg you, give me a child! And if you grant this to me, I will welcome however many you want to give me."

Today Daniela has eight children!

In spite of the war and all the risks involved, Daniela kept her promise. Today, if you walk around Sivric, you will find a bevy of children, (some neighborhoods understood the message and acted accordingly). It's a joy to see! It's also an example for other families, who, unfortunately, are victims of an insidious thought: 'If we have more than two children, we will have to divide our inheritance into more parts, and it won't be enough for them.' What a sad error! Why live as if the Providence of God doesn't exist, or in ignorance of how it works? It is when the step of confidence is made that grace flows down, and it always surprises us.

"Don't be afraid to have children," the Blessed Mother tells us! "The more children you have, the better! You ought to be afraid, instead, of *not* having them when you are *able* to have them … Those who can have children and decide not to have them will regret it grievously in the future," (Messages to Mirjana, 1982).

Is all of Europe, with its incredible human and spiritual riches, going to sink into oblivion and leave its place to others who will remove from its beautiful culture every sign of Christianity? It's not too late to choose life, life as Mary describes to us, true Christian life. All our material goods will be found in a garbage heap one day or another, of that we are sure. Our insurance policies however, (life, health, theft, accident, fire) all kick in *after* misfortune has occurred. For example, health insurance does not prevent sickness, it is only used when you are sick, while our children will be with us always, and will be an immense cause of joy! They will shine without end in a light, which knows no diminishment. Each child is a new creation!

26

An Abortion Refused

"Dear children, today I invite you to decide for God once again and to choose Him before everything and above everything, so that He may work miracles in your life and that day by day your life may become joy with Him. Therefore, little children, pray and do not permit Satan to work in your life through misunderstandings, the non-understanding and nonacceptance of one another. Pray that you may be able to comprehend the greatness and the beauty of the gift of life."

(MESSAGE OF JANUARY 25, 1990)

VALERIE IS AN ACCOUNTANT and lives in Belgium. She came to Medjugorje to give thanks to Our Lady, with her mother and a little boy. Her testimony deserves to be known. Will it save children from the massacre, which is knowingly organized by some doctors? She recounts:

"I found myself pregnant at the age of 29. My family doctor had gone to a conference and could not see me, so I was directed, at 3 weeks of pregnancy, to another doctor whom I did not know. After he carried out the ultrasound, the doctor told me: 'The *fruit* is not good, it is an ectopic pregnancy, and you must go tomorrow to the hospital for an emergency uterine scraping!' When I entered the hospital, I was not convinced that this procedure was necessary. I had a relic of Padre Pio with me. I took it in my hands and while I was praying to him, a very intense inner conviction told me that this procedure was not right and that I should ask for a second opinion.

As I was already wearing the hospital gown and ready to enter the operating room, the voice in my heart would not stop! So I said to the medical assistant that I did not agree with the scraping operation, that it was not right for them to perform it on me, and that I wanted to see my attending physician to have another ultrasound done. My attending physician was in the middle of an operation and was not happy about being interrupted, however I was determined not to have the procedure. Eventually she was free and came to see me. She performed another ultrasound. I was still holding Padre Pio's relic in my hands. I clenched it in my fist because I felt that he was my friend, my anchor in the middle of this unfriendly hospital. The new ultrasound showed that the *fruit* was good, healthy, and safe! My baby was not outside the uterus as the previous doctor had told me. He was actually inside the uterus! But the attending physician informed me that I did not have enough hormones to be able to keep the child. She added that she could not do the scraping since it would result in an abortion, (in Belgium, abortion is illegal). So I was able to escape both the operation and the abortion, and I returned home. I did not undergo hormone treatment and eight months later Jeff was born a perfectly healthy little boy!

"Like his father, Jeff was born on October 1st. He is now 4 years old. His father neither acknowledged him nor saw him because he wanted to avoid having to pay child support. But the Lord allowed Jeff to be born prematurely, on his father's birthday, so that his father will never forget him. As I still live with my parents, Jeff became joy of his grandparents and the household!"

As for Valerie's mother, she admitted that when she learned about the pregnancy, like Valerie who was completely devastated, she and her husband both cried their eyes out. But now, as Jeff's grandmother, she said, "At first, it was a real cross that fell upon us, but the cross became a joy for the family! We never had a boy before, and my husband treated Jeff like his son. Jeff even carries his name. They are very close friends. His grandfather, acting as his father, is just what we needed! God put the little one in our lives and the little one united our lives. His presence among us healed our relationship. It is such a joy!"

Indeed, Jeff's grandmother was radiating while speaking. And I could see it for myself: little Jeff is a darling child. While Caroline and her mother were telling me the story, Jeff jumped around and was excited with every little thing. One day he will learn that he is a survivor, and that many other children do not have the privilege of remaining on earth! Today too many doctors try to take God's place and decide between life and death, often willingly misleading the mother, pretending that the condition of the child is much worse than it really is. I am in a position to say this without hesitation because similar stories come to my ears in Medjugorje much more frequently than they ever did before. In the case of a negative diagnosis, if you are pressured to have an abortion, ask for another examination in a different hospital or clinic! For example, for a Down syndrome child an ultra sound has a 20% margin of error. How many children have been aborted due to that error?

Even if the child has a problem, it is a child! It is your child! He is to be protected and escape death, he has only you!

27

Souha's Most Beautiful Confession

IN AUGUST OF 2010 a group from the Middle East wanted to make a genuine pilgrimage, spending several days in Medjugorje. Among them was a married woman, Souha, whose husband was a gynecologist, and could not join the group because he was working.

Souha had a secret, which stole her peace from her. Shortly after her arrival in Medjugorje she found a priest, and confided in him that she had had an abortion. Diagnosed with Down syndrome while still in the womb, neither she nor her husband wanted to deal with the child. Together they decided to terminate the pregnancy and evacuate the child from the motherly womb. Since her heart was still agitated, Souha asked the priest, "It's not a sin, is it?" The priest answered, "Of course, my daughter, it's a sin! A grave sin!! You have to confess it!" But Souha wasn't convinced, and she was firm in her denial that the abortion was a sin. However, she asked Our Lady to give her a sign to let her know if she should confess this act.

That evening, Souha, and her pilgrim group attended the apparition of the Blessed Mother on the hill with Ivan. The moment Our Lady arrived, Souha, without warning, doubled over, as though she were thrown to the earth. Her entire body was bent over and her nose seemed to be glued to the ground. She remained that way for a long time, and, when she got up after the apparition, her friends saw her crying.

She said to them, "We have to call a priest. I've got to go to confession right away!"

What happened to her during the apparition? We must respect her secret, but the Blessed Mother acted within her. In tears, Souha made the most beautiful confession of her life. She realized the horror of the sin. During the apparition, the Blessed Mother had acted within her. During confession, Souha accepted the mercy of God, and her inner peace was restored. She was free! It was evident to her friends that she was full of immense joy, as never before in her life! "What a contrast, what sudden light on her face," they commented to themselves.

In Medjugorje, some pilgrims have a beautiful tradition. The leader proposes that each one pray in a special way for a fellow pilgrim in the group throughout their journey together. The first or second evening, each person draws the name of another pilgrim from a basket. On that particular evening, out of the 150 people in the group, who should draw the name of Souha and get the job of praying for her, but a little child with Down syndrome!

That very evening, Souha's husband telephoned and, after hearing his wife's story, said to her, "You know, I called you because I was finding it bizarre that you were there praying to God, while I was here carrying out abortions. That just cannot be! I decided to stop today." He, also, was crying on the phone. He sensed that something was happening to his wife, and he was ready to take this enormous step in his professional life. Souha couldn't believe her ears.

Today, Souha, her husband, and their children live in an entirely new way. They put God first. They receive the sacraments, go to Mass almost every day, and give witness to their faith. As for that memorable pilgrimage in 2010, after asking themselves how they could repair such a past, they decided to adopt an orphan.

Many people wonder what happens to children after they are aborted. In Medjugorje, Mary speaks about these babies who are not given the opportunity to be born. She says, "They are with me." Souha's child surely prays a good deal for his parents and for his little companions in today's world who are destined never to see the light of day.

The question that haunts those who have terminated a pregnancy because of a genetic disorder is whether or not the child really had the disorder. Did Souha's child really have Down syndrome? We will not know until we reach Heaven, but as a matter of fact, we have seen more and more examples of false diagnoses. There are many parents who decide to keep their babies whatever their handicap is, and often, the child is born perfectly normal. Our culture of death and the all-out push toward the abortion market never leaves room for false diagnoses! It's something to take into consideration!

Yet, isn't God marvelous! For Souha's family, the Lord turned an evil act into good. That doctor, who from now on will battle to promote life, will not abort thousands of children.

28

He Didn't Want to Get Down on His Knees

"Dear children! In the great love of God, I come to you today to lead you on the way of humility and meekness. The first station on that way, my children, is confession. Reject your arrogance and kneel down before my Son. Comprehend, my children, that you have nothing and you can do nothing. The only thing that is yours and what you possess is sin. Be cleansed and accept meekness and humility. My Son could have won with strength, but He chose meekness, humility and love. Follow my Son and give me your hands so that, together, we may climb the mountain and win. Thank you."

(MESSAGE OF JULY 2, 2007)

PADRE PIO ATTRACTED *crowds* to his confessional. He spent entire days dispensing the sacrament of Reconciliation to sinners. It goes without saying that he saw all kinds! After his death, *L'Osservatore Romano* (the magazine published by the Vatican) wrote about him that, "His confessional was a tribunal of compassion and firmness. Even those he sent away without absolution came back to him, for the most part motivated by the desire to find understanding and peace. A new pathway opened up in their lives, one more devoted to their inward selves."

In his book, *Padre Pio, My Father,* Father Pierino Galeone recounts an actual event in the life of Padre Pio, an event to which he was an eyewitness.[1] It is a story that sheds an interesting light on the mercy of God offered to everyone, and on the psychology of our enemy.

"That day," writes Father Pierino. "Padre Pio was listening to confessions in the sacristy of the old, little church. He was seated in a corner on the right near the small door, which led into the church; and a curtain separated him from it. I could see Padre Pio through a slit in the curtain.

"The people who had presented themselves for confession were waiting in line. I was seated in my chair and, while reading my breviary, I raised my eyes from time to time to see Padre Pio. Through the right side door of the church entered a man of strong stature and proud bearing. His eyes were black, his hair was beginning to gray, and he wore a dark vest and striped trousers. I didn't want to let myself get distracted, so I continued to pray, when an inner voice commanded me, 'Stop and look!' I collected myself and continued to watch.

"Without waiting his turn, after taking several huge strides, the man positioned himself directly in front of the curtain. While another person was confessing his sins, the man stood in front of the person and faced Padre Pio, who, consequently, I could no longer see. Several minutes went by, and then this man disappeared all of a sudden. His legs were pulled out from under him and he went right through the floor. At that same moment, I no longer saw Padre Pio seated on the chair. Instead, Jesus who was young, blond, and handsome was leaning a little against the armrest, His eyes fixed on the man who had been swallowed up from below.

---

[1] Pierino Galeone, Padre.

"I looked again at Padre Pio, he had been standing nearby and took his place again. His face merged with that of Jesus. Then I no longer saw anyone but Padre Pio, and soon his voice called out, 'Hurry up and move!' Among the penitents who were waiting their turn, no one took notice of what had taken place, and they repositioned themselves in line.

"The following year, we were sitting on the veranda, chatting and asking one another if it were true, as a writer seemed to maintain, that after a certain number of thousands of years, the devil and his demons could return to Heaven. Padre Pio listened in silence, but, based on the way he was contorting his face, he did not seem to share the opinion of this author. Someone asked him what he was thinking, and he replied, 'I remember having read one day that a poor, simple priest went to the sacristy to hear confessions. Into the sacristy came a man of strong stature and proud bearing, with black eyes and graying hair, wearing a dark vest and striped trousers. He passed in front of all who were waiting and placed himself in front of the priest to make his confession. The humble confessor invited him to kneel down, but the man said to him, *I can't!* Presuming that this man was sick, the priest did not prohibit the man from having his confession heard, but while listening to him, it seemed to the priest that this person had committed every sin in the world. The priest thought to himself, *There's one who commits all the sins in the world, and Another who takes them all away!* After hearing the confession, he spoke some words of exhortation and asked this peculiar man again to kneel, or at least to bow his head to receive absolution. But the man answered in a harsh, almost tormented, voice, *I can't!* The confessor then said, *My friend, when you put on your trousers in the morning, you bend your head a little, don't you?* The man gave him a look of anger and scorn and answered him with rage, *I am Lucifer; in my kingdom, no one bows his head!*[2]

"Padre Pio ended his story this way, 'As long as Lucifer and his demons do not bend before God, they will never enter into the Kingdom of Heaven!' A little later, Padre Pio got up to retire to his cell. I asked him then, 'My Father, that priest of whom you spoke, in reality it was you, wasn't it? That's in fact what happened to you a year ago in the sacristy. I was there, too!' Padre Pio was very saddened and answered in tears, 'Yes, it's true, that happened to me also, but it is also true that I read the same thing in a book!'"

This testimony of Father Pierino Galeone teaches us—or rather reminds us—about an important fact regarding the schemes of the enemy, and his ultimate goal: to be adored, and to take the place of God Himself. While Jesus was on earth, the enemy tried to trick Jesus. After Jesus' baptism in the Jordan, three times the "other one" tried to lure Jesus into his trap by tempting him with all sorts of glorious gifts. But the ultimate temptation that he placed before Jesus, and that unveiled his greatest wish, was the one that asked Jesus to fall down and worship him. 'You shall worship God, and Him only,' answered Jesus, (Matt.4: 1–11).

Father Tarcisio Cervinara, a colleague of Padre Pio, recounted a similar episode between the saint and the devil.[3]

---

[2] The demon appeared one day to Saint Macarius, the Hermit of Egypt. "All that you do, I do also," Satan said to him. "You fast, and I never eat. You stay awake, and I never sleep.

There is only one thing I can't do that you do." "What is it?"

"Humble myself."

[3] Tarcisio de Cervinara, *The Devil in the Life of Padre Pio*, (Barto: Our Lady of Grace Capuchin Friary, 1993).

Padre Pio was taken aback when a penitent began justifying each of his sins with great ease and great intelligence, making them appear completely natural and normal, and thus void of any malice. Such a confession puzzled Padre Pio, because the horrible sins that this man confessed were portrayed as unimportant and harmless, as though they were trivial. Padre Pio wondered if the man really thought that he could obtain absolution for his sins, while not being sincerely repentant. Thanks to the light of the Holy Spirit, Padre Pio made his penitent pass the test of all tests, the one of humility. It was that test, which permitted him to recognize the true face of this man, who was apparently so pleasant, so refined, so polite; he saw that soon this person would sink into the fiery inferno from which he came.

For us Satan remains the great usurper. Even if he has failed with Jesus, he continues to try desperately to make himself adored, or rather idolized by men, thus capturing for his own profit the extraordinary potential of adoration, which resides in each person and which makes his nobility unique among creatures. How many fall into the trap! If only they knew that true adoration, in spirit and in truth, is that which engenders the greatest joy in the human soul, and the greatest obstacle is pride. "In Heaven," said Maryam, the little Arab. "I saw a lot of faults, but not pride. In Hell, I saw a lot of good qualities, but not humility."[4] The narrow gate through which one enters the Kingdom is that of humility. God pardons all sins in His infinite mercy but he doesn't force anyone. If, through pride, I don't have remorse for my sin, if I am obstinate in holding onto it and refuse to ask for pardon, then I am depriving myself of the mercy which is offered, and I condemn myself to living without God. The

[4] Sister Emmanuel Maillard, *Maryam of Bethlehem.*

tears of Padre Pio are understandable. If only Satan had agreed to kneel down and ask sincerely for forgiveness, he wouldn't be there today!

29

Will Satan Reign in the Vatican?

"My dear children, tonight your Mother warns you that in this time Satan desires you, and is looking for you! A little spiritual emptiness in you is enough for Satan to work in you. For this reason your Mother invites you to begin to pray. May your weapon be prayer! With prayer with the heart, you will overcome Satan. Your Mother invites you to pray for the young people in the whole world."

(MESSAGE TO IVAN SEPTEMBER 5, 1988)

A MEETING TOOK PLACE in Rome in 1917. It was a gathering of Freemasons to celebrate their 200 years of existence. They marched, displaying a flag that depicted the victory of Lucifer over the Archangel Saint Michael. In St.

Peter's Square, they rolled out banners with the inscription: "Satan will reign at the Vatican, and the Pope will be his servant."

But God had His own plan! A young Maximilian Kolbe was cut to the quick by that abominable declaration and came up with a brilliant idea, "It came to my spirit to found an alliance against the Freemasons and other demonic powers," he wrote. "That is how, with the permission of our Rector, the first seven members of the *Militia of the Immaculata* met on October 17, 1917."[1]

Four days after the last apparition at Fatima, which took place on October 13, 1917, these first *Knights of the Immaculata* committed themselves to fight, by their examples, their prayers, their works, and their sufferings, for the conversion of sinners and the return of heretics, schematics, communists, and freemasons to unity with the Church. Their founder never stopped insisting throughout his life that the members of the Militia of the Immaculata achieve this goal more by offering to Jesus their suffering, than by their works.

Brother Maximilian Kolbe was ordained a priest in Rome on April 28, 1918. He returned to Poland during the summer of 1919. Before leaving the Eternal City, he wrote to his mother these beautiful and significant words, "Pray for me,

---

[1] *The Militia of the Immaculata (MI)* is a worldwide evangelization movement founded by St. Maximilian Kolbe in 1917 that encourages total consecration to the Blessed Virgin Mary as a means of spiritual renewal for individuals and society. The MI movement is open to all Catholics over 7 years old. It employs prayer as the main weapon in the spiritual battle with evil. Maximilien Kolbe was canonized in 2008 by Cardinal Stanislaw Dziwisz. For more information see:
http://consecration.com/

Mama, that I grow more and more quickly in love: pray especially that my love be without limit!"

Father Maximilian left Rome in a state of deplorable health. He had contracted painful pulmonary hemorrhages, which made him cough up blood. His superior, Father Kubit, declared, "He is so infected by tuberculosis that the doctors are giving him no more than three months to live." Nevertheless, he was appointed a church history professor at the young age of 25. Although gravely ill, he never complained and, with enthusiasm, he began to propagate the idea of the Militia of the Immaculata within the convent.

But his brothers received the idea with a shrug of the shoulders. So, faced with the indifference of the religious around him, Maximilian turned to lay people for support. The increasing affluence of his listeners led him quickly to found the first Militia of the Immaculata in Poland. Only a few months before founding the Militia in Poland, and weakened by fever, Fr. Maximilien spent a year in the sanatorium in Zakopane at the behest of his superior. Submissive and ever obedient, he rested for hours in a reclining chair, dedicating himself to the apostolate of prayer, and of suffering. He endured these humiliations with patience and gentleness, and later he would have nothing but goodness and tender indulgence towards any who were suffering.

Nothing could ever measure the extraordinary impact that the Militia of the Immaculata and its millions of members had on the life of the Church and the world. In 1943, Father Kolbe himself gave his life for the father of a family in the camp at Auschwitz. In place of that man, Maximilian would die of hunger and thirst, thus offering the utmost concrete example of heroic charity.[2] The flags and the banners of those early days, announcing the reign of Satan over the Church, did not take hold, because the Mother of God listened to her children who were fervently praying for the fall of Satan's plans, and Our Lady's success.

Without any doubt, despite the many spiritual works of those dedicated to the Immaculate Heart of Mary, the threat of Satan's control remains tangible, today more than ever. The saving solution certainly does not rest with our politicians, but rather in each of us whom God calls to holiness, if we agree to hand ourselves over to Him, body and soul. The sacrifice of Father Kolbe has given birth to a considerable number of holy souls who have helped tip the balance. Today Jesus and Mary are seeking holy shepherds like him who will give birth to an innumerable amount of holy sheep. In the desert of this world without peace, Heaven cries out to those of *us* who have received the message. Who will answer?

[2] See other materials about St. Maximilien Kolbe: Patricia Treece, *A man for others: Maximilian Kolbe the Saint of Auschwitz,* (Libertyville: Marytown Press, 1993). Also, Antinio Riccardi, *Saint Maximilian Kolbe: Apostle of Our Difficult Age* (Boston: Pauline Books and Media, 1982).

30

A Valuable Shock for Clement

IN 1976, AT THE time of our great summer assembly in
Paray le Monial (the shrine of the Sacred Heart, in
France), the founder of the Emmanuel Community, Pierre
Goursat, put me in charge of one of the sessions. I was asked
to speak about the Holy Spirit. Of course, while explaining
about spiritual combat, I didn't hide the existence of evil
spirits, and I cited what the Church taught about them.

After my talk, Clément, a very young man who had been
directing the choir for a little while, ran towards me, and said
to me sadly, "Emmanuel, all that you said was good. It really
touched me! But it's too bad you mentioned Satan. Everything you said about him is rubbish! You ought to know that
he's a figment of our imaginations. You spoke of him as
though he truly existed. That spoiled part of your speech. It's
really too bad!"

In these cases, there's only one attitude to have—patience!
Since I knew that no explanation was going to convince him,
I said, "Ah well, Clément, here's what I'm going to do. I'm
going to pray to God that He enlighten us. If Satan exists, let
the Lord show him to you so clearly that you can't doubt.
And if he doesn't exist, may He show that to me!" At these
words, Clément went away in peace, and I began to pray.

On the evening of that same day, Clément ran towards
me again and had barely reached me when he began making
panicky gestures. He cried out to me, "Stop praying! Stop! I
saw him. Yes, him, Satan! It was horrible! Okay, I get it!" In

his emotion, he couldn't manage to say exactly what he had seen; he was still trembling because of it. I admit I was astonished that the Lord had acted so quickly and so forcefully for Clément. But I was not repentant for having prayed in that particular way for him, because this brother, branded for life by this memorable episode, took it upon himself to quite seriously study the Holy Scriptures, and the Church's doctrine on this point.[1]

---

[1] Many people who are tormented by the evil one are asking which prayer of liberation they can pray for themselves, or for others. The majority of exorcists agree that the most efficient prayer is the Promises of Baptism. Of course, we have to pronounce them with faith and sincerely renounce sin so that the evil one has no more hold over us. Here are the promises of Baptism: "Dear brothers and sisters, by the Pascal mystery we have been put in the tomb with Christ in Baptism, so that with him we may live a new life. This is why we renew our profession of faith in the living and true God and in his Son Jesus Christ, in the holy Catholic Church. Therefore:

C. Do you reject Satan?   *R.* I do.

C. And all his works?   *R.* I do.

C. And all his empty promises?   *R.* I do.

C. Do you believe in God, the Father   *R.* I do.
    Almighty, creator of heaven and earth?

C. Do you believe in Jesus Christ, his only Son,   *R.* I do.
    our Lord, who was born of the Virgin Mary
    was crucified, died, and was buried, rose from
    the dead, and is now seated at the right hand
    of the Father?

Knowing the identity of the enemy helps us to identify the dangers that await us on the battlefield of the world. There are some very pernicious cults in the world whose members are well disguised as innocent lambs. These accomplices of Satan are in reality the most unfortunate of men, because they have no future, except to come one day (maybe tomorrow) face to face with their despotic master, and to realize too late that they allowed themselves to be snared by the most subtle and cruel of liars.

That is why we must hope that, before definitively losing themselves those who have made a pact with the Devil can see him for what he truly is and not as he presents himself to them under his false disguises. We have nothing to fear from him if we remain in the state of grace and if we have a regular prayer life. In Medjugorje, Mary tells us "Do not be afraid of Satan, it's not worth it, because with humble prayer and ardent love you can disarm him," (to the prayer group, 1985).

What puts a person in Hell is not sin itself. Heaven is full of sinners (repentant and pardoned sinners)! What puts someone in Hell is being obstinate in sin, not wanting to let go of it, refusing pardon. It is the pride of not wanting to fall

---

C. Do you believe in the Holy Spirit, the holy Catholic Church, the communion of saints, the forgiveness of sins, the resurrection of the body, and life everlasting? *R.* I do.

C. God, the all-powerful Father of our Lord Jesus Christ has given us a new birth by water and the Holy Spirit, and forgiven all our sins. May he also keep us faithful to our Lord Jesus Christ for ever and ever. *R.* Amen.

to one's knees. At that point, God is somewhat disarmed. He infinitely respects the freedom, which He has given to His children, and He will not force anyone to go with Him if that person refuses His invitation.

I really like this piece of wisdom that comes to us from the Great North: An Iroquois grandfather instructed his grandson on the fundamental principles of life in his tribe. He told him that inside every person there are two wolves that are battling against each other in war, a terrible war, without pity. One of the wolves is nasty, evil, angry, jealous, arrogant, lazy, contemptuous, wounding, and bitter. The other wolf is good, loveable, helpful, thoughtful, and prudent. These two wolves are fighting each other constantly. The child then asked his grandfather, "Which wolf is going to win?"

"The one you choose to nurture," answered the grandfather.

A Question Often Asked: How is it Possible That Someone Chooses to Go to Hell?

On this point the teaching of the saints is very enlightening.[2] We learn that at the moment of death, God reveals Himself with great power, and He gives to the soul more graces than He gave to it during the person's entire life. Yet, the soul remains totally free to make its choice—to accept divine mercy, or to reject it; to live for eternity with God, or without Him; to accept Him or to flee. I often ask myself how a human being can choose to go far from God just at the

---

[2] For example, see Maria Faustina Kowalska, *Diary*, §1687.

moment when the Lord reveals Himself to him in the light of His infinite love.

Let's imagine a man who has become accustomed to committing abominable acts. Under the cover of darkness, he ponders and plans his next crimes. His whole being is consumed with hate, impurities of every kind, and the desire to do harm. But death surprises him, and suddenly a great light rises from the shadows. It's time to meet God face to face. It's the hour of truth. The man is taken by surprise. He is caught in the act of plotting against God. What is he instinctively going to do? Without reflection, and with all of his strength, he's going to flee from this light, which is exposing his darkness! He has such fear of it that he begins to run in the opposite direction. He cannot endure it and will do anything to hide from it. In truth, it is himself, and his own horror at the sight of his darkness and weakness, that he cannot endure.

God is light. God is love. God is Loving Light. He calls. He invites. He begs the man, but out of respect for the man's freedom, the Lord will never force him to stay with Him. The one who runs away from God, therefore, throws himself into the abyss where God is absent. That place then exists out of respect for man's freedom. When Vicka and Jakov accompanied Our Lady to Heaven, Hell and Purgatory, she said to them, "Those who go to Hell go there of their own free will. God doesn't put a person in Hell. On the contrary, He sent His own Son so that the world might be saved."[3]

---

[3] See the story of Vicka and Jakov's visit to Heaven, Hell and Purgatory in the January, 1991 issue of the magazine *Triumph of the Heart.* See also Sr. Emmanuel's *The Hidden Child of Medjugorje* and *The Beautiful Story of Medjugorje As Told To Children 7– 97.*

Why does Satan need to work in the shadows? Jesus explains it well in the Gospel of St. John, "And this is the verdict, that the light came into the world, but people preferred darkness to light, because their works were evil," (John, 3: 19).

31

First on the Hit Parade?

"Dear Children, you are ready to commit sin, and to put yourselves in the hand of Satan without reflecting. I call on each one of you to consciously decide for God and against Satan. I am your mother and, therefore, I want to lead you all toward perfect holiness. I want each one of you to be happy here on earth and to be with me in Heaven. That is, dear children, the purpose of my coming here and it's my desire."

(MESSAGE OF MAY 25, 1987)

THERE EXISTS A DEMON so powerful, so seductive that today he would crush even the most virtuous person, if we let him. This demon has no need to be active to succeed, because the simple act of pronouncing his name is sufficient to obtain victory for him. It's a rather long name, longer than the ones we're used to, but this name is so present in our current language that it pronounces itself quite naturally. It seems harmless. It's on the lips of almost every young person; it's whispered in the ear and shouted from the rooftops. This demon takes pride in opening all the doors; it assumes every right. It makes thousands fall, and its popularity ratings seem to get higher each day. It is aware that people have made a cult around it, and that it is given the honor of a king. It lies low under the radar, and is so well regarded that it has obtained entry into the best societies, even into some confessionals. Its name alone is a trap, because it contains within it the excuse of evil. It's a serpent with poisonous venom, disguised as a gentle, compassionate dove. Its name? *Everyone Does It.*

This saying allows everyone to believe that evil is good, and it draws its victims into its curse without even seeming to. Let's not forget that it is written, "Woe unto them who call evil good and good evil," (Is. 5:20).

Is a pregnant woman hesitating to have an abortion? "No problem," her friends say to her. "Go ahead, *everyone does it!*"

A young man goes out with his friends and realizes that they're going to get passed-out-drunk, so he hesitates. Then they say, "C'mon, don't be silly! *Everyone does it!*"

A daughter wears something low-cut and provocative, someone from her family makes a remark about it. "So what!" She says. *"Everyone does it!"*

Someone offers a drug to a teenager who has never even smoked. At first he says "no" but somebody successfully convinces him, because, after all, *"everyone does it!"* A young couple is invited by another couple who says, "Come with us tomorrow, we're going to celebrate a black mass. It will be so interesting." The couple hesitates. Satan isn't really their cup of tea. But, after all, they say to themselves, 'we should tolerate what we don't know, we shouldn't judge, and we should try to stay on top of the newest things.' "Uh," they murmur. "Why not? There'll be many people there. *Everyone's going!*" "What? You haven't tried sex with multiple partners? Where have you been? *Everyone does it!*" How many young girls have sold their virginity at a low price to honor this demon, allowing themselves to be wrecked and ruined for years on end?

But why are you crying out, "Barabbas, Barabbas"? Why would you want to free a criminal? So that he can murder your children? And why do you cry, "Crucify him" to Pilate for Jesus? Wasn't it He who gave sight back to your husband? The response comes, "Don't you see? *Everyone's doing it!*"

I could multiply the examples, but they are too sad. The anguish, the broken lives, the thousands of people with depression, the inner torments of all kinds, the fractured families, the powerlessness to live and work normally, the complete loss of the simple appetite for life, the suicides (attempted and successful), the crimes. The name *Everyone Does It* already carries with it an enormous lie, because in reality, everyone *doesn't* do it!

We are witnessing a massacre, and of course, the youngest and most malleable are the most profoundly affected—naïve as they are about the bitter fruits that await them if they put themselves at the mercy of the worst of modern tyrants, *Mr. Everyone Does It.* But who is warning them with enough love and patience to put them on guard and protect them? Who sets the example? Who spends time with them, listening to the true desires of their hearts and helping them manage their growth in a world that is bombarding them?

Jesus is the answer, for them and for all! He comes to console us from boredom with His infinite kindness, He who knows the uniqueness of each of his creatures. He shows each person how to become what He is: irreplaceable, distinctive, special. There is beauty in differences! Jesus carries within Him our secret image. He cherishes it, and the more we look at Him, the more we become our true selves before Him and before others. "Whoever looks to Him shall be radiant; his face never covered with shame," (Ps. 34). Jesus never said, "Do what everyone else does and you will be happy!" No, He gives an answer, which is neither tricky nor deceptive. He shows us a road, which does not include a cul-de-sac, and He says, "Learn from me, for I am meek and humble of heart, and you will find rest for your souls," (Mt. 11:28–30). And also, "He who follows me will never walk in darkness but will have the light of life," (Jn. 8:12). So why go looking for happiness where it is lost? Isn't Jesus *the way, the truth, and the life,* (Jn. 14:6)?[1]

A Disastrous Practice: Reiki

Promoted by a media culture that has become increasingly new age, Reiki is spreading very rapidly all over the world. Orchestrated with seductive publicity (seductive because it is connected to our wellbeing and everyone wants to be well), Reiki is a supposed method of "healing" that promises rapid results. It is circulating among those who are sick and those who are not, and we cannot ignore its disastrous effects.

---

[1] An unknown author wrote: "Technology has opened up new frontiers, and humanity can follow many different roads. We can fly to the moon or dive into the depths of the ocean. When we started making all these discoveries, we humans dreamt of a new world, like a new Eden, a new Paradise. This time we would create the world with our own hands. It would be a world where man would reach his full potential. The need for God and for a religious faith would be obsolete, a relic of the past. Now, humanity is being confronted with this world it has made, and sees what it has built. Humankind, look carefully, this is what the world looks like without the Heavenly Father.

You can see the road you have chosen. Not only do you see it, but you are afraid. Not only are you afraid, but you realize that you cannot turn back! You are doomed to keep moving forward. New discoveries. New inventions. New entanglements. New opportunities for terrorism, destruction and chaos. Satan has trapped you in your own discoveries. He encouraged you to build your own world independently of the Creator."

Therefore, I feel duty-bound here to raise a flashing red light to warn each one of us.[2]

Reiki is an alternative medicine that uses *universal life energy.* It involves certain powers coming from a *transcendental spirit,* (certainly not the *Holy* Spirit). The technique includes calling down a universal energy on the sick person, and tracing upon him, or over his body, archetypical symbols. The "Reiki Master" (sometimes called a therapist) then visualizes this energy entering into himself through the chakra on the top of his skull. The energy fills his skull and descends into his hands where it overflows from his hand into the patient.

In reality, because the practice of Reiki includes secret symbols from obscure sources, similar to mantras, it opens the door to harmful occult forces. While it is possible to observe a provisional improvement in health on some level, in some cases that improvement quickly gives way to symptoms that often appear in the context of occult practices, even practices of spiritualism like Ouija board.

The practice of Reiki cannot co-exist with our Christian faith. With Jesus, all things are clear! The fact that certain Christians practice it, even Priests and nuns sometimes, does not mean that it is a good thing to do: its snares are subtle. In particular, there are various levels of Reiki Masters. During the initiation ceremonies, séances transmit energy to the reiki master. At the highest levels, the existence of a personal Creator God is denied, and works of the reiki master are performed with *energies,* in the spirit of pantheism. During

---

[2] Read the chapter "Bill's Migraines" in *The Hidden Child of Medjugorje.* For those who know Italian listen to the CD "La Trapola del Reiki" by Tarcisio Mezzetti and Sr. Emmanuel, available at Vocepiu: Milan. www.vocepiu.it.

the third degree of initiation one even calls upon demons in the "spirit of the mountain."

Unfortunately, serious studies on this subject have not yet been disseminated to the general public, but what we know is that the energy and spirits called upon during the initiation rites of a Reiki Master are contrary to the gifts of the Holy Spirit, which are received from God according to His design. Unlike Reiki, the gifts of the Holy Spirit are not transmitted from one person to another, but rather they are free! In Medjugorje, numerous victims of Reiki come to ask for help, because they suffer from oppression, anxieties, insomnia, and other illnesses.

Father Joseph Verlinde, a specialist in the matter explains, "Reiki is an occult practice which is founded upon the major principles of magic. For example, the invocation of spirits from the astrological world with the purpose of exercising, with their collaboration, magical healing powers … It's useless to point out that it is impossible to reconcile such a magical practice (which denies divine transcendence) with a Christian life, which claims to be faithful to Revelation (Scripture, Tradition, Magisterium). And it is not astonishing, either, that these practices, which draw their effectiveness from collaboration with the spirits of the astrological world, lead, both in the mid and long term, to various forms of psychological or spiritual alienation."[3] The National Confer-

---

[3] See the work of Father Joseph-Marie Verlinde on occult practices, which are founded on the major principles of magic, notably "Le Reiki," in the Benedictine Editions table of contents which includes: The Legend of the Discovery of Reiki; A Classic Practice of Magic; The Three Degrees of Reiki; Discernment; An Occult Practice Made Banal; Confirmation of the Magisterium; See the site: http://www.final-age.net.

ence of Catholic Bishops in the U.S. has also published a warning against the practice of Reiki.

See the site:

https://www.la-croix.com/Religion/Actualite/Les-eveques-americains-mettent-en-garde-contre-la-pratique-du-reiki-_NG_-2009-04-27-534080

32

A Great Victory for the Frog!

"Decide for holiness," Mary says to us.

"And don't listen to others."

(MESSAGE TO THE PRAYER GROUP IN 1982)

ONE HUNDRED FROGS WERE gathered at the foot of a high mountain. Basically, they were tired of living in swampy areas and of always being treated as slow and stagnant, so they decided to prove just what they were capable of, and have a race. The object was to reach the summit of a mountain! The truth is, they knew that from higher up they would enjoy a magnificent view and would discover unimagined landscapes. Their vision of the world would finally change. There was nothing like climbing! The sky was clear, with a light breeze, all to their advantage. Each one hoped to bring home a victory.

All excited, they got into line at the foot of the mountain, determined to conquer courageously the many obstacles that awaited them: fatigue, thirst, discouragement, shortness of breath, scratches on their tender skin, and all the difficulties they could expect just from being frogs.

The starting bell sounded, and there they were, launching themselves into the conquest of the mountain. Each one endeavored to leap over obstacles with enthusiasm. But little by little, having to labor hard on a rather steep and rocky slope on the side of the mountain, some of them began to doubt the wisdom of this adventure. They kept their private thoughts to themselves for several minutes. They didn't want any of the other frogs to think they were going to quit in the middle of the race, but, after a new section was conquered only with a huge struggle, they could no longer manage to hold their tongues, and they began to grumble to their neighbors that, after all, the whole thing was more difficult than they had imagined. Words of encouragement were heard from several of them, but the effect did not last.

Before long, all sorts of remarks began pouring out of their mouths, issues of great logical common sense, it seemed: their ideas were simply too big. It would be better to give up. Yet, the majority continued. Halfway up the mountain, great agitation developed within the group. Chattering all at once, they complained about having set the bar too high and of having overestimated their strength. Each one had his own analysis of the situation. They got upset, their voices grew louder, they croaked. It was a cacophony! Finally, the majority declared that they should surrender humbly to the evidence that this mountain was too steep, not accessible to frogs. They should opt for wisdom and renounce the idea of reaching the summit and the hidden, mysterious landscapes they so dearly desired. All of them headed back down the mountain, clopping along, sad and disgruntled, to splash around in the old swamp.

All of them except one little frog who continued to climb, only one. Glancing neither right nor left, little by little he reached the summit. There, he couldn't believe his eyes: the panorama was a thousand times more beautiful and more moving than anything he had ever imagined. He could hardly contain his joy! All his fatigue seemed to evaporate in front of the happiness he felt. Forgetting his weariness and his injuries, he abandoned himself to the wondrous contemplation of the view in front of him.

How was this frog able to climb so high when the others gave up?

Simple: the frog who climbed to the top, was deaf!

A Great Saint of Our Time,
Faustina Kowalska (1905–1938)

Because the frog could not hear the negativity and opinions of the others, he was able to climb to the top of the mountain. In silence, he found strength. St. Faustina Kowalska shared with us unimaginable treasures of wisdom in her *Diary*, which she wrote in obedience to her spiritual father. (May he be blessed!) She hands over to us here one of her secrets, which is healing for us especially, because we live in a century where we are running away from ourselves, escaping into the noise that surrounds us. We are being bombarded! The plethora of electronic messages of all kinds, vain and negative words, multiple contradictory declarations, all modern techniques which ensure that we never listen to our hearts. But let us listen to what Saint Faustina says,

"Silence is a sword in the spiritual struggle. A talkative soul will never attain sanctity. The sword of silence will cut off everything that would like to cling to the soul. We are sensitive to words and quickly want to answer back, without taking any regard as to whether it is God's will that we should speak. A silent soul is strong; no adversities will harm it if it perseveres in silence. The silent soul is capable of attaining the closest union with God. It lives almost always under the inspiration of the Holy Spirit. God works in a silent soul without hindrance."[1]

---

[1] St. Faustina Kowalska, *The Diary, §198 & 477.*

The Opinion of Others

When I lived in Jerusalem, I knew a Dominican who stood out among the other priests of his order. His name, Paul Dreyfus, clearly pointed to his Jewish origins. As an adolescent, he discovered the Gospels, and, fascinated by the person of Jesus, he followed Him. But it wasn't until during WWII (1939–45) that he was Baptized in a concentration camp. He entered the Dominican order in 1947. He was part of the very famous Jerusalem Bible Institute, on the Street of Prophets, very close to our convent. I had chosen him from among a thousand to be my spiritual director and confessor. Why did I choose him?

A specialist in Judeo-Christian relations and a very fine interpreter of scripture, it was exciting to listen to him.[2] As Jesus said of Nathanial, Father Dreyfus was a true Israelite, a man without artifice, not very talkative, who had the courage to be himself, without compromise. He went right to the heart of things without embellishment and couldn't care less about what others might think of him. He didn't care, so much so, that he intentionally lived a form of poverty that wasn't always practiced in that noble friary of worldwide renown. His inner sense of freedom had a somewhat rebellious character to it. He already stuck out physically: his shoes were worn and often had holes. He dragged his feet (his legs often bothered him), and, as for his socks, there was always one falling down and wrinkled around his ankle. His Dominican robe was always askew, either to the right or the

---

[2] He is the author of a work honored by the Academie Francaise: "Did Jesus know He was God?" Cerf Editions, 1984.

left, his hood hung halfway around his neck, and he kept his head down to protect himself even more from useless worldly contact. He delighted us. In addition, he possessed a truly pure and humble heart. We loved him dearly.

One day, during an official reception where ambassadors and other persons of high rank were aglow in the spotlight, Father Dreyfus stood there, too, with his brothers, still dressed absent-mindedly, wearing the same old shoes with lamentably gaping holes. That day, as was his custom, he wore a blank look, his mouth a little open, certain of not attracting any of the compliments, which overflowed at that type of meeting. (He would have delighted Pope Frances!)

It was then that an event occurred which will remain forever etched in my memory: one of the attendees, full of evangelical zeal, approached the Father Superior and whispered in his ear: "I congratulate you, Father. I see that right in the heart of your community, you welcome even the handicapped!" Father Dreyfus was one of the most brilliant minds in the entire Jerusalem Bible Institute!

33

Getting Away from Dependencies

CÉLINE TELLS A STORY that might inspire many people suffering from a dependency. For years, Céline lived the messages of Our Lady, to the best of her ability, and she took particular care not to omit the message about fasting two days a week, Wednesdays and Fridays. She had, indeed, experienced the fruits of fasting, but she was very sad about being unable to give up coffee on those two mornings. Her reason wasn't trivial: if she didn't have coffee, her brain was foggy, and she fell asleep at her computer, or at church during Mass. In short, the result was not pretty. That didn't prevent her from feeling deep in her heart that even coffee ought to disappear from her life if she was going to fully live out the message of fasting, and she believed Our Lady was waiting for her to give it up. Despite her previous experiences, she prayed for the grace to deprive herself of coffee, but it never worked.

One day, during her hour of adoration before the Blessed Sacrament, an idea came to mind, and, without reflecting on it for more than a second, she heard herself saying to the Blessed Mother, "Okay, I won't have anymore coffee, but you know the disastrous consequences of those times I've fallen asleep, so *you* be my coffee! Make everything happen the way it would if I were having coffee. Take charge of preventing me from falling asleep while standing up!"

Céline had to admit that Our Lady accepted the proposed bargain and that she did her work very well! For months,

Céline affirms, coffee disappeared from her menu not only on the days of fasting, but also on other days, a change, which has tangibly improved her health and her presence of mind at work! She laughed when she told us this story. "I don't know if Mary has received this *be my coffee* type of demand often, but in any case, she accepted it!"

Advice to lovers of coffee or other edible goods: consume with moderation—chocolate is no exception!

Rosie and 24 Hours of the Gospa

In our house, "Bethlehem," in Medjugorje, we try to live the messages of Mary, which also means struggling against our worst tendencies. Believe me, it's not easy! The volunteers who come to share our lives and stay with us for a year or two under the guidance of Our Lady, often experience surprising things. In reality, the Mother of God works actively in the hearts, bodies, and spirits of those who surrender themselves to her school of prayer and thought. She has no time to waste. She does in several months' work that which would be difficult to accomplish in several years under other circumstances. It's intense! She always aims to give back to her child his essential beauty, the beauty which God the Creator fashioned with love from the very first day, which has been damaged in the world over the course of years past.

For three years a young American woman from New Jersey joined us to be my special assistant. A lot of you know her—it's Rosie! See photo pg 215. Now, Rosie suffered from a very bad habit, but I'll let her tell the story:

"For years I smoked one pack of cigarettes a day. I had often tried to stop, but each attempt ended in failure. It seemed too difficult, and I had come to believe that I just didn't have the grace. I used to tell myself: 'It's not that I don't want to stop, but my body needs it. In any case, if I stop, I'll be impossible to live with!'

"On June 24, 2009, I decided to offer a gift to the Gospa for the 25th anniversary of her apparitions in Medjugorje. I knew it would be difficult not to smoke for an entire day, so I thought that would be the most beautiful gift I could offer her. That day, during the apparition at 6:40 P.M., I made up my mind. I said to myself, 'Okay, I will not smoke until the apparition tomorrow, June 25th, the day we celebrate the anniversary of the apparitions.' But stopping definitively was out of the question for me.

"Not smoking for a day seemed feasible, as long as I knew I could go back to my cigarettes the next day. I knew nothing about *the 24 hours of the Gospa* or how it worked.[1] Sister Emmanuel said nothing about it to me, and her CD on the subject wasn't available in English. The day went by very slowly, but I kept my gift to Our Lady in mind. As a matter of fact, that was all I thought about, because the desire to smoke that cigarette in the evening became greater and greater. To sum it up, I was dealing with the crisis of withdrawal. Then the long-expected moment came. I was finally going to be able to smoke a cigarette. My thoughts were fixed on the pleasure and satisfaction it would bring me. But what a surprise! As soon as I filled my lungs with smoke, the taste of it was repugnant to me! I immediately threw the cigarette away, thinking I was sick.

"I returned right away to the house to tell the others what had happened, certain that the next cigarette would be better. But I had the same reaction, one of profound disgust. It was

---

[1] Sr Emmanuel's CD "The 24 hours of the Gospa" explains how to prepare a gift to be given to Our Lady the next day at the hour of the apparition.

the same for all the cigarettes that followed that day. I found it truly strange. So I told myself that the Blessed Mother didn't want me to smoke anymore. The next day, every time I tried to smoke the same thing happened. Sr Emmanuel told me "Don't be silly, don't you understand that Our Lady has rewarded you for giving up this bad habit? Seize the grace!"

"I haven't smoked since that day, so it's been more than 6 years. During the weeks that followed the day I stopped, a strange phenomenon occurred. I can't explain it scientifically, but I see it as a time of purification. I couldn't stop spitting out thick mucus, brown and black, which kept coming up constantly. It was disgusting. Before, I didn't have any idea about what tobacco was depositing in my body. Some say it takes seven years for a smoker to get rid of this pollution after they've stopped smoking. The Gospa was quicker for me. She made it all come out in record time! Now I feel so much better! Before, I had trouble climbing the mountains. I came back exhausted every time. Now I climb them without getting out of breath. I even pray better, and I no longer have to apologize to my friends for leaving their company to go out to smoke!

"The Gospa took care of it all for me. I thought I was giving her something, but actually it was she who gave me a beautiful gift! Typical of her …"

Rosie, the American assistant to Sister Emmanuel

34

When Jesus Comes into Our Hearts

"Every Christian life is a Mass and every soul is a host."

(THE VENERABLE MARTHA ROBIN)

IN MEDJUGORJE, THE CENTRAL event of the day is not the apparition of the Mother of God, as you might expect, but the evening Mass. The two realities intermingle in a magnificent way. Twenty minutes before the Mass, while the rosary is being said, Our Lady appears to the visionaries. She invites all those who do not see her to welcome her into their hearts as if they did see her, then she accompanies them to Mass to experience it with them. Let's not forget that she gives to the "non-visionaries" like us the same graces that she gives to the visionaries when they receive the apparition, as long as we open our hearts to her coming!

One day, I asked the visionary, Vicka, if Mary had ever given any particular message about Holy Communion. I was not disappointed with the answer! Here it is, "Dear children, when you have received my Son Jesus into your heart through Holy Communion, and you return to your seat, don't look at others. Don't judge the priest! Dear children, kneel down (health permitting) and stay there at least 10 minutes, and speak with my Son whatever is in your heart!"

A great joy came over me when I discovered that message! Then I said to myself, '10 minutes? The faithful might find that a little long. What can be done so that the message is received and followed willingly?' So I asked Vicka that question in order to prompt her (because, after all, she delivers other interesting messages), and also because I wanted to play the devil's advocate for those who might raise their eyebrows at 10 minutes.

"Vicka," I said to her. "Are you sure thatOur Lady specified 10 minutes exactly?"

"No," she answered me. "She didn't say 10 minutes, she said at least 10 minutes, minimum 10 minutes! Because Our Lady said, 'That moment is the most sacred moment of your life, dear children, when my Son Jesus comes alive into your hearts! Welcome Him! Let Him enter! Take time for Jesus!'"

I had my answer, and I could transmit it with confidence while adding, "It's the Blessed Mother who said it!" In the parish of Medugorje, the evening program includes those 10 minutes of prayer which Our Lady asked for after the Mass. It's the time when we say the 7 Our Father's, 7 Hail Mary's, and 7 Glory Be's.

When Jesus comes in Holy Communion, He is extremely happy, as are those who are in love when they go to meet the person they love. He not only prepares to give Himself completely to our hearts—the most sublime of gifts—but He also gathers up innumerable blessings, graces, gifts, and favors that He intends to pour out into our hearts. But what happens when he finds a closed heart? For example, when a person has followed those receiving Holy Communion out of habit, without saying a prayer, or making a single act of love toward Jesus, that person has no real interest in Him, his door is closed to the Lord in Holy Communion. What does Jesus do when confronted with a closed door? Certainly, He respects our freedom. He will wait and wait and wait. He will hope against all hope that the door will finally open to welcome Him, not only Him, but all of the gifts He bears as well. But at the end of the Mass, seeing that there is nothing for Him in this heart, He will draw Himself away without having depositing into this heart all the graces and gifts that he had so lovingly prepared. It goes without saying that His heart is shattered with grief. We can't imagine the pain of such a heart, which is nothing but love, a heart which rejoiced in giving its riches, and which leaves scorned, ignored, counted for nothing ... and the person remains empty because he has missed his *rendez-vous* with his God.

One day, in the 1980s, the inner locutionist, Jelena Vasijl, stood in front of St James' church after mass.[1] Then she shared a vision of Jesus that she had had after Holy Communion, "I saw Jesus with his arms loaded with gifts. He looked deeply sad and he told me, 'Look at these gifts. I brought them to give to those who would welcome me in Holy Communion. But I could give nothing. You need to know that when those who receive Me in Holy Communion go back to their seats, they often make the sign of the cross and dismiss Me immediately!'"

How many times during Mass is Jesus maltreated like this! He said to Sister Faustina, "Oh, how painful it is to Me that souls so seldom unite themselves to Me in Holy Communion! I wait for souls, and they are indifferent toward Me. I love them tenderly and sincerely, and they distrust Me! I want to lavish My graces on them, and they do not want to

---

[1] Jelena Visijl was in charge of the prayer group created by the Blessed Mother in 1982. She was not receiving apparitions, but rather internal phrases and visions from Jesus and Mary that she saw in her heart. These phrases and visions are some of the most beautiful messages of Medjugorje for young people who want to study at the school of Mary. See the DVDs and CDs about the prayer group, "St. Malo Retreat" by Sr. Emmanuel. See also "Other works by the author" on page 397

accept them. They treat Me as a dead object, whereas My heart is full of love and mercy."[2]

On the other hand, if Jesus is welcomed into an open heart, a heart well-prepared, which has taken care to be purified by frequent confession, a heart which rejoices sincerely in receiving its Lord and its dearest Friend, then He finds delight in this heart. As He said to Sister Faustina: "My delight is to come into the human soul through Holy Communion, in order to unite Myself with this soul and to communicate to it all my graces."[3] And also, "Write for consecrated persons that my delight is to come into their hearts through Holy Communion."[4] We might be astonished that Jesus speaks of delight, when He comes into a soul in the state of grace! I think that we share with Him this passionate desire for all who love to cry out from their whole being, 'I truly believe that You are the Savior, and that the joy of a savior is to save.' Surely, inside us, He will always find something to save!

After He has entered into this open heart, what does He do there? His joy is to change us, to purify us, to console us, and He particularly excels in transformative actions. Basically, he transforms us into Himself, nothing less! In other words, everything He has and everything He is becomes ours. If Jesus has chosen a food such as bread for us to have communion with Him, it's not by chance. He could have chosen another way. But that food gives us a perfect physical image of how He operates mystically in our souls.

---

[2] Maria Faustina Kowalska, *Diary,* §1447.

[3] Ibid., §1385.

[4] Ibid., §1683.

If I eat a piece of fruit, that fruit will be transformed after several hours, and it will become Sister Emmanuel, (so to speak)! All my cells will be reached by this food. They will be fortified and renewed by it. Without my conscious awareness, the fruit will nourish all the parts of my body: my brain, my blood, my eyes, my feet, and all my organs. So, we understand that in eating food, our own body does the work of assimilation and of transformation. I digest the fruit and my metabolism makes its nutrients available to my cells.

When I take the Body of Christ in Communion, the operation is both similar and different. It is not I who transforms Jesus into myself. (The poor thing, that would be the end of everything!) Rather, just the opposite, it is He who breathes into me and transforms me into Himself. This mystery of union and intimacy between the soul of Christ and the human soul is immense! So immense that even the angels prostrate themselves before such splendor! For, even though the angels enjoy great light and many gifts emblematic of their nature as angels, it was not given to them to receive the Body of Christ. That privilege is accorded to the human race.

If Jesus transforms us into Himself (of course he does that with the opening of our hearts and our desire for Him), then we can say that Holy Communion helps us take giant steps forward along our way to sainthood. For, if Jesus gives us His joy, His peace, His mercy, His strength, His love, His light, and all His attributes, He is communicating to us also His own sanctity. He makes us divine, nothing less! A number of mystics who have seen Heaven report that the happiest and most glorious among the elect are those who on Earth received each day the Body of Christ, and have permitted it to live in the center of their very being. If we absorb every day the sanctity and the glory of Christ, why would we be surprised that in Heaven this immense weight of glory is resplendent from its beautiful light? The mystic Martha Robin, who lived without food except that of the Eucharist for fifty years, declared, "Our degree of glory and of happiness in Heaven will be proportional to the quality of our Holy Communions on Earth."

Jesus said to Sister Faustina, "See, I have left my heavenly throne to become united with you. What you see is just a tiny part, and already your soul swoons with love. How amazed will your heart be when you see Me in all My glory. But I want to tell you that eternal life must begin already here on Earth through Holy Communion. Each Holy Communion makes you more capable of communing with God throughout eternity."[5]

Who could spurn such a future for his eternity?

We understand, then, why the Mother of God, who received the Body of her own Son every day from the hands of St. John, invites us to take time with Him to let Him accomplish His work of transformation in us!

I really like the words of a little seven-year-old girl who had just made her First Holy Communion. After the Mass, her mother asked her, "Are you happy, Sweetheart, that you received Jesus into your heart today?"

"Oh, yes, Mommy," the child replied. "And you know what I did with Jesus?"

"No, tell me."

"Well, when Jesus came, I took the key to my heart and I locked Him inside! That way, He'll never be able to leave!" Then she added these magnificent words: "That way Jesus and I will always be together!" That child had never read a theology book about the Eucharist, but she understood

---

[5] Ibid., § 1810.

everything! When Jesus enters into our hearts, two lovers meet each other, and embrace. What else is there to understand?

I also like to think about a very simple gesture. Take a glass and fill it with water. Put it on a dresser or any other support, which is at eye level. Take another glass and fill it with a little red wine. Then, very, very gently, pour into the water a little of the wine—just a few drops—and observe attentively what happens: the wine makes its way into the water. It passes through little by little, outlining a dancing path, but finally blends so much with the water that it becomes impossible to separate the two. The two elements are now one. This observation explains—although in an imperfect way—what happens in Holy Communion when we welcome Jesus with love. The union of the divine soul with ours is so intimate, so profound, that we are absorbed into God and God into us; we are inseparable.

Spiritual Holy Communion

For various reasons, some of the faithful cannot get to Mass, or, if they can, they are not in a state to receive Holy Communion (for example, if they are not yet baptized, or if they are not in a state of grace, etc.). In that case, they can make a spiritual Holy Communion or a Communion of desire. They can approach the priest with arms crossed over their chests as a sign that they cannot receive Holy Communion, and the priest will give them a blessing. Knowing how to practically receive spiritual Holy Communion can be confusing. Just know that it is sufficient to open your heart to Christ, and invite Him to come in. Then, all too happy to be invited for once by someone, Jesus will answer the call quickly. He will communicate to your heart the same graces that are in a sacramental Holy Communion.

All the saints have incorporated spiritual Holy Communions into their daily lives. That is why they have moved so quickly along the path to sainthood. The Blessed Mother used to make a constant spiritual Holy Communion to console Jesus from all the closed doors He ran into and which He still runs into today, even in the heart of the Church. When the faithful realize that this possibility is offered to them, many seize it with joy and begin to invite Jesus very often into their everyday life. Then they are surprised to notice great changes in their lives.

Why not perform a little test tonight, when you put your cell phone down on your bedside table? Ask yourself this: today, how many times have I called my friends, and how many times have I called Jesus? Calling Jesus has many advantages: the call is free, you don't need to re-charge the batteries, and you never get an answering machine! And how can you even take into account the treasures of grace that are accorded to you!

Chrissey, Kristin, Sister and Kim
while on mission in California in 2004

35

Natuzza Saw Purgatory

"I desire, little children, for each of you to fall in love with
eternal life which is your future, and for all worldly things to
be a help for you to draw you closer to God the Creator. I am
with you for this long because you are on the wrong path."

(MESSAGE OF JANUARY 25, 2009)

NATUZZA (1924–2009) HAD scarcely returned home to The
Father when the diocesan cause for her beatification
was initiated. No fewer than seven bishops and 120 priests
concelebrated her funeral rites. This simple country woman,
wife of a carpenter, mother of five and a grandmother, had a
formidable impact in Calabria, where she was born, and in

all of Italy. Today, testimonials about her even resound throughout the entire world.[1]

In the very heart of simple family life, and immersed in the poverty of her region, which is economically disadvantaged, Natuzza lived out a very particular relationship with Heaven. Among the multiple charisms she exercised, one can cite the fact that she knew the content of a book simply by taking it into her hands, because she knew neither how to read nor to write. She was capable of saying, for example, "On page 48, there is theological error," which could then be quickly verified. What's more, she could see the state of certain souls, and could counsel them in the right way. She had the gift of bilocation, and came to people who were suffering to comfort them and help them turn themselves towards the Lord. Sometimes these persons even found themselves healed. At the age of 11, she visited her father, who had left for Argentina to earn a living for his family. Natuzza constantly recited prayers of the most simple kind from her Christian heritage. Jesus visited her often, sharing the needs of His Church, for which Natuzza would sacrifice herself without hesitation.

One day, when she was physically suffering a great deal, and she asked Jesus to lighten her cross a little. Jesus listened to her with benevolence. But he returned to her some time later and said to her, "I tried to find a soul who would accept carrying this cross in your place, out of love for Me, and for My Church, so I could lift it from you. But none of the souls I asked accepted it, so I came back to you. Do you want to continue carrying this cross? I have need of this offering to save a great number of souls." Aware now that Jesus had

---

[1] See the site:
http://www.patriziacattaneo.com/natuzza_evolo.html

failed in his requests to other souls, who nevertheless called themselves his friends, she was overcome and accepted with all her heart the continued carrying of that cross.[2] She lived very poorly and always refused the gifts of the faithful. Her bishop said, "She is patient, of great faith, obeys the Church, and never allows herself to be tempted by money, which could make her a millionaire, considering the crowds who run after her."

At the age of 15, she began to see those who had died, and to converse with them. Her familiarity with them was such that people called her *the radio station of the other world.* She helped souls who were suffering in Purgatory and knew why they had to stay there for purification.

One of my friends from Sicily, Carlo, a man from a traditional Catholic family, kept up a beautiful friendship with Natuzza. He loved to visit her and talk to her about the things of God, because, he said, he always came away very happy and refueled for continuing on his journey. He had a brother, Renzo, who, like him, had been raised in a purely

---

[2] It is important to underline here that it is never suffering in itself that saves souls, rather love. It is out of pure love for Christ that Natuzza accepted to carry certain crosses, knowing the redemptive value of them. In Medjugorje, the Virgin Mary said, "Dear children, very few people have understood the great value of suffering, when it is offered to Jesus!" (Words spoken to Vicka in 1982) See also the message given by the Virgin Mary on May 13, 1917 to the three little shepherds of Fatima, "Do you wish to offer yourselves to God, to bear all the sufferings that he would wish to send to you, as an act of reparation for the sins by which he is offended, and of supplication for the conversion of sinners?" And Saint Paul writes, "I complete in my body what is lacking to the passion of Christ, for his body, which is the Church," (Col 1:24).

Christian tradition, but who, for reasons known to him alone, let go little by little, and gave up the practice of his faith. Among his children, he had a very brilliant son who promised to have a wonderful professional future. In the course of his engineering studies, his heart was taken hold of by a very strong call to the priesthood. After some time of intense prayer to test that vocation, he spoke of it to his parents, knowing that the idea might be badly received. Indeed, his father, Renzo, became very angry and said to him with all the paternal authority proper to his Italian culture, "I didn't pay for your engineering studies to have you end up a priest! You will be an engineer, Son, and that's it!" The son had to bend to the decision of his father, and with great sadness he abandoned his plan for the priesthood, finished his studies at the top of his class, and got married.

Carlo prayed a great deal for his brother Renzo, knowing that he was leading a life not well conformed to pleasing the Lord. Money had taken a great place in his life, with all kinds of imaginable snares.

Several years later, he was killed in a car accident. Carlo, very anxious about the eternal fate of his brother, went to the house of his friend Natuzza to ask her to pray for him. He also wanted to ask her if she had any knowledge about the final fate of his brother in the after-life. He came into Natuzza's little shack and, as he was getting ready to greet her, she didn't even give him the time to open his mouth, crying out right away, "You must pray hard for your brother, Renzo! Because he's in the deepest part of Purgatory, and he's suffering terribly!" Dumbfounded, Carlo asked her in a low voice, "My God!! Why?" "Because he prevented his son from following the call of God."

Then Natuzza, who used to see in spirit realities, which stayed hidden to other eyes, explained to him that God had called this young man to the priesthood to bring back a great number of souls. Even one priest more or less in the Church makes a huge difference in the economy of salvation. But Renzo did not accept that, and he opposed the plan of God. "Parents," Natuzza used to say. "Bear great responsibility before God when they prevent their children from following their conscience, and oblige them to take other routes. Children do not belong to their parents first, but to God." Carlo still trembled with emotion when he recounted that episode to me at the time of his visit to Medjugorje several months later.

Some people become unsettled when reading this story. Our modern society focuses so much on the things of this world, as though they will endure forever! Don't forget: we have only this time of our earthly lives to prepare for all of eternity! Wanting to invest for our children is an excellent thing, but don't forget that among the banks that are proposed to us, the bank of the Heart of Jesus is the only one which multiplies investments to infinity!

36

Pornography, a Modern Leprosy

"My children, do not deviate from the way on which I am leading you. Do not recklessly walk into perdition."

(Message of May 2, 2013)

A LEBANESE PRIEST, WHO is a friend of ours and comes often to Medjugorje, received a special grace to help souls in confession. He shared this very enlightening testimony with us:

A couple came to see him because their 7-year old son was not well at all. In the past, his health had always been good and he was successful in school, but then everything collapsed! The child was continually sick and none of the consulting doctors could find the source of the problem. Also, his grades were falling and it was as if he had lost all motivation and even his ability to study. Then, the worried parents consulted several psychologists with their child, but it was to no avail.

Eventually, they came to our friend and asked him to speak with the child. However, the priest asked them to leave the boy outside as he wanted to speak with them first. After a few basic questions about their habits and behaviors at home, the priest discovered with amazement that for some time both parents had been indulging in pornography when the child was not with them. They considered this activity as one distraction among others, and they had become addicted. Because they were married they thought that pornography would gratify their sexual passions without falling in the sin of adultery. This is a subtle snare. As if the sacrament of marriage released the couple from all moral responsibility in the practice of impurity, as if the sacrament permitted them to safely welcome the unclean spirit, Asmodeus, the killer of couples.[1]

The priest exclaimed to the parents of the child, "What are you doing? Stop that immediately! Don't you know that in doing this you are committing a very serious sin? Go to confession! You have opened a door to the evil one and you let him enter in your home, you allow him to attack your family. Through pornography Satan destroys marriages!" Addressing the man, he said, "You are the head of the family according to God's plan, but by indulging in pornography you are losing your fatherly grace and you are destroying what God entrusted to you!" Addressing the woman, he said, "You are damaging yourself and damaging the way your husband looks at you. In reality, you are making your husband distant from you and running the risk of losing him! And you wonder why your child is sick and crushed? He is paying a heavy price for your sin. So stop this, it is not too late! Pornography makes families sick!"

By the grace of God, and in spite of the addiction they already had, the couple decided to put an end to their perverted habit and they had the courage to abandon it. They threw all of their pornographic media in the garbage. Soon after, without any medical care, the child recovered his health and regained his motivation at school and his enthusiasm for

---

[1] Asmodeus is the name of the demon in the book of Tobit that tormented Sarah, killing all of her 7 husbands after they consummated their marriage. This demon is still at work today as a destroyer of families, (Tobit 3:8).

life. He experienced a kind of rebirth. It was high time for
this to happen![2] The couple is now well aware of the snare in
which they were trapped and they can witness that to other
families who are at risk.

In Rome, this priest has been asked to write a report for
exorcists on the effects of pornography. After his many years
of ministering to people in similar situations, this priest has
noticed that if a man indulges in pornography, many times
the result is that his wife starts to suffer serious troubles in
her reproductive system. It is not rare to see her affected by
infections or worse, cancer of the reproductive organs. As for
the affection shared by the couple, it frequently happens
when a woman indulges in pornography that she starts
turning away from her husband, and falls into the arms of
another man. This is because the sin to which she opened the
door worked in her and pushed her away from her husband.
Sometimes she develops hatred for her husband without any
cause and she tries to get rid of him. Similar things happen
on the husband's side. Why? Because this sin of impurity
produces in the heart of the married couple the fruit of
death, all the more significant since sexuality touches the root
of life. Healthy sexuality created by God bears the fruit of
life. Perverted sexuality, inspired by the destroyer, gives death.
"The wage of sin is death and the gift of God is eternal life,"
says St. Paul.[3] As in the snowball effect, this evil extends the

---

[2] This does not mean that any time a child is sick or disturbed that
it is due to a sin of the parents. There are many different causes
of illness. However, it is always valuable to remove serious sin
from the heart of the family, especially when there is an unex-
plainable malady there.

[3] Rom 6:23

damage done to the heart, and the couple ends up filing for divorce.

Moreover, the practice of pornography makes people lose the blessing given by God on material things in the family. It facilitates the structural destruction of the family. People lose their concentration, become lazy, and are not able to work as before. The young people who give free reign to pornography become disturbed and their intelligence is darkened. They are attacked by fear, and they become nervous and even have panic attacks. They fall away from God and are likely to wander aimlessly, always seeking new excitement. Pornography is like the mother of adultery, from which many other grave sins come, (Gal 5:19–20).

Pornography is harmful to all the aspects of the human person because it carries in it Satanic messages of destruction. It is no wonder that it is publicized and promoted by sects that worship Satan.

Closing the Door to Evil

During one of my missions in Italy, a man came up to me and joyfully said: "Sister Emmanuel, I'm so happy. I made a pilgrimage to Medjugorje this year, and I experienced a beautiful conversion! I abandoned almost all my sins!"

"Almost?" I asked him

"Yes, almost all! I only held onto one." "Why did you hold onto this one?"

"Because I like this one. It gives me pleasure." I lowered my head for a moment to gather my thoughts, because I didn't want to answer in the wrong way. Then I asked him, "How can you voluntarily hold onto a sin?

"But I let go of all the others! There was only one left …"
"We're all sinners, but it's one thing to fall through weakness

and another to actually want to continue to sin. When you receive Jesus in the Eucharist, you are saying to Him that you love Him, that you adore Him, that you are happy to know Him. How can you at the same time slap Him in the face so cruelly?"

He looked at me with shock and questioned me saying, "Slapping him?"

"What was it that nailed Jesus on the cross? I'm telling you, my sin, your sins and the sins of everyone. And you have decided to continue nailing him by voluntarily holding onto a sin?"

"Oh, my God! I never even gave that a thought!"

"Thank God that you think about that today! You know, wanting to keep a grave sin is like keeping a door open for the Devil, who is all too happy to have his little private entrance to your house. That way, he can work his destruction on you, on your family, on your health, on your life, and you are not even aware of where the trouble is coming from."

"Okay, I'm going to do everything I can to leave that sin behind! Pray for me!" That man was totally sincere. He simply lacked basic information!

There is today such an ignorance of the Christian faith that the most basic realities escape the consciences of a great number of 'believers.' Satan lulls these consciences to sleep, by distracting them with earthly attractions, and the search for worldy well-being. St. John of the Cross wept with compassion for the many souls abandoned to themselves, dangerously adrift, when all of them were called to a high degree of holiness. What a waste!

Our Lady never ceases to call us to be witnesses, apostles, and missionaries, because she sees clearly that the harvest is more abundant than ever. The suffering, which results from grave sins (sins that are sometimes even enshrined within our laws), is abysmal for her children who do not yet know the love of God. Legislatures and governments bear a heavy responsibility before God. The words of St. Paul, "The wage of sin is death," do not have an expiration date. They are still true today. Our culture of death is in the process of throwing millions of children and young people into agony. So Mary comes to Medjugorje to cry out to us that our true peace is in Jesus alone. Since she has been listened to only by a few, she arranged for the Lord Himself to express himself during the apparition of Christmas, December 25, 2012, "I am your peace," He said. "Live my commandments!" The visionary Marija told us that when He said that He was standing on the arm of his Mother (although He was a new-born) and spoke with authority! He had the voice of a child who had reached the age of reason.

In the Gospel, Jesus said, "If you want to enter into life, observe the commandments."[4]

Visionary Marija Pavlovic-Lunetti shares Our Lady's message

[4] Matt 19:17

The Death of the Wolf

This parable describes the way sin hurts the soul. In Alaska, the Eskimos have a unique way of living and protecting themselves. When there is a danger of wolves, the Eskimos scope out the whole area around where they have had sight of the wolf. Then, they take a 10–12 inch knife blade and cover it in blood and then they freeze it. Again they cover it with blood and freeze it. They do this a third and fourth time. Once this process is finished, they take the blade to the site where the wolf's tracks have been located. They lodge the blade in the ground so that it cannot be moved, and they sprinkle blood around it in order to attract the wolf. Then they wait.

When the wolf comes around, he likes what he sees and he likes what he smells. He first licks the blood on the snow. Attracted by what he tastes, he draws closer to the blade. He begins to lick it. He licks through the first layer and then through the second. By the time he reaches the third layer, his tongue becomes numb due to the ice. Little does he know what waits for him beneath that last layer of blood! He licks and licks without realizing that he begins to cut his tongue to pieces. By the time he finishes and takes one last gulp, he swallows his own tongue and inevitably chokes to death. The next day the Eskimos come and pick up the carcass and enjoy safety once again.

Like wolves, we are attracted, affected, and eventually destroyed by sin. We seek immediate pleasure—this is the problem of our society, which is especially affecting the youth. The media makes the habit of calling what is good, evil and what is evil, good. As the tongue of the wolf becomes numb by the frozen blood, in the same way the world of today has become numb to sin. People do not know what sin is anymore and do not recognize where evil is; they do not believe that sin exists. Sin is attractive. We like what we see. We like what we smell. We blindly follow our senses and in so doing we find the blade hidden there. Without Jesus in our life, before long, we will end up like the wolf.

Last May, Our Lady said, "I, as a mother, desire to save you from restlessness, despair, and eternal exile. My Son, by His death on the cross, showed how much He loves you. He sacrificed Himself for your sake and the sake of your sins. Do not keep rejecting His sacrifice and do not keep renewing His sufferings with your sins! Do not keep shutting the doors of Heaven to yourselves!" And in June she said, "My children, great is the responsibility upon you. I desire that by your example you help sinners regain their sight, enrich their poor souls, and bring them back into my embrace. Therefore, pray, pray, fast and confess regularly. If receiving my Son in the Eucharist is the center of your life, then do not be afraid, you can do everything."

37

Blessed Be That Table

"Today bring to me the souls of priests and religious, and immerse them in My unfathomable mercy. It was they who gave Me the strength to endure My bitter Passion. Through them, as through channels, My mercy flows out upon mankind."

(DIARY OF ST FAUSTINA, § 1212)

FATHER ROBERT WAS NO exception to the rule. Like all priests, he was familiar with the harshness of spiritual combat, and he knew from experience that the enemy of the human race would be happy to destroy him, him and his priesthood, today more than ever. A priest is so precious in the plan of God! That is why Our Lady invites us not only to pray for our shepherds, but also to watch over them.[1] The sheep ought to watch over their shepherds? Isn't that proof that the world is upside down?

In order to give us a little insight into the type of suffering priests must endure today, Father Robert shared with us his own experience in the exercise of his priesthood, and the pitfalls that have threatened him. To begin the story it is important to note that today this old, American priest achieves miracles in confession for the pilgrims of Medjugor-

---

[1] "My Children, my Son has given you shepherds, watch over them, and pray for them! Thank you," (May 2, 2013).

je, but it is also helpful to cast a rather indiscrete glance at his past, with his permission, of course. Here's his story:

"When I was ordained a priest, I made a promise to the Lord, with the agreement of my spiritual director. My commitment was that there would always be a table between me and the person who might come to me for advice or for other things, the idea being that this would protect me. That promise has never been easy to keep, but I have kept it, thanks be to God. That table has saved me!

"One day, a woman came to me, because she needed to talk to a priest about her very complicated family situation. She had barely arrived before I began to feel a very strong attraction to her. Because of her problem, she came to me often, looking for the comfort in me that she could find nowhere else. Very quickly, I fell in love with her, I mean really in love! I had all the symptoms of a man infatuated with a woman. She began to inhabit my thoughts, to invade all my feelings, my emotions, etc. I couldn't seem to control this overwhelming feeling. Every time she visited, I had a strong desire to take her into my arms, or even to reveal my feelings. But between us there was this table. Oh, how I hated that table! How many times I wanted to turn it around, to knock it upside down. However, the table never budged from its place.

"This torture lasted three years. And then one day, the woman arrived as usual, and, to my great surprise, I realized when I looked at her that I no longer felt anything for her. All my feelings of love had left me; it had disappeared as fast as it had come! I did not recognize myself. I didn't even see what could have been so attractive! What a relief! I continued to help this parishioner the best I could, but with this great and marvelous freedom of heart that a brother can have towards a simple sister in Christ. I understood then that these feelings of love were a trap that the enemy had set to destroy my priesthood. But the preventative grace of Jesus, starting at my ordination, had inspired me to make that promise—to set up a table. How far I was from imagining then that this table was going to save my priestly vocation! Or rather that Jesus Himself, by my promise to remain vigilant, was to save me from disaster!"

After that experience, Father Robert carried out his priestly vocation with a special charism to care for tormented persons. He received the gift of "seeing" what was not going right with them, and of getting to the bottom of the evil through his prayer, to uproot it. How many hearts has he helped? How many lives has he saved by praying and witnessing to the mercy of God? What a loss for so many, many suffering hearts his fall would have been! Today, he is a happy priest who is preparing himself to meet the Lord, full of the joy for having been able to serve the Church humbly and to remain a priest in the midst of the waves. Blessed be that table!

Certain women, willing to do harm to priests, have specialized in "the fall of priests," sometimes using occult activities. We can only pray and fast for those poor souls! "Do not touch my anointed ones," says the Lord. "Do not harm my prophets!" (*Ps. 105: 15*) "Touch not my anointed, and to my prophets do no harm," (1 Chronicles 16: 22).

If Father Robert knew enough to foresee his own protection right from his ordination, we also, we lay people, can place "tables" to protect our priests, and find concrete ways to avoid the situations that could make them fall. Isn't that a means of "watching over them" as Our Lady asked us to?

I Would Still Be a Priest Today!

" … Merciful and gracious is the Lord, slow to anger, abounding in kindness. God does not always rebuke, nurses no lasting anger, has not dealt with us as our sins merit, nor requited us as our deeds deserve. … As a father has compassion on his sons, so the Lord has compassion for he who fears him. For he knows how we are formed, remembers that we are dust … But the Lord's kindness is forever, for he who fears him. He favors the sons of their sons of those who kept his covenant, who take care to fulfill its precepts …"

(PSALM 103)

Father Kevin Scallon, a Lazarist, who often accompanies Sister Briege McKenna on her missions, leads marvelous retreats for priests in Ireland and all over the world. During his stay with us in September of 2013, he recounted for us this sad story: A priest came to find him and confide in him that, during an inner crisis due to an overload of work, he had let go of his priesthood. "I went to find the Provincial of my order," he said, "to complain to him. I was being crushed with work, and I couldn't do it anymore. I told him I was thinking of leaving the priesthood. Then, without even trying to talk with me, to listen a minute, or to try to help me, my Superior told me that he was going to arrange for my return to the laity as soon as possible. Now, if that man had taken just a little bit of time to look at my situation, to listen to me, and to take into consideration my state of extreme fatigue, I'm sure I would still be a priest today. I know it, I would have remained a priest!"

That story hurts. And it's not rare. Oh, Lord, multiply in Your Church good fathers of families, good priests, and good bishops; increase in them the feeling of fatherhood, so that all your shepherds will be living icons of the heart of the Father![2]

I gleaned the following testimony from Sr Briege McKenna that enlivens our hope in this domain, "I felt the Lord saying to me, 'I that you wish go throughout the whole world, and that you say to my people that the priesthood is the gift given to them so that they may be fed and strengthened. I wish you to call my priests to intercede, to love the priesthood, and to venerate this sacrament. When my people will come to love, venerate and give thanks for the priesthood, priestly vocations will blossom in their midst. Then it

---

[2] Priests have need of our protection more than ever before, because there are, of course, the first targets of the enemy. Forced by God to reveal to Maryam of Bethlehem his snares and techniques, Satan admitted, "For us [the evil spirits], to triumph over a priest or a religious soul, means more to us than perverting an entire city." The fact is, thousands of souls depend mystically first of all upon priests, and also upon religious souls. If only by celebrating his daily Mass, one single priest who is faithful draws a multitude of sinners to Jesus and to salvation. The Enemy knows what is at stake for souls, he is terrorized by the power of priests and he wants to destroy them. This is why they have such need of our prayers. May they take hold of Mary's hand with all their heart, then they will walk in security.

Venerable Marthe Robin prayed in these words: "O my God, keep all your priests on your holy way. Do not allow the attractions of the world and the desires of the flesh to have the slightest hold over them. Make them all more and more apostles, more unshakeable in their faith, more faithful to their ministry, and may your adorable will always be accomplished fully in them."

will be a joy for young people to say *yes* to this calling, because then they will be supported by their communities and their families.'"

Mirjana Knows

"My Children, my apostles, help me open paths for my Son. Once again I invite you to pray for your shepherds. At their sides, I will triumph. I thank you."

(MESSAGE TO MIRJANA)

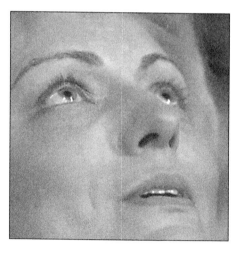

Visionary Mirjana in ecstasy

On February 9, 2013, the visionary Mirjana participated in a prayer meeting of priests in Italy in the Church of Santa Maria Maggiore of Trieste. In attendance was the Archbishop of Trieste, Monsignor Giampaolo Crepaldi. During the course of her testimony, Mirjana declared vehemently:

"As your sister, I beg you—because I know all that the Holy Mother is preparing for us—Love! Love your priests! Help them, pray for them, especially for our Holy Father! For him especially who, in these times in which we live, has great need of your help, of our help, of our prayers, of our love, and not of our judgments!

Because if tomorrow you find yourself in front of God and He asks you, 'How is it that you felt worthy to judge? Who are you?' How will you answer Him?

"That is why, as a sister, I beg you, ask God for the gift of love! When you have the gift of love, you never judge, you never criticize, because in each person you see Jesus, and you always find a justification. And even when someone does harm to you, you find a justification, you find an excuse, because for you, in your life, God comes first. Everything else passes away, only God remains. We are only sure of one thing: that we will find ourselves before God, and when we are there, will we raise our heads or lower them? I beg you, pray also for us, the visionaries, so that we can do all that God wants of us, but in a right way, because it is so easy to be mistaken. As for me, I will pray for you with all my heart."

Like Ivanka and Jakov, Mirjana also received her 10 secrets. She knows, therefore, a great deal about the future of the world, which gives her words remarkable weight.

A Truly Good Mother

It often happens that mothers are the inspiration and protecting angels of priests. I know a Lebanese priest, Father Mansour Labaki, whose story is typical. When he celebrated his first Mass, his mother offered him the most beautiful host one could imagine. It was delicately made by hand, in a beautiful golden color like fields of wheat, and enormous. He exclaimed then, "Mama, where did you find such a host?" The mother explained its origin. When he was a child, her son had confided to his family that he felt a call from Jesus to become a priest. She was very happy about it and decided to support this nascent vocation by offering both small and large sacrifices. She begged God to make her son a holy priest in His Church.

To concretize her maternal and spiritual help, she took a vase and decided to drop into it a grain of wheat each time she offered a sacrifice to God. Shortly before he was to celebrate his first Mass, she said to herself, "I'll grind these grains of wheat, and with the flour I'll make a large, flat cake, which will be his first host."

And so she did. When Father Labaki heard the story from his mother, he was overwhelmed! Each particle of the Body of Christ that he was going to take into his priestly hands would come from an offering of his mother! And she had kept this precious secret for so many years, sacrificing in silence for the priestly vocation of her son! Later, Father Labaki was put in charge of the formation of priests. His books are true marvels!

May his story inspire many mothers and spark the vocations of "spiritual mothers" so that good priests will multiply in our world!

38

The Lesson of the Fiji Islands

FATHER LAMBERTUS SOMAR HAS been a priest for 50 years. I met him during my mission in Jakarta in March of 2014. An Indonesian by origin, he was first sent as a pastor to a very difficult parish in the Fiji islands. No one hid from him the intractable side of this town, where previous pastors had worked so hard without ever succeeding in attracting people to the church. When Father Lambertus heard these details, he said to himself, 'No problem. I'm young. I'm bound to find a way to change this village!' And he set off for the conquest of this half-dead parish, confident in his talents as a preacher.

Shortly after his arrival, he was hit by the endemic local problems. People were drinking enormous amounts of alcohol, which lead to other deadly tendencies and that rendered them deaf to the preaching of the Gospel. One can imagine the damage within the families as well. Religion was of hardly any interest to them. Each day Father celebrated Mass in the presence of a single person, sometimes two, as many as three parishioners came on his best days! He tried every means of persuasion—going into their families, trying to gather young people—but nothing worked. His church remained empty. After several months of exercising his ministry without any apparent result, in spite of all his efforts, he began to get discouraged. One day, he took God to task and said to Him, "Lord, I'm giving you one year to change my parish, because I just can't stand celebrating daily

Mass anymore all alone. If nothing happens at the end of one year, I'll leave."

A year went by without the slightest change. Father Lambertus celebrated Mass each day all alone, while his parishioners indulged themselves in their various activities. The two worlds were simply not coming together.

The deadline arrived, and on that day, faithful to the challenge he had issued to God, Father Lambertus celebrated his last Mass all alone in the pitiful empty church. Since the church would be without a priest, he took care to consume the last host, unable to leave the Blessed Sacrament behind him. After the Mass he went to his house to make the last preparations for departure. He tied his knapsack to his bike rack and got onto his bike to go to the neighboring city and leave the Fijis. He had cycled only a few meters away from his house, when a man came running towards him, shouting, "Father, don't leave! A man fell from a palm tree and he's dying. He needs to make a confession and receive Holy Communion before he dies."

'Holy Communion?' thought the priest. 'But I don't have anymore hosts! And the idea of celebrating one more Mass all alone doesn't exactly make me happy.' But then he thought, 'Oh, well, if this man goes to heaven because of his confession and this Holy Communion, he'll certainly pray for me! So, okay, I'll celebrate Mass for him!'

He went back to his house, put down his knapsack, and left for the church to celebrate Mass. While he was putting on his priestly vestments in the sacristy, he heard an odd racket in the church—voices and noises never before heard in this holy place. Surprise! He opened the curtain, which separated the sacristy from the church and received the shock of his life! Contrary to all expectations, the church was full to the brim! Dumbstruck, the priest stood for a moment, frozen. He couldn't believe his eyes: the people had brought the dying man in on a pallet, and the man was lying there right in the middle of the main aisle. On that day, all the parishioners religiously followed the Mass. Who among them could have guessed that one year ago at exactly that hour, Father Lambertus had provoked God by saying to Him, "I'm giving You one year to act!"

Almost trembling, Father celebrated Mass, overwhelmed by this masterful response of the Lord. In the end the man did not die, and it was obvious to Fr. Lambertus that the Lord had His plan all along. He made use of the slippery palm tree, and the country man's fall to set in operation the major incident which was needed to bring His children back to His heart. On the days that followed, parishioners continued to fill the church, so much so that Father Lambertus had a hard time getting into the rhythm of administering all the sacraments they were demanding. "When it is the right time, I will act quickly," says Holy Scripture! Since that time, the church has always been full. During the three years that followed this event, Father Lambertus celebrated 500 baptisms. What more needs to be said?

Today, this old priest of 80 years, still very alert, recounted this memorable episode to me while laughing at himself. He sees both the humor and the love of God. In his naïveté as a young priest, didn't he say to himself, 'I am going to make it there!'? But he needed to understand that only God changes the hearts and that we are all poor, useless servants. That day, he realized that the true shepherd of his parish was Jesus, and not himself. He learned at his own expense that souls are conquered by the grace of the Holy Spirit, with a lot of prayer and profound humility. Later on, Father Lambertus was endowed with the great gifts of preaching and of healing, but he will never forget his first "client," the man who fell from the palm tree!

The moral of the story: if you want God to take over your work, don't make Him wait a year, but ask Him to do it starting today! He will be happy to take your affairs into His hands, or rather, permit you to collaborate humbly with His own divine affairs.

I was 7 Years Old When He was Arrested

In March of 2010, I took advantage of a trip to Singapore to return to China. There, I was struck by the depth of faith among many Christians.

In a village in central China, where I was received, a Catholic family resided. During the Cultural Revolution in the 1960s, the uncle of the family, who was a priest, had been arrested and put into jail. No one knew how long he would be in jail, and whether or not he would even return. His parishioners and family feared the worst. After 15 years he came home, but for 5 years he was under house arrest. He had barely returned when he undertook the rebuilding of his parish in the village and gathered together his faithful flock. Among his nieces and nephews, who lived with him at the time, as is the custom in the traditional Chinese families, there were two priests and one religious. When I asked one of the priests how he had received his priestly vocation, he answered me, "I was 7 years old when my uncle was arrested and led to prison. They came to get him at the house. I saw him leave with my own eyes. We couldn't say anything. That day, I received my vocation as a priest!"

Then I suggested that he write something about his uncle, who had since passed away, because giving a testimony about such courage is always magnificent. However, sobriety of words is a characteristic of people who have lived under Communism. "It's not worth the trouble," he answered me quite calmly. "As a priest, his case is not really special. Here, lots of Christian families have gone through the same thing!"

Now that is something to meditate on—in China, Christian families and priests suffer for their faith!

A Priestly Heart Prays

"I love You, oh my God, and my only desire is to love You until the last breath of my life. I love You, oh infinitely loveable God, and I would rather die loving You than to live a single instant without loving You … I love You, oh my God, and I desire heaven only to have the happiness of loving You perfectly. I love You, oh my God, and I fear Hell only because there, one will never have the sweet consolation to love You.

Oh, my God, if my tongue cannot say at every moment that I love You, at least I want my heart to repeat it to You as many times as I breathe. Ah! Give me the grace to suffer in loving You, of loving You in suffering, and of dying one day in loving You and in feeling that I love You. And the more I approach my end, the more I entreat You to increase my love and perfect it. Amen."[1]

---

[1] *Act of Love* by St. John Marie Vianney, the curé of Ars and patron saint of priests.

39

The Chinese Bishop

"Dear children, as my eyes are looking at you, my soul is seeking those souls with whom it desires to be one—the souls who have understood the importance of prayer for those of my children who have not come to know the love of the Heavenly Father. I am calling you because I need you. Accept the mission and do not be afraid, I will strengthen you. I will fill you with my graces. With my love I will protect you from the evil spirit. I will be with you. With my presence I will console you in difficult moments"

(MESSAGE OF SEPTEMBER 2, 2012)

DURING A TRIP TO CHINA, I visited the province of Herbei in the northern part of the country. There, my friends familiarized me with a figure who is dear to them, that of their bishop, Monsignor Raymond Wang Chong-Lin, born into Heaven a little before my arrival in 2012.

Arrested as a priest in 1958, and a prisoner for 21 years, he suffered a great deal and was not able to go back home until 1979. He was consecrated a bishop in 1983, but his diocese was what we call in French "ex sanguine," which means there was no life force, no blood in the diocese: no priests, no religious, no convents, not even a church or a presbytery, nothing. He made a pilgrimage to the Shrine of Our Lady of Graces in the Shanxi province, for the purpose of imploring help from the Blessed Mother. He had an overflowing love for her. He used to say to his friends, "You know how noble the call to become a bishop is, and how heavy that responsibility is. All I can do is turn it all over to the Virgin Mary! She is the Mother of God, the Mother of the Church, and also my beloved Mother. The Church has made me a bishop, but here the Church has nothing! No land, no seminarians, not even a room. What a poor shepherd I am! What does the Mother of God want?"

He had heard about the Shrine of Our Lady of Graces in Bansishan, where Our Lady had been appearing since 1982, and he decided to go there. He remembers,

"A voice seemed to urge me to go to see my Mother there, in Bansishan. We prayed the rosary on our knees, and during the prayer, she appeared to me near the church, dressed in white with a blue sash. I looked into her eyes and she looked into my eyes. Oh, Mother, if only you could always keep your eyes fixed on me! The next day, I celebrated Mass in the church for her intentions. It was a very important Mass for me, because at that moment I offered up my entire diocese with its 60,000 faithful. I consecrated them to Our Lady, and I offered myself up as well. I said to her, "Since I have nothing, I can't do anything. So I consecrate my diocese to you, my Mother. Take care of it yourself!" My Mother said, "My Child, don't worry, I will take care of you just as I took care of my Son Jesus."

And so it was! The Blessed Mother granted the request of this confident son, because the number of priests and seminarians began to multiply. Within a short time, 1985, Monsignor Raymond Wang Chong-Lin was able to create a seminary, restart the Congregation of Saint Therese, open an orphanage, found a vocation center, start a program of formation for laypeople, and many other wonderful things to support the Church.

This bishop had been able to do the impossible! In his radical poverty and his solitude, he prayed with faith. He consecrated everything to the Mother of God and abandoned himself to her with the confidence of a child. He knew that she would take the work of her Son to heart more than anyone.

Today, how many of those consecrated to religious life face similar situations of privation, emptiness, and solitude! They are tempted to surrender in front of the tremendous task ahead. But Our Lady is ready to do miracles, whenever it's about the work of her Son and the salvation of Her children. For many years in Medjugorje as well, she has been trying to make us fall to our knees!

Faced with the threats which weigh heavily on the future of humanity, with political and social implications which profoundly disturb us, the Blessed Mother always encourages us not to be afraid, especially when, from a human point of view, we would have good reason to be afraid. It's true that huge waves are shaking the boat of Peter! Everywhere Catholics are increasingly persecuted. Many governments want to impose impious laws, and, despite all the interventions of Heaven, the number of true believers is relatively feeble compared with the immense crowd of "those who do not yet know the love of God" and of those who want nothing to do with Him.

It's time for the perseverance of the saints! During our time of trial, practicing joy and confidence permits us to hasten the hour of the complete victory of our God over the forces of evil. Among all the organizations man has created, only one has survived over the course of centuries: the Church! And that is despite the sinners we are! Why? Because Jesus is the Head of it! And, besides, for His Church, Jesus made Peter a promise, which was unique in history: "The gates of Hell shall not prevail against it," (Matthew 16:13–

18). The Church has a future! So, what are we afraid of? "If God is for us, who shall be against us?" says Saint Paul.[1] Our job is to remain with Him and in Him, not to leave the boat when He seems to be sleeping, and never to disconnect ourselves from His grace.

For a long time, Our Lady has been indicating the path to follow. But it's important to point out that for a little while now she has been using the future tense to explain her action, as though she wants to prepare us for something ahead. "I *WILL* fortify you." "I *WILL* fill you with my graces." "With my love, I *WILL* protect you from the evil spirit." "I *WILL* be with you." "By my presence, I *WILL* console you in difficult moments," (9/2/12). "I *WILL* be by your side." "I *WILL* pray to the Heavenly Father that the light of eternal truth and love enlightens you,"(2/2/13). Why the use of the future? Is she hiding something from us? Like a mother who spares her child from listening to certain words when he is still too small and fragile, is the Virgin Mary sparing us in her revelations because of our lack of spiritual maturity? Yes, she has said it clearly many times: "Dear Children, I have still other messages to give you, but I cannot give them to you now, because you haven't yet begun to live the messages that I have already given to you."

Let's prepare ourselves through her, quite simply, by putting ourselves humbly in her hands. She is counting on us more than ever for the arrival of the *new times!*

---

[1] Roman 8:31

Slovenia Seized the Blessing!

"Many people now live without faith; some don't even want to hear about Jesus, but they still want peace and satisfaction! Children, here is the reason why I need your prayer: prayer is the only way to save the human race."

(MESSAGE OF JULY 30, 1987)

In April, 2014, while on my mission to Ljubljana, I discovered with joy a people very attached to the Blessed Mother. Slovenia is a very small country in the northern part of the former Yugoslavia. You cross through it to get to Croatia or Herzegovinia. Its mountainous landscapes call to mind the splendid beauty of Austria, its neighbor. There are only two million inhabitants, but it enjoys a strong personality in the heart of the Balkans. Much like the rest of the region, Slovenia has undergone bloody persecutions over the course of these last centuries, first with the Islamic invasion, then with the Second World War, and following that, the rapid growth of Communism. The numerous mass graves discovered in recent years show that the Slovenians were tortured or simply shot by the hundreds of thousands, and there is no way to enumerate the atrocious sufferings of which they were the victim.

But one day, the bishop of Ljubljana, Monsignor Gregorij Rozman, was inspired by the Holy Spirit to take an initiative which spared his country from being part of the terrible war of the Balkans (1991–1995) that broke out in the other provinces of the former Yugoslavia, such as Bosnia-Herzegovinia, where Medjugorje is located.

Let's look back a little. In 1917, at Fatima, Our Lady said to three little shepherds, "If you do what I tell you, there will be peace. But if you do not do it, Russia will extend its errors throughout the world, the pope will suffer greatly, entire nations will disappear, and there will be an even more terrible war ..." She offered the remedy to prevent that: consecration to the Sacred Heart of Jesus and to her Immaculate Heart. This consecration the Virgin called for had to be lived out first by individuals, then in families and parishes, and finally, in nations. In Europe, only Portugal achieved this consecration, and as a matter of fact, that country did not undergo a Nazi invasion. The experts still can't explain why Hitler did not rush into Portugal, a prey so easy to capture.

Fortified by this example, with the approval of Pope Pius XII, and ignoring the pressures against him, Monsignor Gregorij Rozman placed all his trust in the promises of peace made by Mary at Fatima; he decided in 1943 to officially consecrate his diocese and the whole nation to the Immaculate Heart of Mary, and through her, to the Sacred Heart of Jesus. To the surprise of everyone, hundreds of thousands of the faithful arrived from all parts of the country at the Marian Shrine in Rakovnik, near Ljubljana, to experience this magnificent celebration. From January onwards, they had been preparing themselves through the practice of the 5 first Saturdays of the month, recommended by Mary in Fatima.[2]

---

[2] On December 10, 1925, the Virgin Mary spoke the following words to Sr. Lucia at Pentevedra, in Spain, "See, my daughter, my Heart encircled by thorns with which ungrateful men pierce it at every moment by their blasphemies and ingratitude. Do you, at least, strive to console me. Tell them that I promise to assist at the hour of death with the graces necessary for salvation all those who, in order to make reparation to me, on the First Saturday of

And that day, the last Sunday of May, 1943, the soul of the Slovenian people regained its strength and courage, and hope was reborn.

Despite the Communist persecution, which lasted nearly 50 years, the Slovenian people remained faithful to Christ and to his Mother. Many believers renewed their consecration each day and thus found the strength to persevere in the middle of chaos. After the fall of Communism, when the terrible war of the Balkans broke out in 1991, the enemy stayed only three days in Slovenia, then left the area to go further into Croatia. Why this retreat? Slovenia had been consecrated to Jesus and to Mary. It belonged to them. It's clear that the enemy did not feel at all comfortable there!

The horrors brought by the conflict in the other provinces of Yugoslavia are incalculable. The concentration camps, the bloodshed, the crimes of all kinds, the agony of decimated families, the numerous young people wounded by the war and prevented from supporting their families, not to mention the interior wounds of hatred and lack of forgiveness which continue to poison hearts today. If we consider what dramas Slovenia escaped, how can we not give thanks to the Virgin for her maternal protection?

During the first year of their independence, 1992, the faithful reunited at the national Shrine of Mary Help of Christians in Brezje on the Feast of the Assumption to thank Mary for having obtained for them—miraculously, we might say—the recognition of their independence, in spite of all the opposition. They re-consecrated themselves on that day, and

---

five successive months, go to confession, receive Holy Communion, say five decades of the Rosary, and keep me company for a quarter of an hour, meditating on the fifteen mysteries of the Rosary."

since then, they have renewed this consecration each year on August 15th. This act has greatly contributed to the purification and revitalization of the Church in Slovenia, in fidelity to the Gospel.

Readers, take note! Other countries can very well choose their own protection, not the protection promised by the dubious speeches of politicians, but the protection that comes to us from on high—protection that is divine, solid, unswerving, freely given, peaceful, and not bloodthirsty! Already we have seen both private and public initiatives for consecration take root in many countries, following in the footsteps of Lebanon. Answering the call of Mary, Lebanon renews the consecration of the entire country every year! May these initiatives multiply everywhere on earth, until evil is crushed by love.

40

The Master Is Here and He Is Calling You

"Dear children! Also today I am with you and I am looking at you and blessing you, and I am not losing hope that this world will change for the good and that peace will reign in the hearts of men. Joy will begin to reign in the world because you have opened yourselves to my call and to God's love. The Holy Spirit is changing a multitude of those who have said 'yes.' Therefore I desire to say to you: thank you for having responded to my call."

(MESSAGE OF JANUARY 25, 2011)

O NE DAY, WHEN I was praying at the grotto of Lourdes, a young man accosted me and demanded, "How is it that you come to Lourdes when you live in Medjugorje, where Our Lady is still appearing?" Funny question! To answer him, since we had the time, I allowed myself to flashback to when I first came to Lourdes, since, for me, it is like an old acquaintance that one loves and returns to, just to bask in the joy of knowing you are home.

Every summer we used to go as a family to the Atlantic coast of France, near Saint Jean de Luz (only a 2 hour drive away). On the way, my father would take us to spend a day at Lourdes, to pray there and to bathe in the famous pools. During the car ride, we would pray the rosary. How I bless my parents for that tradition, it is one of many that they kept alive in us for so many years! Considering all the trials that my family has endured, that anchoring in the heart of Mary has saved us from many evils, and strongly united us. I was a long way from suspecting then what role the Virgin of Lourdes would play in my vocation. But let's go back …

In March of 1976, Pierre Goursat, the shepherd and founder of the Emmanuel Prayer Group, to which I belonged, came to pray with me. He finished the prayer by saying, "You need to leave Paris for a few days and pray in a peaceful place. I'm sure Jesus will speak to your heart." I complied and left for the convent of the Sisters of Zion Contemplatives near Paris.

In April of 1976, I found myself in front of the Blessed Sacrament, exposed in their chapel. There the Lord Jesus called upon me to consecrate myself completely to Him, through clear and humble words that I heard in my heart. I remember it as though it were yesterday. Several things struck me during that very particular and short time, which separated His call for me to become His spouse, and my response, which also had to be clear. It would be either *yes* or *no.* In essence, Jesus knew me well, and He knew how to go about reaching me! Freedom, innocence, and love, those are the things that he showed me at that moment. It is only now that I understand it, from a distance.

Jesus let me be completely free. No pressure, no "sentimental blackmail," no insistence even. I could say *yes* or *no* with the same ease.

Jesus spoke to me like a poor person, and not like a rich person, who would have tried to seduce me with beautiful promises.

Jesus showed me such love that my heart could do nothing but melt. The message was crystal clear: no one in the world would ever be able to love me the way He loved me.

It touched me so much that within a minute I fell for Him, and I gave him my *yes,* a yes rough and raw, and He

accepted it. My life really changed dramatically at that moment. When I think again about that minute of silence
during which Jesus was waiting for my answer, and with
what ease I could have said *no,* I give thanks for having
chosen the *yes!* And what if I had said no?! I would rather not
think about it. I had no idea then what plan He had for my
life. I knew only one thing: that I was going to spend my
whole life with Him and for Him. And that thought alone
filled me with joy. I had confidence in the future. He had
already concocted His plan. I didn't have to worry about it.
Today, as His plan for me reveals itself a little more each day,
I realize with gratitude that it was first and foremost He who
said *yes* that day, since He remains faithful beyond all we
could ever hope. He took my little *yes,* so fragile and so often
mixed, and continues to take it just as it is, in order to transform it, to make it like his own yes and present it to the
Father.

When I see the world today, the conflicts, the divorces,
the agonies of broken families, the distress of so many
youths, and especially the lack of true peace in the great
majority of hearts, how I thank my Lord for having asked of
me that sacrifice on that particular day, and for being content
with my little *yes,* fragile but sincere, for bringing me into
His boat … and what a boat! Waves flow into it sometimes,
storms make it pitch hard, but it doesn't sink. Jesus is in it.

I am certain of this: to say yes to God is to leap blindly
into the most beautiful adventure that one can live on this
earth. Whatever our call, unique, of course, for each of us,
we will never regret having said yes to God!

In Mary's message above, the Gospa delivers to us, in a
way, her own testimony. That's because her entire school of
love, founded in Medjugorje to prepare us for new times, is
in reality the adventure of *her yes,* of His *yes* to her—pure,
complete, with no turning back–which has illuminated the

world! She simply invites us to share it with her, to hide our poor *yes* in hers, in other words, to enter into her happiness. Today, she invites us to nestle against her maternal heart and to enter with her into the multitude of those who say YES!

I was 28 at the time of this call from Jesus, and it was up to me to figure out the practical details of how this new path would be with Him. Many advised me, "Go see this place, go see that place!" No, I wasn't anxious to test out many convents. Besides, my call wasn't about a convent, but rather, about belonging to a group of men and women who were renewed in the Holy Spirit, who would be in the movement called the Charismatic Renewal, such as I had experienced at the time of my conversion five years earlier.[1]

Two months later, in June of 1976, I discovered the new Community called the *Lion of Judah and of the Slain Lamb* in the French region of Tarn.[2] From my very first contact with these young people, their prayer, the beauty of their liturgy, their eschatological spirit, and their connection to the mystery of Israel struck me. The life that was lived there corresponded well with my aspirations. However, I needed a truly concrete sign from Heaven in order to make my decision. At the end of my brief stay as a "visitor," I had to go to Lourdes for the great gathering of Pentecost organized by the Emmanuel Prayer Group, to which I had belonged since my conversion. I prepared for this Pentecost by saying a novena to the Holy Spirit, asking Him to enlighten me about the place in life chosen by Jesus for me.

---

[1] See Chapter 4 in *The Hidden Child of Medjugorje*.

[2] *The Lion of Judah* is the first name given to the community, which became "The Beatitudes" in 1992.

As soon as I arrived in Lourdes, I hurried towards the Grotto where Mary appeared to Bernadette in 1858. The exact spot where Bernadette prostrated herself when she saw Our Lady is indicated on the ground, so I threw myself right on top of it, just as Bernadette had done. I prayed to the Virgin with fervor, thanking her for my being there, and I explained my situation as a child would to his mother.[3] After praying for a long time, with my face to the ground, the pain in my back forced me to get up. As soon as I stood up, I understood!

Our Lady did not answer me with words, even less with a vision. (She never does that with me, and I refrain from asking it of her!) But during my prayer, she acted without my even perceiving it. She imperceptibly inclined my heart towards the will of God so well that, when I got up my question had disappeared. It had truly vanished! A great peace came over me. I had passed over to the other side. I was already a member of the *Lion of Judah.* She had mysteriously given me that belonging; it was clear, indisputable. I was like a child who was put to bed in one house and awakened in another. It was typical of the ways of Our Mother: humble and hidden, but how profound and efficient!

---

[3] Even if Mary no longer appears there, Lourdes remains a place where she is always present. She offers everyone there her maternal and transforming love and sometimes heals us of our infirmities. As at Fatima or at Guadalupe, she is simply there, that's all, that's huge! For France, Lourdes is an incomparable treasure. Especially when our governments do everything to remove God from all the most vital fields of society. Poor things! Trying to remove our Creator and Savior has never worked, they should obtain that information. Jesus and Mary have their plan, and Lourdes is part of it.

In my joy, I thanked her, but I had to get the approval of the founder of Emmanuel, Pierre Goursat, also present at Lourdes.[4] Since he had entrusted to me several responsibilities in Paris, he could have said to me, "No way. You stay with us!" But this very inspired man of God answered me in peace, "Yes, that community suits you very well, go there!" I also needed the approval of the founder of the *Lion of Judah,* Ephraïm. That posed no problems, and I was able to enter into the community during the summer of 1976. I am still there today, thanks be to God.

---

[4] Pierre Goursat, died in 1991. He was declared *Servant of God,* to the great joy of those who knew and loved him. A Diocesan inquiry is open with a view toward his beatification.

41

The Gentleness of Mary
in Mother Makaria

YURI GAGARIN WAS BORN on March 9th 1934 in a little village in northwest Russia. His parents worked on a kolkhoz, or collective farm. His father, Alexei Ivanovitch Gagarin, was a carpenter. His mother, Anna Timofeievna Matveieva, had the job of milk maid. She was the daughter of a family of engineers in St. Petersburg. Life was hard in their village as it lacked both electricity and running water.

In 1941, the war with Nazi Germany broke out. Yuri, the third child of the Gagarins, was then 7 years old. The village was bombed and the little resources they had were depleted by refugees who rushed in after the Battle of Smolensk. Despite the risks, Yuri, like other little children of the village, turned to carrying out minor sabotages of the German war machine. One day, an event left its mark on him, an event that would play an important role in his future. A Soviet fighter plane landed near the village, and a rescue plane came to pick up the pilots. The children of the village, attracted by the spectacle, hurried to the spot. Yuri was fascinated by the plane, all the more so because one of the pilots took the time to show him how the controls in the cockpit worked.

The child grew more and more captivated by planes and grew up with a passion for them. Long after the war ended, on April 12, 1961, Yuri became the first man to make a flight into space, taking part in the Vostok mission launched by the Soviet space program. In 106 minutes, this young cosmonaut made a trip around the world! It was Yuri's hour of glory. He received the medal of the Order of Lenin, and the Russian hero was known around the world from that day forward.

A little while later, his mother, Anna, who was a devout Christian, received a wonderful privilege from heaven. 80 kilometers from her village lived a great Russian Orthodox "saint," Mother Makaria who lived from 1922 until 1993. She was one of those souls still hidden from the eyes of our Western culture, even though her nearly perfect configuration to Christ made her extremely holy. She was born in the little village of Karpovoka, in an area just west of Moscow. Right from childhood it was obvious that she had been given the gifts of continual prayer and healing. Overflowing with compassion, she led an exceptionally ascetic life and went so far as to take upon herself various evils and sicknesses of those who came to her for help. Russia knew great misery at the time, and many people rushed to the house of Mother Makaria to solicit her prayers. And, actually, many of them found healing there. Anna Gagurin was no exception. She came often to see Mother Makaria and, in fact, was linked to her in true friendship.

One day Anna spoke to her son Yuri about this holy, ascetic woman, and described to him the alarming state of poverty she was in because she wasn't able to manage on her meager pension. Moved with compassion, Yuri decided to pay her a visit and give her a little help. When he arrived at her humble dwelling, he found himself so at peace in her presence that he decided to come back to see her from time to time. His last meeting with Mother Makaria took place at the beginning of March, 1968. About that meeting, Makaria said, "We talked a long time together. Yuri was a good and simple man, like a child. That day, I told him, 'Yuri, don't fly anymore. You should not fly anymore!'

Yuri Gagarin didn't take those words very seriously, and on March 27, 1968, ignoring the precious advice of his saintly friend, the space hero decided to fly anyway and took off into the sky. But a terrible accident awaited him that day—a fatal accident. Yuri was only 34 years old. The cause of the accident was never really clear, but some inquiries concluded that the plane had been deliberately sabotaged.

Devastated by the brutal death of her son, Anna went again to Mother Makaria's house and asked her if, before the accident, she had knowledge of the misfortune that would happen to her son. To Anna's great surprise, Mother Makaria told her that yes, she did know. So Anna exclaimed,

"But why didn't you tell him?"

"I learned about doing that from the Blessed Virgin," Mother Makaria answered.

It's astonishing and remarkable that Our Lady, through the mouth of Makaria, had told Yuri not to fly with such meekness, given the seriousness of what was threatening him. She could have told him with authority, "Above all, do what I tell you. If you don't, you'll die!" But he didn't make anything of it. She had simply said, "Don't fly, you should not fly!" Yuri was free to listen to the message or to not listen to it. Why didn't he grasp it, knowing that this holy woman, radiating love, had very special charisms?

It's the same in Medjugorje. For so many years, Our Lady has spoken to us gently in her motherly language, very tenderly but also very clear. She doesn't say to us, "If you don't fast on Wednesdays and Fridays, misfortune will come upon you!" She doesn't say to us, "If you don't pray for the unbelievers, they will end up devouring you!" She doesn't tell us, "If you don't abandon your sins and go to confession, you are playing games with the enemy, and it will be easy for him to devour you at the last hour!" She doesn't raise her voice to try to convince us. She did not come to threaten us or to frighten us, but to show us the way of salvation that is her son Jesus.

Today many of her children read her messages with a distracted heart, without entering into their depth. Like Yuri, people pick and choose them. If we lead our lives that way, we lose the blessing of God on our lives, and we do harm to ourselves. Reading the episode about Mother Makaria, some people might reproach her at not having expressed the danger of death more clearly. However, the error is not on the side of the Blessed Mother, because her message is transparent, more than crystal clear. No, the problem resides rather on the side of the man, who, wrapped up in his passions and material wellbeing, allows his conscience to fall asleep, and becomes deaf to the plea of Heaven. That's a malady of the soul that is widespread today in our hyped-up and stressed-out Western culture!

That is why the Mother of God says to us, *"My children, again, in a motherly way, I implore you to stop for a moment and to reflect on yourselves and on the transience of this, your earthly life. Then reflect on eternity and the eternal beatitude. What do you want? Which way do you want to set out on?"* (Message to Mirjiana July 2, 2012).

The Field of Watermelons

As long as we are looking into the personality of the Mother of God, I can't resist the urge to slip in here an episode of her life from a local tradition in Egypt that deeply touches me.

During my trip to the fabulous countryside of southern Egypt in 2011, my friends from Cairo and I made a stop in the village of Kousseya, near Assiout. In that village, a little church attracts many Egyptians and foreigners, because quite frequently miracles occur for those who pray there. The village is also known for being the same village where the Holy Family stayed for a little while after fleeing Bethlehem. An ancient, local tradition has it that Joseph and Mary had gotten wind of the fact that spies sent by Herod just arrived in the region looking for them. So, they had to flee very quickly. (Such was their life of political refugees at that time, the life of very poor nomads, entirely dependent on Divine Providence.) As they were leaving the village, the Blessed Mother saw a man planting watermelon seeds in his field. She approached him and asked for a favor. "It might be," she said, "that some men come to you and ask you if you've seen a foreign family with a tiny little boy. You could answer them, 'Yes they passed by close to my field, during the time when I was sowing watermelon seeds.'"

The next day, the man came to work in his field, and to his great surprise he saw that all his watermelons had grown during the night! They were ready to be picked and consumed! He was just beginning to harvest them when some of Herod's men approached him. The men questioned him,

"We're looking for a foreign family with a tiny little boy. Have you seen them?"

"Yes, the man answered. I've seen them!" "When did they go through here?"

"When I was sowing these watermelon seeds!"[1]

It was the absolute truth! I am so deeply touched by that story because even if it doesn't carry the official stamp of an historic document, it is a beautiful description of the candor of Mary! We also find in it signs of the special protection the

---

[1] After the sowing, it takes watermelons in Egypt four months to grow before they can be harvested.

Heavenly Father gave to this little nuclear family that was so invaluable for the work of salvation, and yet so despised by men! The inhabitants of the village point out that Mary, thanks of course to the Infant Jesus who accompanied her, performed this miracle so that the farmer would not have to lie, while giving an answer that protected them. The miraculous harvest was her way of paying back the farmer for his help.

In the midst of all the tragedies and dramas that touch the Christians of Egypt today, we hear them pray, "Lord Jesus, remember that Egypt protected you when you were little, so now protect Egypt!" Let us unite our fervent prayers to theirs![2]

---

[2] Christian Egypt is teeming with such memories about the journey of the Holy Family. Of course, some are authentic, others are not; still others mix truth and legend. It is impossible to verify them because they belong to oral tradition, to that precious ancestral memory transmitted by the word of mouth for two thousand years and which lives deep in the hearts of Egyptians. They consider this oral tradition their "sacred history."

42

Carolina and the Tears of a Son

"Dear children, God does not want you lukewarm and undecided, but that you totally surrender to Him. You know that I love you and that I burn out of love for you. Therefore, dear children, you also decide for love so that you will burn out of love and daily experience God's love. Dear children, decide for love so that love prevails in all of you, but not human love, rather God's love."

(MESSAGE OF NOVEMBER 20, 1996)

WHO COULD EVER EVANGELIZE me more on divine love than Carolina? This American friend has seven children between the ages of 6 and 22. As an associate with our apostolate in the United States, she invited me to speak at her church and to do a radio program that she hosts each week.

First of all, as a bonus, her household is like a little paradise, where husband and children live in great freedom while still remaining attentive to one another. Joy reigns, humor abounds; it is good to live in Carolina's home. Gradually, as the children came along, small living spaces were added to the main part of the house, encroaching on the garden and giving to the whole area the look of the most charming village. But the confidences shared by Carolina demonstrate that the cross truly exists everywhere.

Steven, the oldest son, the "big brother," who was the pride of all because of his talents and his kindness, had to leave the family nest and go to Rome because he thought he had a vocation to the priesthood. He chose the Pontifical Gregorian University for his formation in theology. After several months of study, love came knocking at his door. She was a marvelous young French woman, Esther, who was also a student in Rome. She revealed to our Steven some previously unsuspected dimensions of his heart. A change of direction for his future plans was in the air! While the Tiber was sending forth its waters to flow under the bridges of Rome, love grew between Steven and Esther, a strong and reciprocal love that grew more intense day by day, so much so that plans for marriage were taking shape. The two decided to finish their studies before forming a family. Esther did not know God, but she had nothing against Him, and remained open to Steven's beliefs. He, as a Christian, wanted to live chastity before marriage, and Esther accepted it with courage, out of love for him, an act that brought a new quality to their relationship. Their love took the high road with much happiness.

But one day, Esther set off on a trip to France, and, not far from Marseille, she was the victim of a serious car accident. When he was notified, Steven took the first flight to Marseille and found her in the hospital, in Intensive Care, at the point of death. She could no longer speak but remained completely conscious; although she could open her eyes, her situation was very serious. All day long, Steven held her hand. He knew her hours were numbered. He spoke to her gently and prayed as he had never prayed before. Then, during the night, Esther left him to go home to her Father.

That morning, Carolina received a telephone call she will never forget, "Mom, I want to die!" Both of them, mother and son, had broken hearts. Steven repeated the same words even when his sobs left him with almost no voice, "Mom, I want to die. But at the same time, I want to live, to become the man she thought I could be." And the mother, seeing her son's fiancé taken so abruptly, shared with him his hallucinating descent into that terrible purgatory where the human heart finds itself crushed to the point of screaming. All her maternal feelings were being tortured. Only the name of Jesus escaped from her lips from time to time in the course of this intimate conversation between mother and son.

For a while, Steven returned to his family in America. He kept quiet. He wandered from one room to another. He tried to survive. Carolina guessed it all, and she made sure not to leave him alone too long with his grief. One day, when she was coming into the living room, she saw him ready to burst into tears and let all his sorrow be released. To spare him the embarrassment of being heard, she turned up the sound of the television so the noise would cover the moans of her son. Discretely, she went into the next room to iron her clothes. She felt the grief of her child, and she began to pray.

What prayer did this mother find to send up to God? What was she going to ask for her child? What desire did she carry in her heart for him?

It is here that I want to interrupt the story. Listen well to the prayer of this Christian mother, who wants the happiness of her son so much and who sees it crushed by this ordeal.

"Lord Jesus, You see my son. He is overcome with grief, and me, his mother, I am overcome along with him. Lord Jesus, don't spare him any of the trials he must live through to become the saint that You hope he will become. Don't take away a single ounce of the trials that he must live through to become the great saint that he can be under Your plan!"

When Carolina told me that she had prayed in this way, I saw Mary at the foot of the cross. Mary, who never tried to suppress the cross; Mary, who had for her Son not a human love, but a divine love. Mary loved her son divinely. She took no steps before Pilate to prevent his condemnation, or before the Sanhedrin, or before Herod, or before the High Priests of Jerusalem. She made no noise. She started no petition. She knew that her Son had to go through it all to accomplish his mission as Savior. She did not try to take the cross from Him, but she helped him carry it. She carried it along with him through her compassionate love.

Here you have the difference between human love and divine love! It is this divine love that the Holy Spirit wants to infuse in our hearts, so that, day after day, it blossoms in us to its fullness.

What is the definition of divine love? To love divinely is not only to desire the greatest happiness for the beloved, but also to give oneself over to serving that greatest happiness, to help it grow, without looking to take any personal gain. It is to sacrifice oneself to help the beloved become the best he can be in the eyes of God, his Creator. It is to help him realize all the potential love of which he is capable, and to become, in that way, the saint he is destined to be in this world and for all eternity. The saint is the one who, in his heart, has the fullness of love. So nothing is too costly, nothing is too inaccessible for the one who loves genuinely, without receiving anything in return and without egotism. There is no personal agenda there. Only true love performs miracles. If we achieve the potential of love that God has placed in us, we will be crazy with love! Why live beneath our means?

Mary gives us the splendid example of a heart totally abandoned to love, because no obstacle ever stopped her journey with Jesus. She never said, "This is too much!" or "That's going too far!" or "I can't do it anymore!" or "I'm not capable!" No, the eyes of her heart were fixed on her Son, and she never gave a thought to looking at herself. Continuing this example, my friend Carolina abandoned herself to

God for the good of her children, offering her joys and sufferings for their journey towards sainthood. She wanted to build on The Rock, on eternity.

"Only love is efficient," says Our Lady. "Love performs miracles. Love will give you unity with my Son and the victory of my heart. Therefore, my children, love!" (Message of September 2, 2008).

While Carolina was agonizing with her son, with all the feelings of a mother, she held onto that extraordinary hope that his suffering was not in vain. God would know how to use it for her family and well beyond her family, for whomever He saw in His wisdom.

In Medjugorje, the Virgin Mary confided something to one of the visionaries that may seem shocking at first glance, but which corroborates what my poor words are trying to get across. Mary said to her, "When I was standing at the foot of the cross of my Son, I experienced the greatest joy of my life, at the same time as the greatest sorrow." Why *that* joy? She saw Jesus accomplishing the ultimate goal of His coming on Earth, she saw Him achieving fully his mission, she was proud of Him! He was in the act of conquering evil and the author of evil forever. She was seeing with her own eyes God's plan fulfilled: the salvation of the entire humanity!

Of course, her joy was not in the fact of seeing her son suffer–which would be sadism—no, her joy was seeing her Son win the victory! On Golgotha, she saw Heaven opened up for every one of us; and the gaze of the Most Pure took in the most atrocious suffering the earth can bear—the cross of the Son—only to look beyond it and see the fruit of this suffering: our eternal happiness. That was the cause of her joy.

When we say to someone, "I love you," Jesus asks us, "Would you give your life for that person?"

43

The Sister of the Stable

"I have always wanted to be a saint, but alas, when comparing myself to the saints, I have always had to concede that between them and me there is the same difference that exists between a mountain whose summit is lost from sight and an insignificant grain of sand that is trampled underfoot by passersby. Instead of being discouraged, I said to myself, 'The Good Lord would not inspire desires that were not able to be realized, therefore, despite my littleness, I can aspire to holiness.' It is impossible for me to improve myself, I have to bear with myself as I am, with all my imperfections, but I want to find the means to go to heaven by a little way that is very straight, very short, a little way that is completely new. The elevator that must lift me up to heaven is your arms, O Jesus! For this, I don't need to get bigger, on the contrary, I have to remain little, and to become so more and more."

(St Therese of the Child Jesus)

THE CURÉ OF ARS often repeated, "Humility is to virtue what a chain is to a rosary. Take away the chain and the beads scatter. Take away humility and all the virtues disappear." He loved to quote St. Macarius, the hermit of the Thebaid region of Egypt who tells the story that one day Satan appeared to him and said, "Everything you do, I can do also. You fast and I never eat. You stay awake and I never sleep. There's only one thing I can't do that you do."

"Oh, and what is that?" "To humble myself."

That's a remarkable fact that calls for reflection, all the more so since the Gospa (especially through Mirjana) never stops exhorting us to pray for our priests. "Pray for your shepherds," she says. "Priests don't need your judgments. They need your prayers, your help, and your love. Today, it is difficult for a priest to remain faithful," (Message to Mirjana, 1982).

A famous German bishop, Monsignor Ketteler, recounts this event, which impacted him profoundly. God revealed to him that a nun was sacrificing her life for him, and that the fruitfulness of his ministry was due to her prayers. He was shown the face of this nun. But he didn't know where she lived. During his pastoral visits to the convents of his diocese, he always asked to see all the sisters. That way, he thought he'd recognize her. One day, he visited some nuns in a neighboring city and celebrated Mass in their chapel. The distribution of Holy Communion had finished when his eyes rested on a lone nun. He turned white and froze for a minute, but getting hold of himself, he gave Holy Communion to this sister who didn't seem aware of anything. Then he calmly ended the Mass.

He asked the Mother Superior to introduce him to all the sisters. But, not finding the one he was looking for, he asked, "Are all the sisters here?" The superior said, "Your Excellency, I called them all to come, but actually one is missing. She takes care of the stable in such an exemplary way that, in her zeal, she sometimes forgets other things." "I want to meet this sister," insisted the bishop.

A little later, the sister arrived. The bishop again turned white and asked to be left alone with her. He asked her: "Do you know me?"

"I have never seen you Your Excellency."

"What is the devotion that you like to practice the most?"
"The devotion to the Sacred Heart of Jesus," was her answer.
"It appears that you have the hardest job in the convent," he
continued.

"Oh, no, Your Excellency," she replied. "Although, I have
to admit that it repulses me sometimes."

"What do you do when you are attacked with temptations?" "I have gotten into the habit of completing every task
that is difficult for me through the love of God and with joy.
And I offer that up for a soul on this earth. It's up to God to
choose which soul will be the beneficiary. I offer my hour of
adoration of the Blessed Sacrament each evening for that
soul."

"And how did you come up with the idea to offer all that
for a soul?" The sister answered, "It's a habit I got into at
school. The priest taught us that we should pray for others
the way we pray for our own families. He also said, 'It's very
important to pray for the souls in danger of being lost. But
since God alone knows who has most need of it, the best
thing to do is to offer prayers to the Sacred Heart of Jesus,
trusting in his wisdom.' That's what I have done, and I have
always believed that God found the right soul." "Do you
want to know for which soul you are praying?"

"Oh, no. That's not necessary!"

By the time they left each other, the bishop had not unveiled his secret.

44

Spiritual Motherhood

"While he was still speaking to the people, behold, his mother and his brothers stood outside, asking to speak to him. But he replied to the man who told him, 'Who is my mother, and who are my brothers?' And stretching out his hand toward his disciples, he said, 'Here are my mother and my brothers! For whoever does the will of my Father in heaven is my brother and sister and mother.'"

(MT 12:46–50)

HOW COULD JESUS SAY, "Here is my mother" to those women who, there in front of him, were avidly drinking in every word he spoke? Jesus sometimes identified himself with certain persons. For example, to the lowly he said, "Whatever you do to the least of these little ones, you do it to me," (Mt 25:40). Or, to those who were persecuted because of his name he said, "Saul, Saul, why are you persecuting me?" (Acts 22:7). But here, he identifies certain women with his own mother, Mary, she who, par excellence, had always "done the will of my Father in Heaven." Jesus does not say that they are "like my mother." No, it is infinitely more powerful, since he says that they are "a mother" for him, without the "like." We shall never be able to fully sound the depths of this identification!

Great indeed is this mystery of Mary's divine motherhood! What else is a mother, but one who brings to birth? In her divine motherhood, Mary gave birth to the Son of God in the flesh, but her role as mother did not stop there. She also gave birth to him in his vocation as Savior and his mission as High Priest. She was so at one with the Father's plan for him that at the moment of his Passion, she did not oppose the Cross, but rather, she helped her Son to carry it. Through her loving compassion towards him, she endured all his sufferings with him, and in doing so she participated in his work of redemption.

This, then, is the authentic mission of woman with regard to man. From the time of Genesis, Eve was given to Adam as a *helper.*[1]

Mary, the New Eve, is there beside Jesus, the New Adam, to work with him. The Redeemer had need of this feminine presence, which was full of love, prayer and sacrifice. Mary, however, does not reserve for herself this privilege of helping Jesus in his mission. She is seeking out those souls who want to become one with her soul.[2] She is searching for mothers for her Son, and not only for Jesus, but also mothers for priests, her Son's preference. Every priestly vocation has need of prayer and sacrifice in order to blossom, grow, and bear fruit. We are dealing with an extraordinary invitation from the Mother of God, to every woman who wishes to claim her beautiful Marian virtues, and live out her motherhood geared toward Jesus!

---

[1] See Genesis 2:18. The Hebrew word ezer is much broader in meaning than the simple idea of a helper. It refers to an assistant, a support, a partner, and also to the type of help and support that God himself brings to man.

[2] "Dear children, as my eyes are looking at you, my soul is seeking those souls with whom it desires to be one … Accept the mission and do not be afraid!" (Message given to Mirjana on September 2, 2012)

"Here is my mother …" These words of Jesus have creative power!

The history of the Church offers us many magnificent examples of holy women, canonized or not, who took this preferential love for the person of Jesus to the extreme. These 'spiritual mothers' had the great privilege of becoming his intimate friends, with whom He could share His needs, His desires, His joys, His secret sorrows, and His suffering in the face of the world's indifference. They have been stationed, like angels, at the side of certain priests who have had key roles to play in the Church. Let us take a look at some of them.

Barbara

When my friends from Zagreb told me how their parents lived under Communism, (which officially collapsed in Yugoslavia in 1991) I was struck by the heroism of certain women whose son or sons had been imprisoned simply for being Catholic, and for refusing to renounce their faith. The example that moved me most deeply was that of a certain woman named Barbara, the mother of eight children.

Since the parents of my friends had known her, I was able to gather this testimony first-hand.

They told me that while her son, Alojzije, was suffering in prison, Barbara would do anything to visit him, to encourage him, and to bring him consolation. In those days, the regulations were enough to deter even the most fearless of women! To reach the cell of the prisoner, the mother first had to undress in a room at the entry of the prison, present herself in the simplest of underwear, and endure all kinds of similar humiliations, even in the harsh winters of Zagreb, where the temperatures sometimes fall to ten degrees below zero.

She loved Jesus above all and went about her everyday tasks with simplicity. Wise and humble, like many Croatian women, with her feet firmly on the ground, the description of her made me think of certain traits of the perfect woman in the Book of Proverbs, "The virtuous woman—who can find her? She is far beyond the price of pearls. Her husband's heart has confidence in her; from her he will derive no little profit. Advantage and not hurt she brings him all the days of her life. She procures wool, and flax, and does her work with eager hands. She is like those merchant ships, bringing food from afar. She rises while it is still dark, and gives food to her household, and tasks to her servants," (Prov. 31:10–15). Barbara's husband was a farmer in Croatia and did well enough financially.

Alojzije Viktor, Barbara's fifth child, was baptized in the church at Krasic, on May 9, 1898, the day after his birth. That day Barbara made a sort of tacit pact with Jesus, a very special vow that she recognized as coming from the Holy Spirit. She hoped so much to see one of her sons become a priest! She asked for this grace especially through the intercession of Mary, to whom she was very devoted. In her deep love for the mystery of the Eucharist, she saw the priesthood as the grace of all graces. To be able to give a priest to the Church represented for her the preeminent gift, something divine! As her part of the bargain, in order to obtain such a gift from God, she committed herself to praying every day and fasting three times a week, with no time limit. This decision was not the result of a sort of pious lack of consideration. She knew that being a priest could become dangerous in the future, and, indeed, the era that followed proved her intuition accurate. In those times, a priest was subject to humiliation and persecution, even possible martyrdom.

Only the parish priest of Krasic knew about Barbara's secret vow, and he approved of it. She had confided in neither

her husband nor in any of her children, though they could see that she was fasting. Moreover, she did not want to influence her son's vocational choice, a free choice that he alone was to make if he recognized a call from deep in his heart. God heard Barbara's request and granted it. During the summer of 1931, Alojzije received the sacrament of Holy Orders and celebrated his first Mass in Krasic. Barbara had fasted and prayed for thirty-two years! Following tradition, Alojzije reserved his first blessing for his mother. The parish priest then whispered into Barbara's ear, "Now that your son is a priest, you have been given what you desired. You can stop fasting." To which she replied in a resolute voice, "Certainly not. On the contrary, I am going to fast and pray all the more in the future, because I'm asking God that my son become a holy priest!"

After enduring the Fascist rule of the Nazis, Croatia passed into the hands of the Communists, and serious persecutions followed. Alojzije stood out for his unshakeable faith and his tenacity, not to mention his exceptional intelligence. In 1934, four years after his ordination, he was consecrated a bishop and became the youngest bishop in the world. Barbara's sacrifice was quite obviously bearing fruit! For Alojzije, his mother's example of faith and the support of her prayer, as well as her affection, were beacons that illuminated his way. Faithful to the heritage he had received from her, he always kept a rosary in his hand. Some of his sayings have become famous, for example, "When everything is taken away from you, you still have your two hands to pray with!"

A painful way of the cross was in store for him. Alojzije was threatened, accused of being an enemy of the people and a traitor to his country. In 1946, after a mock trial, he was incarcerated. He was condemned to sixteen years in prison with forced labor. His crime? His refusal to hand over the Catholics of Croatia to the Communist powers who were seeking to separate them from Rome. His courage and his steadfastness did nothing less than prevent a schism! If the Croatian parish of Medjugorje still exists today, if it has been able to remain Catholic and welcome millions of the faithful, let us not forget that it is thanks to those who paid with their blood for their fidelity to Rome and the Apostolic succession!

Through her hidden sacrifice, Barbara inspired the heroic fidelity of her son, Alojzije. Thanks to her motherly help, he received the strength and courage to stand up to all these attacks. She had to walk the way of the cross with him, in the way that only the heart of a mother can! She died in 1948 at the age of eighty-two, while her son was still being held, and she never saw in this life the double glory that would crown her efforts. In 1953 Pope Pius XII, who knew of the whole situation, named Alojzije Stepinac, Cardinal of Zagreb, even though he was still being held in custody. Alojzije entered into his heavenly reward in January of 1960, two years before the end of his sentence In 1997 John Paul II beatified this remarkable man who offered his life to safeguard the Catholics of Yugoslavia from schism![3]

Perhaps today, from his heavenly vantage point, Saint John Paul II might be saying to himself that he could also have beatified the little, hidden mother, Barbara. She was a chosen soul, who had given birth, not only in the flesh, but

---

[3] The tomb of the Blessed Cardinal is located in the Cathedral of Zagreb. The Croatian people come every day to pray to their hero and ask for his intercession. After having suffered through the Communist era, Croatia has still had to face other evils in their own days, due to the consequences of the war, internal crises, as well as governments that are more or less hostile to the Christian faith.

also spiritually, to a national hero and a saint and martyr of such caliber![4]

Sometimes, in the course of my missions, I make an appeal to those in the assembly, and I say to them, "look at what this mother obtained for her son! That is true maternal love! Who among the mothers here would like to pray like Barbara and ask Jesus for the honor of being able to count a priest among their sons, if such is His will? If there are some mothers here who would like to do this, let them kneel down and we will all pray for them and the priests will give them a blessing."

How many times, after a period of silence, have I been able to observe with wonder and with tears in my eyes, a number of women in the audience fall humbly to their knees, one after the other! The first time was in Kuching, in Malaysia. There, twenty or so women got down on their knees and prayed. But after the conference, a woman said to me in a rather rough tone of voice, "I only have one son, and I don't want him to be a priest because he has to continue the family name!" I replied, "The Virgin Mary had only one son as well, and she gave him! His name is above every name! And in Heaven, priests will also have a name above every other name, because in celebrating the Mysteries, they are other Christs. Think about it!"

The enemy seeks to destroy the image of the priest according to God's plan by laying before us, in the media, the sins of some of them, and making us forget the heroic self-gift and the sanctity of so many priests. Every family desires God's blessing on themselves and on their descendants, and

---

[4] Cardinal Kuharic of Zagreb (1919–2002) used to say, "One cannot understand Stepinac or his heroic life without knowing his mother."

they are right to do so. Then surely, the best way to draw down this blessing is to invite the Giver of all Blessings to come in the midst of the family as its King. Let us open wide our doors to the One who is the source of all blessings and who desires so much to give Himself to us through His priests! Are they not Christ Himself when they give the sacraments? Are our priests not our treasure, ladders that lead us upwards towards Heaven?

Blessed Cardinal Alojzije Stepinac during his trial in 1946.

Maria Bordoni (1916–1978)

Maria Bordoni during a pilgrimage to Lourdes.
© *Opera Mater Dei, Castel Gandolfo*

In the course of his years of captivity, God gave to Stepinac another spiritual mother, but in a completely different way. Her name was Maria Bordoni, the foundress of the 'Mater Dei' Institute, who at that time lived with her Sisters at Castel Gandolfo, near Rome. Since then the Church has proclaimed her Servant of God.

Maria was a mystical soul, every bit as great as she was hidden, completely permeated by the priestly spirit, which inspired her to offer herself to God as a victim-soul for the clergy. She often prayed during the night for the Church, for the Holy Father, for priests and for persecuted Christians. The Blessed Mother spoke to her soul, and, during the night, would take her in bilocation to visit places of misery and also to Eastern Block countries during the time of Communism, in order to bring consolation to those who were suffering in prisons and camps.

During one of these bilocation events, the Blessed Virgin showed her a priest in prison, sitting on a chair. He was bent over with his arms leaning on his knees, and the beads of his rosary were slipping through his fingers. He was praying. Our Lady then said to Maria, "Do you see this beloved son of mine? He is suffering a great deal. Pray for this beloved son of mine. His name is Alojzije Stepinac." It was Cardinal Stepinac while he was being held in custody in Zagreb.[5]

Even after his captivity, Cardinal Stepinac was held under house arrest for nine more years in his hometown. Thirty guards kept careful watch over him. He died in 1960, forgiving all those who had wronged him.

When Pope John Paul II beatified this martyr bishop in Croatia, in 1997, the Sisters of Maria Bordoni recalled having heard his name in the stories she told about him, and reading about him in the writings of their foundress. While searching through her spiritual notes they found a recording of this "visit of consolation" she made to Cardinal Stepinac. In visiting Stepinac, Maria Bordoni lived out her desire. She wrote, "I would like to be like the lamp that burns at the altar and is slowly consumed before the Lord's tabernacle, for the Church and the Holy Father, and for all priests and missionaries."[6]

---

[5] The Sisters of her Institute confirmed this to the priests of the Community Family of Mary in March of 2010.

[6] On this topic, see the magazine Triumph of the Heart, August 2010.

Sister Faustina Kowalska (1905–1938)

This wonderful Polish saint, who was to fill the entire world with her messages on the Divine Mercy, complained to Jesus one day that Poland didn't have any great saints like the ones she saw from other countries. Jesus answered her, "That saint will be you!"

In her *Diary,* Saint Faustina relates just how much she wanted to help priests, not only by her fervent prayers, but also by a thousand other ways that she imagined in the generosity of her heart. Heaven accorded her a rare favor to help her accomplish her goal, that of having a spiritual father of great worth, Father Mickael Soposcko. He knew just how to guide her during the last years of her life. (This priest was himself beatified by Cardinal Dziwisz in 2008.) Seeing all that he endured in order to carry out the mission of Mercy, she decided to render him a service, in the way a mystic would! She wrote, "One time, a priest asked me to pray for his intentions. I promised to pray and I asked him for a mortification I could do on his behalf. When I received permission for a certain mortification, I felt in my soul an inclination to surrender everything on this day for the good of that priest, all the graces that the Divine Goodness intended for me. I prayed that the Lord Jesus accord to me all the suffering and all the afflictions, interior and exterior, that this priest had to suffer on that day.

"God accepted, in part, my desire, and right away there began to emerge from who-knows-where all sorts of difficulties and aggravations to the point that one sister said aloud that the Lord Jesus must be behind it, if everyone was tormenting Sister Faustina. And the facts that people put forward were so lacking in foundation that half the sisters believed them and half denied them, and me, I offered it all in silence for that priest.

"But this wasn't all. I endured interior suffering. First a sort of discouragement and an aversion to the other sisters came over me. Then, a kind of doubt began to trouble me that I couldn't resolve through prayer. I was preoccupied by a host of different things. And when I entered the chapel, very fatigued, a strange sadness oppressed my soul, and I began to cry quietly. Then I heard this voice in my soul, 'My daughter, why are you crying? It is you who offered to take on these sufferings. You should know that this is only a small part of what you accepted for that soul. He suffers a great deal more!'

"I asked the Lord, 'Why are you acting in this way towards that priest?' The Lord answered that it was in view of the triple-crown that was destined for him: virginity, the priesthood, and martyrdom. At that instant, a great joy invaded my soul, knowing the great glory that priest would receive in Heaven. Right away I said a *Te Deum* for the special share of divine grace that allowed me to learn that this is the way God acts with those whom He wants near Him; so, all our suffering is nothing in comparison to what awaits us in Heaven."[7]

Like Therese of the Child Jesus, when it was a matter of bringing souls closer to her Lord, Faustina did not shy away from any hardship or any torment! She wrote, "Oh, Love eternal, I desire that all the souls You created know You. I would like to become a priest and speak without ceasing of Your mercy for those sinful souls plunged into despair. I would like to become a missionary and carry the light of

[7] Diary, § 596.

faith into primitive countries to make you known to souls, and be slain for them, to die a martyr, the way You died for me and for those souls. Oh, Jesus, I know perfectly well that I could be a priest, a missionary, a preacher, that I could die a martyr, reducing myself to nothing and abandoning myself completely for the love of You, Jesus, and for the love of immortal souls. Great love can transform little things into great things, and it is only love that gives value to our actions. And the purer our love becomes, the less there will be within us for the flames of suffering to feed upon, and the suffering will cease to be a suffering; suffering for us will become a delight. By the grace of God, I have now received this disposition of heart which means that I am never so happy as when I suffer for Jesus, whom I love with every beat of my heart."[8]

All spiritual motherhood is rooted in the love of Christ! The Virgin Mary gives us the most beautiful example. According to the writings of Marthe Robin, before suffering his Passion, Jesus spoke at length to his Mother and revealed to her all that would happen to him. She was filled with dread and asked to be able to die with him. But Jesus would not allow it, for the Father's will was quite otherwise. At the Cross, Mary was to receive a motherhood that would enlarge her heart still more, to new dimensions that were immense, and grand! Her motherly love would then embrace the whole world, with all generations, past, present and future. Mary was to become the mother of all mankind, beginning with the apostle John. Jesus explained to her that the apostles would have need of her after his departure and that he was counting on her to accompany them with her prayer and her motherly solicitude. We can easily guess how much the

[8] Diary § 302.

presence of such a Mother among the apostles, who were still young in the faith, must have reminded them of their dear Jesus, of his spirit, his words, his attitudes with regard to people and events! Not to mention the "family" testimony that Mary was able to bring them and that has inspired some parts of the Gospels, particularly the Infancy Narratives. In this last dialogue with his mother, Jesus also implored her to take care of Mary Magdalene, as she was still fragile.

And he added, "She loves me more than the apostles."[9]

The Blessed Mother accepted to live a new motherhood for her Son. She was to give birth to him again in each one of us. In effect, Jesus was no longer going to be simply this Man-God that she had known in his humanity, limited in time and space. After his Resurrection he would become universally present in the world through his Church. For Mary, each human creature would become her child, and priests in an especially privileged way, since in their priesthood they are *other Christs* (*persona Christi*) in the exercising of the sacraments. Her motherly heart was going to resonate with each human heart, for Jesus says to us all today, "Behold your Mother." It is significant that in the original Greek version of John's Gospel, it is written, "Jesus, seeing THE MOTHER and the disciple he loved standing near her, he said to *the Mother*, 'Woman, behold your son'"![10] This title or name, "the Mother," indicates that Mary was no longer just *His* mother, already it points to Mary's universal motherhood!

---

[9] Extracts from Marthe Robin's notebooks, published in French by the Foyers de Charite. Marthe Robin: Journal, 2013. Biography available in English: Raymond Peyret, Marthe Robin: The Cross and the Joy (Alba House, 1983).

[10] Jn 19:26

This is spiritual motherhood *par excellence,* and it is one of the many splendors of the vocation of woman since the Creation. The *Virgin Most Pure* is sharing her vocation with all women: religious and laywomen, single women, those who are sick, and those souls that wish to be attuned to her maternal heart, and have a share in its riches. The Little Flower, St Therese, understood this very well when she said, "The Mother's treasure belongs to her child." It is not asked of every spiritual mother to take upon themselves the sufferings of priests as St Faustina and several others have done, because the beauty of God's work resides also in its incredible diversity. Nor is it a question of asking for the stigmata in order to better resemble the Crucified Christ. Definitely not! Jesus and Mary propose this grace when they judge it to be fitting for the soul, and they adapt this special charism to the deepest parts of that person's personality. The universal aspect that shines out in all spiritual mothers, is their unbounded and unconditional love for Christ. Could Mary make them a greater gift?

Venerable Marthe Robin (1902–1981)

This exceptional woman, whom I had the grace of meeting five times, lived the gift of spiritual motherhood for all souls, and especially for priests, to the absolute extreme. She ate nothing, she drank nothing and she never slept. What did she spend her time doing during those fifty years of total immobilization in her little bed? She was offering up her suffering, and offering herself to the Father. She was living out, like none other, the grace of her baptism and the *royal priesthood of the faithful* that is conferred on us at that moment.

Every week, on Thursday evening, Jesus would come to her and invite her to live his Passion one more time. He needed it in order to complete His work of redemption, as St. Paul so clearly wrote, "In my flesh I complete what is lacking in Christ's afflictions, for the sake of His Body, that is, the Church," (Col. 1:24). Every week Jesus would call upon Marthe one more time to be a *co-redemptrix*.[11] But, knowing the agonies that awaited her, Marthe would stall. It was impossible! She did not feel she had the courage for it; it was beyond her strength. Having received her negative response, Jesus exited the room leaving Marthe totally free to decide. Not long after, Marthe's heavenly Mother, her "Maman Cherie" (beloved mama), appeared to Marthe. The miracle of love occurred, and renewing her trust in the power

---

[11] St. John Paul II used this title, Co-Redemptrix, to describe the Mother of Jesus on six occasions during his post Vatican II pontificate. On September 8, 1982, Feast of the Birth of Mary, within the context of a papal address to the sick, John Paul II called Mary the "Co-redemptrix of humanity"; November 4, 1984 the Pope called his Mother the "Co-redemptrix" in a general audience; At a Marian sanctuary in Guayaquil, Ecuador, on January 31, 1985, JPII delivered a homily in which he professed the Co-redemptrix title within a penetrating theological commentary of scriptural and conciliar teaching on Coredemption; Palm Sunday 1985, during World Youth Day, he addressed the youth invoking the aid of Mary under the title of "the Co-redemptrix"; On March 24, 1990, in the context of the sick, to volunteers of Lourdes the Pope called upon the aid of Mary under the title "Co-redemptrix"; In commemorating the sixth centenary of the canonization of St. Bridget of Sweden on October 6, 1991, John Paul II used "Co-redemptrix" as a title and role understood by this fourteenth century mystic. For more information on the title "co-redemptrix" see: Dr. Mark Miravalle's work, "The Pope of Mary Co-Redemptrix" December 30, 2011.

of divine grace for her, Marthe gave her full and generous 'yes,' accepting to live through this new Pascal Triduum with Jesus. This process took place in the same order every week. It is very consoling for us to see that each week Marthe first expressed her dread and recoiled before the cross, and only afterwards, gave her loving assent. In all those fifty years she never allowed 'no' to be her last word! During the days that followed her passion, from Monday onwards, Marthe would once again receive people who were there on retreat. When they met her, they would find the most joyful woman in the world. Positive and cheerful, she never missed an opportunity for a bit of humor. My younger sister, who was a student at the Foyer of Charity, said that when she was with the school children, Marthe would sometimes burst out laughing like a child. Her deep union with Jesus filled her with such love that by simply being in contact with people, they changed and regained their taste for life, and left happier and more determined.

Only in Heaven will we see the many wonderful fruits of Marthe's offerings and sacrifices. I believe that even I can attest to her greatness since she also saved me from a wretched end. In fact, a little after my conversion, after having walked through a minefield of certain occult practices, Marthe said to the priest who was helping me, "She has come back from far!"

What Jesus was seeking from Marthe, was a continual offering of herself to Him, and to the Father, especially for priests. Marthe offered herself in this way in reparation for all the desecrations and sacrileges that are committed every day in the Church. "Fear nothing," he said to her. "I am with you and you are all Mine. Long have I searched for a soul who would consent to represent the whole of humanity before me—a soul upon which I might impose My divine will and manifest My desires! A soul into which I might pour out unceasingly my loving desires for my priests, and the thoughts of my heart for my priests and for sinners—A soul that would live only from us and for us in our divinity of love! And that soul is you, My beloved, to whom I have given the total and ineffable gift of My life. You, in whom I have truly substituted Myself, in whom I continue and complete Myself more fully every day, you whom I have freely chosen for us and for them. I want you to be constantly occupied with My Father and with Me. I want you to be only with us and in us, as we are always in you and with you. I want to absorb you so fully in Me that I am totally in your place and in all things with all the attributes and perfections of My divinity, to the point of being but one in suffering and in love. You in Me and I in you entirely."

About such a union, Marthe said, "While I was thus all absorbed in God, I felt the divine blood of Jesus falling in large drops from His face and gushing from His heart towards me. They then flowed through my whole being, flooding me with graces and with divine life, filling me with Him, with His love for the Father and for souls, identifying me with him, substituting me for Him so as to pour out His grace upon the whole Church and, it seemed to me, over the whole world and upon all souls, to purify them, to regenerate them, to heal them, to increase the divine life within them, or, to restore it to them, and to prepare them for the life of glory in Heaven."

Jesus gave Marthe an understanding of the immense love with which He loves His priests, and all that He wishes to do for them. He showed her the preferential love He had for each one of them, and all that He expected from them. He also revealed to her how she should help all of them, "to deliver them from evil and draw them out of sin, to bring them back to their sublime and most holy ministry; to purify them, to sanctify them, to divinize them for their fruitful life as apostles, to unite them to Him, who wants to live and continue Himself in them and through them in all His members." He said to Marthe, "My beloved, tell all of them that all their actions, even the least of them, must be, above all else, animated essentially by the intention of praising and glorifying God, much more than by their desires for their own advantages and even for their salvation."

Marthe could see priests in spirit, and sometimes she would begin to sob at the sight of the interior state of certain priests who were celebrating Mass. Jesus said to her, "My priests, my priests, give me everything *for them!* My mother and I love them so much!" Jesus also gave Marthe the understanding that priests had a real need for everything He was going to do in her for them. Then Marthe had only one desire, to let herself be transformed into a little host as an offering to the Father to bring back to His heart, in union with Jesus, this multitude of priests that Jesus wanted to sanctify, and the thousands of souls that he wanted to sanctify through His priests.

In Medjugorje, Our Lady asks the same thing in her own way, speaking of the triumph of her immaculate heart she said, "My children, my apostles, help me to open the paths to my Son. Once again I call you to pray for your shepherds. Alongside them, I will triumph!" (Message given to Mirjana on October 2, 2010.)

Mother Yvonne-Aimée of Malestroit (1901–1951)[12]

Yvonne-Aimée was one of the greatest mystics in the last century. A French religious of the Congregation of Augustinians, she was favored with many wonderful charisms, as though God derived pleasure in bestowing all of them upon her. What characterizes her is her extraordinary love for God, and neighbor. Christ wished to entrust priests to her, for whom He asked her to offer prayer and sacrifice.

At the age of three, Yvonne found in her grandmother a friend who would often speak to her about Jesus and the saints. This awakened in the child the desire to love Jesus above all else, and to become a saint herself.

When she received her First Holy Communion at the age of nine, Yvonne was overjoyed. Father Questel, SJ, who

---

[12] The cause for the beatification of Yvonne-Aimée was opened on March 25, 2005, by Bishop Gourvès of Vannes.

discerned a great depth and spiritual maturity in her, suggested to her that she make a promise to Jesus that she would pray and make sacrifices every day for priests. He wrote, "Ask Jesus also, to attach to your soul, in a special way, the soul of a child who is called to become a priest, without wishing to know his name or in what country he lives. Pray for him every day and sanctify yourself for his vocation and his priesthood." Yvonne made this two-fold promise without hesitation. From that moment onwards, her motherhood towards priests began. She was still only a child.

When she was twenty-two years old, Yvonne's friend, Jeanne, asked her to pray for her nephew, Paul Labutte, who wished to become a priest. Yvonne agreed, but it wasn't until 1941, when Yvonne was already forty years old, that Jesus revealed to her that Father Paul Labutte was the priest for whom she had offered herself when she was nine years old.

In 1926, five years before the priestly ordination of Paul Labutte, Yvonne and Paul saw each other for the first time, without knowing God's designs on their future spiritual union. One year later, a friendship began. Paul recalled that moment, "I knew nothing about her at that time, but I had a strong intuition that she was a girl who was genuine, to the very core of her being. For me, Yvonne-Aimée was an older sister in whom I had absolute trust. In short, I used to ask her for advice, and at the same time, I was the younger brother to whom, at times, she would confide some aspects of her personal life and of her missions in the service of Jesus the King."

Periodically they met in the Augustinian convent located in Malestroit, France, where Yvonne entered on March 18, 1927.

During the Second World War, Father Labutte was wounded in combat. Sister Yvonne-Aimée invited him to recuperate in Malestroit. He remained there from March until July of 1941, and was a witness to the numerous mystical graces that were received by his spiritual mother. In their conversations, she recounted how, while she was in bilocation, she had been able to assist him several times in the past, without his knowing it.

One of these bilocations took place in 1940 in Wintzenheim HautRhin, France. Father Labutte lay in the grips of severe influenza. Interiorly he turned to Yvonne to implore her aid and comfort, which she joyfully bestowed upon him. She told him the story a year later, "One night, in Alsace, you were in a room, restless and feverish. I can still see the cream-colored bed, the gray and green blankets and your torn shoes on the rug beside the bed. Jesus said to me, 'Go. He is suffering.' So I came."

Yvonne was able to bring relief to the sick priest and strengthen him, without father even realizing at the time from where the help came. With good reason does he say about Yvonne, "Before she even knew me, she was my spiritual mother." Jesus gave Yvonne a confirmation of this motherhood. He said, "I give him to you more than a child to its mother, since you have paid for him more by prayers and sacrifices than a mother would generally do for the soul of her child. Keep him. Guide him!"

Father Labutte was often a consolation and a support for Yvonne as well. In 1943, she was saved from death in an extraordinary way, thanks to her spiritual son. Mother Yvonne was a thorn in the side for the Nazis, because the convent hospital at Malestroit, where she was Superior, offered refuge and aid to everyone, without distinction. When she left for Paris on January 24, 1943, she knew she was in danger. As it happened, she was arrested by the Gestapo on the morning of February 16th. When Father Labutte was informed of this, he immediately left for Paris. Mother

Aimée appeared to him in the subway and said, "Pray! Pray! If you don't pray hard enough, I will be taken to Germany this evening. Tell no one!"

Frantic with worry, Father Labutte went and cast himself at Our Lady's feet at the Rue du Bac to beg for the release of his spiritual mother. That evening, upon his return to Malestroit, he asked to go into Yvonne's office to pray the rosary there for her intentions. Suddenly he heard a muffled sound behind him and, turning in fright, saw Yvonne standing near the desk, her back stained with blood and extremely exhausted. Years earlier, in a prophetic dream, Yvonne had foreseen what would taken place, "I saw myself in prison, and an angel came to deliver me." It was, in fact, through a supernatural intervention that she was liberated at the last minute and brought to her home, just before she was to be deported to Germany.

Yvonne's spiritual motherhood extended well beyond her magnificent friendship with Fr. Labutte. It included *numerous* priests, both known and unknown to her. At the age of twenty, she heard the voice of Jesus for the first time. He called her three times by her name, like the young Samuel in the Old Testament. Then he showed her a cross and asked in a gentle voice, "Do you wish to carry it?"

"Oh, yes, Lord," she replied.

"Be a surrendered soul," Jesus said. "Accept the trials that I will send you as the greatest of graces and the greatest of favors given to souls that I love. Accept them without complaining, without examining their nature or their duration, without taking pride in them. Pay no attention to whatever mortifies or humiliates you. Look at Me. I love you."

One year later, Our Lord showed her in a vision the horrors that would befall humanity during World War II. Speaking gravely, but still with gentleness, He entreated her, "Pray,

pray a great deal, especially for priests and for prisoners." He often showed his beloved the places where there were people about to offend Him deeply. He sent her to the homes of people who had stolen hosts with the intention of desecrating them, entrusting to her the task of bringing them back. He would also let her know when priests were in danger, and send her to them to save them from sin.

On January 16, 1925, in a letter to Father Crété, she wrote, "I had gone into a church to make a visit to the Blessed Sacrament when I understood, all of a sudden, that I had to go to the priest who was a short distance from me and tell him not to go where he was intending to go that evening, because he would fall. He was overcome with emotion and surprise, since he alone knew his plans. He asked me how I knew what I had just told him. I answered that it had been revealed to me as I was praying, and that I had come immediately to see him. He thanked me very much."

Certain priests caused her a great deal of suffering. One of them, who had given her his trust, later spoke calumny against her, accusing her of being a false mystic. During a vision on July 6, 1923, Jesus gave her to understand the following, "Under the pretext of defending my glory, he will act against my will and pierce your heart with a sword. However, you will have friendly hearts to defend you, but doubts will afflict people's minds. As of this moment, accept this trial. The time of calamity during which this trial will come to you will help powerfully in saving the world. Stay closely united to me and pray, so that, in fidelity to grace, the one who will break you may become a friend again." This prophecy became a reality in 1943, and Mother Yvonne accepted the trial calmly, without a word of justification. She had been praying for him for 20 years! After four months, the priest asked for her forgiveness on his knees.

In the last years of her life, Mother Yvonne was in a state of total exhaustion. Her untiring devotion combined with different physical illnesses such as breast cancer made it understandable. Nevertheless, she transmitted to her Sisters, and to all who came seeking her advice, the joy of living and a profound peace.

After suffering a stroke, Mother Yvonne entered into eternal life on February 3, 1951.

Filiola (1888–1976)

Filiola can be counted among those extremely simple people that Heaven sometimes chooses, in order to entrust them with secrets that elude the cleverest among us. Each time she complained to Jesus that she was not the most suitable person for the mission he had entrusted to her, He replied that, in this way, everyone would understand that His messages did not come from her, but from Heaven. Filiola, who was born in Alsatia, France, did not even know how to speak French properly. She had learned it in the working class neighborhoods of Paris and often used slang to describe the most sublime mystical experiences. One day, seeing Jesus in His passion and covered with blood, she said to him, "Well, they sure fixed you!"

Here are a few extracts from her numerous writings: "The entire Church is suffering now more than ever. But Jesus lets me see the secret of His merciful goodness. The Spirit of God as a whole is going to act to the stupefaction of mankind. France is going to suffer a great blow, for the Sacred Heart of Jesus is so scorned, the Sacred Humanity of Jesus is so disfigured, torn apart by His own people! Jesus allowed me to see such great hypocrisy in minds and hearts. Jesus is Good, but the Holy Spirit is going to sweep everything away with his sword of fire. Oh, they had it coming!"[13]

"Oh, France is going to suffer for her lack of faith in Jesus, and in his sacred humanity. France is going to be humiliated. Her pride will suffer, but Jesus will reign through his most sacred humanity. The world no longer knows where to turn. People are looking for a person to confide in. They are defending their own wellbeing and souls are being lost …"

"Those faithful to Jesus, and to His Spirit, to His love, are few. But Jesus will build with them! Jesus lets me see a light that is so beautiful, that it is a nameless power. How consoling it is! Jesus is seeking out poor souls caught in the mud, in order to clothe them with His love … Jesus will reign through these little ones! With these little ones, Jesus will rebuild His Church that is suffering so greatly. The Spirit of Jesus will reign in His Church, which has been torn apart … I dare not write of it. The Church is even sicker than the world. The Church has been lead into the lion's den … Satan is more active than ever. And they are following him, like lambs for the slaughter. Oh, the fools! But God has his ways. Satan seeks to demolish and God builds in silence."

Filiola evokes the responsibility of the clergy and the hierarchy. "To be responsible for the whole Church of Jesus Christ, that's no small thing! Oh, the whole Church is not a thing for one's amusement! Jesus let me feel the whole Church in His heart. Where have they led the Church? O my Jesus, have pity, they have not understood. (Oh, I had never seen Jesus look like that!) O my God, have pity on those who have wavered. Do not punish them as they deserve. Oh, I

---

[13] Extracts from the book, Filiola, Chemins de Lumière' Téqui, 1999, 04/29/1974.

understand, it is a grave matter; they have lost so many souls! They have allowed the Church to be torn apart, the entire body of the sacred humanity of Jesus. They have even gone so far as trampling God entirely. Oh, the villains! But, my Jesus, Your love is greater than everything; do not look at what we are, look only at what You are. Blot out all the abominations; pour out your Precious Blood over them, so that God sees only You, His beloved Son!"

Jesus said to her, "My little one, I love it so much when you write! Your simplicity consoles my Heart that is suffering so much in its Church. I have not come to tear down but to build … My little daughter, my love wishes to have need of you to support the Church that is suffering so much." Filiola added, "Satan and his henchmen think they have triumphed. Yes, for a time, God permits this. He wants to have need of them to open the eyes of the blind. But before that, blood will be shed, and this blood will open the eyes of the fools … Divine love itself wants to save the world from satanic tyranny. And God makes use of the whip that we ourselves have twisted together through our lack of faith, and our infidelity!"

Filiola asked Jesus what would happen to His faithful ones. He answered, "My little one, I am making of them a formidable rampart in order to push back the enemy," (6/13/1975). Filiola responded, "Oh, my Jesus, how can the Church regain the light in the midst of such disorder?" Jesus then showed her a vision, and she responded, "Oh my Jesus, is that what the cleaning of Your Church is going to be like? My Jesus, I don't dare to write any more."

Filiola saw masses of souls who were seeking help, stretching out their arms towards the *Apostles of Light*. "The enemy is gaining ground. Everything could have been otherwise! I am sick at heart for France. But the Church will triumph despite Satan and his henchmen," (17/06/1975).

During the night of the sixth to the seventh of June 1975, the evening of the Feast of the Sacred Heart, Filiola received an extraordinary favor. Jesus gave her the gift of His own Heart. The prophetic mission of Filiola would come to depend a great deal on this exceptional mystical grace. With Jesus' heart beating within her, she could feel two of the realities that belong to this Heart, as if they were her own: firstly, she saw in spirit all the sins of the clergy and of consecrated souls, which made her suffer enormously, and she cried out toward the One who is mercy. "My daughter," Jesus said to her. "Let My heart pray in your heart." Secondly, she had a prophetic knowledge of what Jesus called the *Church of Light* and the magnificent new pentecost that He was preparing. "My daughter, look! There will be the new pentecost!" Filiola even saw some of those who are now being formed in secret by Christ, to be apostles of His Church, which will be regenerated from within, the foundation of his victory. She was able to meet some of them, and encourage them and sometimes she would transmit to them directives coming from Heaven.

Filiola lived out her spiritual motherhood in profound solitude. Married to an unkind man who mocked her, we could say that she had only Jesus as an interlocutor and friend. A few pious people of her parish gave her some support, but she had need of this solitude to embrace the entire earth with her prayer. Seeing the evil that was being done, and the good that was being prepared in secret, Filiola allowed the Heart of Jesus to stir within her. Both joy and sorrow were intermingled with such intensity, that only a special grace enabled her to bear it. It was in this way that she became the mother of a great number of souls. On the day of her death, Venerable Marthe Robin declared that she had seen a great star rise up to Heaven from out of France.

45

The Forgotten Prophesy
of Joseph Ratzinger

"Renew prayer in the family. Gather together in prayer
groups, both big and small. Do not call down God's anger
upon your adversaries, but bless them and pray for them.
Prayer groups, even if they are only made up of two people,
are places of grace and are little lights for those who are in
darkness."

(MESSAGE GIVEN TO FATHER FRANZ SPELIC
AT KURESCEK ON JULY 6, 1991)[1]

FEBRUARY 18, 2013, THE big Italian newspaper, *La Stampa,*
published the prophesy of a certain Joseph Ratzinger. At
the end of the 1960s, during the troubled period just after
the Second Vatican Council, and the events of May 1968, a
young theologian, Joseph Ratzinger, gave a few talks on the
future of Christianity. He compared our modern era to that
of the French Revolution and of the "Enlightenment," when
the Church was the target of various powers that sought to
destroy it. These powers had already confiscated the Church's
properties, her convents, and her places of worship and they

---

[1] Father Franz Spelic of Kurescek (Slovenia), a converted communist who received the stigmata, died on April 10, 2012, received apparitions of Our Lady until 1998, recognized by the
Archbishop of Ljubjana, Aloïs Sostar.

were actively trying to eradicate religious orders. And so it is that in our own time the presence of these "powers that seek to destroy the Church" are visible for all to see! The war is waged primarily through the media, but also encompasses laws and decrees that distort the meaning of marriage and the goodness of family. In France for example, how many churches or places of worship are totally abandoned?

This prophetic vision can be summarized in a few lines. Professor, at the time, Ratzinger had the intuition that "from this crisis will emerge a Church which will have lost a great deal: buildings, adherents, priests, and social privileges to name a few. It will be a Church re-dimensioned with many fewer of the faithful, who have been obliged to abandon most of the places of worship constructed over the course of centuries. It will be a Church of very few Catholics, having a minor influence on political choices, humbled, and forced to start over. But it will also be a Church which, through this massive disruption, will find itself again and will be reborn simplified, more vigorous and missionary."

What Ratzinger described in his days had to be accomplished over time, following a long process. He said, "There will be small groups which will make the Church come alive again, minor movements which will put faith back at the center of their hopes. It will be a more spiritual church, renouncing all political pretensions and all flirtation with the left or right. Because it is poor, it will become once more the Church of the needy. When that happens, men will discover that they live in a world of indescribable solitude. They will have lost the vision of God and will be horrified by their indigence.

"Then, and only then," concluded Ratzinger, "will they see the little flock of believers as something completely new. They will discover it as a hope for themselves, an answer always secretly hoped for."

I can't help but connect these prophetic words of a young Joseph Ratzinger (who never suspected for a second that he would become Pope) and a message from the Blessed Mother given in Medjugorje, which seems to me to have also passed unnoticed, "Dear children, I desire to thank you for making my plan realizable. Each of you is important ... Prayer groups are powerful, and through them I can see, little children, that the Holy Spirit is at work in the world ..." (Message of June 25, 2004).

It is significant that Mary did *not* say that the Church is strong, the Vatican is strong, the parishes are strong, or the family is strong. Rather, she said, "The prayer groups are strong."[2] Why does she put so much hope in these little prayer groups? What signs can we read today that might put us onto the path of a feasible response? I am not a prophet, far from it. But I do not want to disappoint Christ who has reproached his contemporaries for not knowing how to read the signs of the times and for missing out on the message, which was offered to them. What follows here, then, is my personal interpretation of events observed for many years, dialogues with believers from all countries, of messages listened to, and of intuitions received in prayer. I want to point out that Our Lady and the Lord have never appeared to me. I am a simple, "normal" Christian. I am giving here my personal opinion in all simplicity.

[2] "Prayer groups are necessary in all parishes," (April 11, 1982). "Renew prayer in your families and form prayer groups. In this way, you will experience joy in prayer and togetherness. All those who pray and are members of prayer groups are open to God's will in their hearts and joyfully witness God's love. I am with you ..." (September 25, 2000).

In Medjugorje Our Lady has spoken to us several times about a *new time, a time of spring,* and no one would guess the beauties this time is holding for us.[3] I believe that we don't have any idea, and that it is too soon to even have the slightest notion, because our modern ways of staying secure will have also disappeared and will be based on other values. While waiting for this time of peace, it seems to me that great disruptions are being prepared for the world and for the Church, and we are seeing the first signs of that. We live presently in a time of such flagrant disobedience to God that the world will bring upon itself consequences it can't even measure because of its blindness. But, for all that, God does not let go; His love remains unchanged, and His mercy is immeasurable. He is patient. He calls. He warns. He sends the Virgin Mary to instill the Gospel in our hearts. He gives graces as never seen before. However, we are still not satisfied with all that. A great majority of the world continues to ignore it.

When the Queen of Peace arrived in Medjugorje in 1981, she defined her mission with these words, "I have come in order to bring you closer to the Heart of God!" But could she have failed? On October 25, 2008, 27 years later, she observed that, "the world is distancing itself more each day from the Heart of God." Mystics recognized by the Church

---

[3] "Dear children! Decide for God, for peace and for the good. May every hatred and jealousy disappear from your life and your thoughts, and may there only dwell love for God and for your neighbor. Thus, and only thus shall you be able to discern the signs of the time. I am with you and I guide you into a new time, a time which God gives you as grace so that you may get to know him more. Thank you for having responded to my call," (January 25, 1993).

who have produced undeniable fruits (like VEeneralbe Maryam of Bethlehem, Blessed Marthe Robin, Filiola, Servant of God Marcel Van, and so many others), have helped us to understand that a purification of the world is required, just as has always been the case in the history of the Judeo-Christian people. In August 2012, the visionary Ivan Dragicevic, said on Radio-Maria in Italy, "When the secrets of Medjugorje are revealed, the Church will find itself in a great persecution and a great suffering, and this suffering has already begun."

During this time of purifying trial, it's conceivable that we could find in our churches, in place of the cross, signs foreign to our Christian faith, such as the Islamic crescent, symbols of Communism, or emblems of Freemasonry.

Here's what I'm getting at: it's possible that at that time, under threat and in great distress, many will deny their faith. Many, but not all! This wave of trials could come upon us very suddenly, spontaneously, like the one that happened in the time of Noah. At that time people ate. They drank. They got married. And when the flood arrived, it took everyone by surprise. Well, not everyone. Some of the faithful were deemed righteous before God, and His blessing protected them. The same goes for the time we're living in today. God will recognize His own, and His blessing will express itself by interventions that we have never or only rarely known before, interventions adapted to the specific trials of today. Those who will benefit from this will surely have the heart to share their goods with those who do not know God. In Medjugorje, God has already performed signs, like multiplications of food and other commodities. It is as if to prepare us not to be afraid of famines. It is not that multiplications are anything new! But who today still thinks about them actually happening in the Church? Divine Providence is so little solicited! If one day there are no more medications, God will be capable of curing us in another way. If the air is too polluted and toxic, He will have us breathe in a different way. We will escape the sight of the evildoers and no electronic chip will be able to find us and stop us.[4] If some of us are called to die as a martyr, others will enjoy a very special protection, as the history of the Church shows. Edith Stein died in the Auschwitz concentration camp, for example, and Mother Yvonne-Aimee escaped from the hands of the Nazis by finding herself carried from her jail to her residence without knowing how it happened. Some people enjoy special graces! Didn't Jesus say to His apostles, "those who have believed … will pick up serpents, and if they drink any deadly poison, it will do them no harm …"?[5] The arm of God has not gotten any shorter!

I believe that the future of the Church lies in these small, very modest, unassuming groups that will remain hidden to the eyes of the enemy, and will escape him. They will slip through his fingers, or pass through the mesh of the fowler's snare, because they will be so small. They will live in the presence of Mary, who will help them and cover them with

---

[4] Today, a lot of information concerning our health is stored in the microchip that is inserted into our social security cards, or credit cards. In France, driving permits holding a microchip are being proposed. I've heard that all of our driving infringements, accidents, fines, etc. will be recorded there. Tomorrow will it be an intra-corporeal microchip that will be 'proposed,' or 'imposed' upon us? It will store all of our personal information, even our political and religious ideas! A remote computer would be able to command these chips in order to influence, or even direct our behavior. What safeguards will be in place to protect us from the violation of our freedom and of our conscience? Let us be on our guard, and pray!

[5] Mark 16:18

her motherly mantle. They will have the power of the humble, and the freedom of those who have nothing to lose, because they will have given everything, consecrated everything. They will have things to suffer, it is true, but they know that they will be held in God's hand, and they will help those who run the risk of reaching the point of despair. Saint Louis-Marie Grignion de Montfort gave a prophetic description of them when he spoke about the 'apostles of the last times.'[6] The little Marcel Van also spoke of them.[7]

Medjugorje holds a place of prime importance in the formation of these little groups. Yet again, on May 2, 2014, the Virgin Mary reminded us, "My apostles, pray and act. Bring the light and do not lose hope. I am with you." We do not yet know the content of the secrets that are to be revealed during the visionaries' lifetimes, but we can guess that if there are secrets, it is because there are things of importance for the world that have yet to be revealed. There is only one attitude to have before these mysteries, and that is an attitude of trusting prayer. "Do not speak about the secrets," Mary says to us, "but pray!"

---

[6] Read Saint Louis-Marie Grignion de Montfort's True Devotion to Mary. He writes, "The return in glory of Jesus will be preceded by a time of Pentecost, a time of the Holy Spirit and of Mary. Since God became man through Mary, it is also through her that he will bring his work to completion. Apostles will rise up, formed by Mary, and assiduous in following her teaching. Like a blazing fire they will enflame the world with divine love."

[7] Preface by Cardinal Schonborn, Marcel Van: Conversations (Herefordshire: Gracewing, 2008). A splendid book!

This photo has been taken in a restaurant of Linz (Austria), in 1991, during a meeting where more than 300 priests discussed their experiences of confessions in Medjugorje. Upon his return, Father Slavko told Nasa Ognjista, a Croatian monthly (XXI, 1991), that he and Cardinal Ratzinger had a long conversation about Medjugorje and the cardinal had told him that "the Church does not want to repress anything that is bringing good spiritual fruits."

46

The Conversion of a President

"All things are possible for he who believes!"

(Mκ 9:23)

Gustáv Husák, Prague, 1978. © Gustáv Husák—oríznuto.

BISHOP PAUL MARIA HNILICA, S.J., a very dear friend of mine whose cause for Beatification has been opened, once told me the following story, "The former Czechoslovakian President, Gustáv Husák, was born in 1913 into a deeply religious family, but he became a fiercely atheistic communist. False accusations were made against him and he was condemned to life in prison. He spent almost ten years in prison under the Communist regime. His wife, the former actress and stage manager, Magda Lokvencoca, died as a result of reprisals and persecution.

"In 1973, he was awarded the Order of Lenin for the second time, as well as the Order of Clement Gottwald for the rebuilding of the socialist fatherland. Two years later he became President of Czechoslovakia.

"After the 'Velvet Revolution' in November, 1989, and the collapse of Communism that followed, Gustáv Husák resigned as President. Great indeed was the surprise amongst those who had known him, to learn that on November 18, 1991, this hardened atheist had passed away after having received the last rites and Holy Communion! He himself had asked the nurse who was caring for him to send for a priest."

Bishop Hnilica continued, "During a presentation that I gave in a retirement home for priests in Pezinok, near Bratislava, I mentioned this most unexpected conversion in these words, 'Divine Mercy is inconceivable, is it not? Who has not asked themselves with wonderment how it could be possible for a diehard militant atheistic communist, like Gustáv Husák, to ask for the last rites before his death?'

"At these words, one of the priests present stood up and corrected me, saying, 'But your Excellency, there is nothing surprising about this! I knew Gustáv well at the time of our university studies. As students, to the great joy of his mother, who was a firm believer, we made together the First Nine Fridays of the month dedicated to the Sacred Heart!'"[1]

It's astounding that Jesus made this promise to St. Marguerite-Marie Alacoque, "I promise you in the excessive mercy of My Heart that My all-powerful love will grant to all

---

[1] A devotion that Jesus revealed to a French mystic, Saint Marguerite-Marie Alacoque who lived from 1647–1690.

those who take Holy Communion on the First Friday in nine consecutive months, the grace of final penance; they shall not die in My disgrace nor without receiving the Sacraments. My Divine heart shall be their safe refuge in this last hour."[2]

---

[2] See the May-June 2007 edition of the magazine Triumph of the Heart, no. 31.

47

Struck by the Holy Spirit

Jesus said to Sr. Faustina, "Tell souls that they must look for consolation at the tribunal of the Divine Mercy. There, the greatest miracles will keep repeating without ceasing. It is sufficient simply to cast oneself in faith at the feet of the one who is taking my place and tell him his wretchedness, and the miracle of the Divine Mercy will manifest itself in all its fullness. Even if that soul is like a decomposing cadaver and even if, humanly speaking, there is no longer any hope of returning to life and all seems lost, it is not that way with God. The miracle of Divine Mercy will bring that soul back to life in all its fullness. Oh! Unhappy are those who are not profiting now from this miracle of the Divine Mercy. In vain will you call; it will be too late!"

(DIARY OF ST FAUSTINA, §1448)

BATTISTINA IS VERY MUCH an Italian woman of today. She is a 47 year old internet based accountant. When her partner, who she lived with, invited her to go to Medjugorje, she wasn't interested. But one morning in her car, she heard a Marian hymn playing on Radio Maria, the same song which, for years, used to irritate her whenever she was looking for a radio station. Unexpectedly, this song overwhelmed her. Tears began to flow in an uninterrupted stream for no apparent reason. It was uncontrollable. She understood that Our Lady was inviting her. But I'll let her tell the story:

"Ever since I made a pilgrimage to Medjugorje in July of 2012, everything in my life has changed. Nothing is the same as it was before! My conversion took place during adoration of the Blessed Sacrament. We were outside, gathered by the thousands around the Rotunda. Suddenly I found myself on my knees, and I had the impression that I was holding my living heart in my hands. I saw my entire life passing before my eyes. I saw very clearly what was good and what was bad, and everything that had seemed good before became bad in front of my eyes. I began to feel enormous pain about my divorce. How could I have broken a promise made before God? These words echoed in my mind, 'What God has united, let no man separate,' (Matt 19:6).

"I understood then that my present serenity was only in my head, because my heart was frozen. I had always imagined myself as a 'righteous' person, and a poor victim. But in that moment, in front of the Blessed Sacrament, I saw how hard my heart had been. I saw the suffering that my four children, my father and my stepparents had endured, and I saw, especially, that I was not at all a victim. In reality, I had never forgiven anyone. When my oldest daughter was 9 years old she was enrolled in religious education lessons, and she insisted on making her First Communion. I told her it didn't make any sense to do so. To make matters worse, I didn't even have my last child baptized! In that same moment I saw all the New Age books that I had bought over years. I wondered to myself, 'How could I have spent all that time reading and trying to discover myself when those things only ended up turning me away from God and from my family?'

"The pain in my heart became sharper and sharper, and before long I found myself face down on the ground. I was saying, 'Lord, let me die here because I am not worthy to lift my head from the ground.' Then I felt something like a great, loving embrace accompanied by an inner joy that did not belong to this world. I said to myself, 'For eighteen years I thought I had given everything to my children, but in fact I had given them nothing, because I had not given them *that*. So if I were to stay here and pray for them for the rest of my life, would that be better than anything I could do by returning home? If I, as the mother, the soul of the house, had cultivated prayer instead of cultivating useless things, my children would have a united family today!'

"When we decide to throw off the cross of marriage, we put it on the shoulders of our children. I sensed at that moment that I had to remain tied to my promise of fidelity in marriage, and I decided to take the vow of chastity. I offered that to God so that a thousand families would not separate. My companion felt the same way. And he told me that now we had to consecrate ourselves to it entirely. After returning to my home, I went to confession often. Some priests, presented with my choice of chastity, told me that it wasn't necessary. Other priests told me that it was a pure invention on our part, but I was very sure and very decided, because the sacrifice seemed so little to me compared with the infinite mercy I had received.

"My children thought I had gone crazy because I went to Mass, and I hung a crucifix in the living room. My oldest daughter was very irritated by my enthusiasm, and she said to me, "So what do you make of all that you told us for 18 years?"

"I'm sorry," I told her, "I was mistaken!"

"In November, I returned to Medjugorje with my 4 children, so that they also could understand, and I had great hope that they would encounter the Lord. I observed them from a distance, and, while waiting, I thought, 'But if I, their mother, with the little bit of love I'm capable of, am so happy to see my children pray, how much happier is our Mother in

Heaven? And how unhappy she must be for children who become lost!'

"During that pilgrimage, the hearts of all my children were touched. We studied the Catechism together. Nine months later, the youngest, who was 10 years old at the time, was baptized, and all my children received their First Holy Communions at the same celebration. That was the most beautiful day of my life! It was as though I saw them all reborn at the same time. My companion and I stayed together, living like brother and sister for a year. But each day I asked God for the ability to understand His will, whether we ought to remain close in order to support each other, or whether we should separate completely. I held this ambivalent feeling in my heart for a long time, but, little by little, the Lord made sure that our work distanced us from each other.

"After my conversion, I contacted my ex-husband. For nine years every one of our phone calls had ended in a shouting match. It was so bad that for a whole year we didn't even talk, and he only communicated with me through the children. After I recognized my faults, I considered his errors a consequence of my own, so my bitterness evaporated. It was I who asked for forgiveness! Little by little I began to feel the deep bond of marriage, sealed by God, and I felt married again. But I didn't understand. I asked a priest if it was good to feel married like that, even if my husband was attached to another person and had a son. The priest answered, 'The sacrament of marriage is indissoluble before God.'

"Today, I found again this love that I thought had been reduced to nothing, or had never even existed. It was totally intact in the depths of my heart. I keep it in its purity and I pray each day for the conversion of my ex-husband and for both our families. I thank Jesus and Mary for the infinite grace that my family receives each day, and I continue to move forward along the road of conversion."

48

Families, Don't Let Yourselves Be Destroyed

"Dear children, with all my heart and soul full of faith and love in the Heavenly Father, I gave my Son to you and am giving Him to you anew. My Son has brought you, the people of the entire world, to know the only true God and His love. He has led you on the way of truth and made you brothers and sisters. Therefore, my children, do not wander, do not close your heart before that truth, hope and love. Everything around you is passing and everything is falling apart, only the glory of God remains. Therefore, renounce everything that distances you from the Lord. Adore Him alone, because He is the only true God. I am with you and I will remain with you. I am especially praying for the shepherds that they may be worthy representatives of my Son and may lead you with love on the way of truth. Thank you."

(MESSAGE OF SEPTEMBER 2, 2011)

WHY DOES THE FAMILY seem to be falling apart? Why is Satan so hell-bent on destroying it? What is it about the family that bothers him? It's as clear as day: If he destroys it, he will have destroyed humanity, and that is his number one plan, because he hates the human race. Divinely instituted, the family is a splendid reality, whose beauty and grandeur he cannot tolerate. The family shines out as the jewel of God's creation, as His cherished child, His masterpiece. The family unit allows the human race to exist, because it is within it that life is conceived, brought to birth, nurtured and multiplied. Without the intimacy of the family unit, the human race would be quickly swept off the face of the earth. The greatness of the family has its source in the very life of the Trinity, in the relationship between the three Divine Persons. A family is such a beautiful treasure! Even the Son of God Himself wanted to be brought up in a family!

When God created the world, each day He contemplated the work of His hands. For the first five days *"He saw that it was good"*! But, on the evening of the sixth day, as He looked upon His masterpiece, man and woman, *"He saw that it was very good"* (*Genesis. 1:31*)! The splendor of the Creator, who made us in His own image, is reflected in the love shared between spouses, in sexuality as God intended it, in their fruitfulness, in the respective roles of father and mother with regard to their children, and in being of mutual help to each other. But Satan is jealous. The very fact that he is raging against the union of man and woman to such a degree is a clear indication for us of the unique value of the family. Why would he concentrate his most powerful weapons of destruction on a reality that has no value? He's not stupid!

The visionaries of Medjugorje are unanimous: Our Lady suffers greatly in her heart, because she sees such an overwhelming amount of problems, conflicts, heartbreaks, betrayals, and dramas of every kind weighing down upon families today. Therefore, she is warning us, "Dear children, today as never before, Satan wants to destroy your families." She goes on, "He never sleeps, but works night and day."

Whether we like it or not, we are all on a battlefield. And what a raging battle it is! If the one who finds himself there is unaware of the enemy's identity and the weapons that Satan uses, he has very little chance of making it through, he is as good as defeated. That is why for so many years our Heavenly Mother has been coming to tell us again and again what battle we are fighting and what weapons will enable us to win the victory.

If Our Lady is specifically saying that Satan is out to destroy the family "as never before," it means that the situation is serious. For if we recall the harm caused by the enemy in centuries past and the extent of his cruelty, what is this saying about his present day action? Mary loves us too much to abandon us to the carnage. That is why she is accompanying us like an attentive and infinitely loving Mother, but she is also educating us and showing us the effective resources at our disposal. Looking to places on the other side of the world for sophisticated weapons or pursuing complicated initiatives is useless. Looking to atheist politicians is useless. No, the weapons our Mother offers us are of astonishing, even childlike simplicity. Apart from God Himself, who knows better than she the sensitive points and weaknesses of the enemy?

The first weapon advocated by the Mother of God, the indispensable weapon, is family prayer. "Pray in your family, dear children, and pray for the family," she tells us. "Family prayer is the remedy to heal the world today," (message to Ivan on Podbrdo, July 2013). Then she continues by explaining why family prayer is so powerful in protecting the family and making it grow. When the members of a family join together for prayer, Jesus comes into that house. It's in the Gospel! Jesus tells us, "Where two or three are gathered in My name, I am among them," (Matthew 18:20). In reality, the goal of family prayer is precisely to have Jesus arrive in the home! And religious, don't think Our Lady has forgotten you, or that you are let off the hook! When Mary speaks of the "family," we can assume that she is also including religious families and communities. And when Jesus has arrived, what else do we need?

If the family prays each day, Jesus honors the invitation that is given to Him, and He remains among His own. I don't see how Jesus could say to these people, "Okay, now that the prayer is over, I'll pack my bag and wish you a good night. See you tomorrow!" Jesus truly dwells in the home where people pray each day, and as you might guess, He accomplishes a divine work there, as it is written, "My Father goes on working, and so do I."

What is the work that Jesus accomplishes? With immense happiness, He shares His treasures with those who are His own. He distributes them liberally. He gives peace to one, consolation to another, healing to a third, repentance, the courage to forgive, the joy of living, etc. He minimizes the number of viruses that are destroying the family: hate, jealousy, envy, refusal of forgiveness, and let's not forget such disastrous practices as occultism or pornography which are spreading like poisonous mushrooms, and whose destructive effects no longer need proving. Moreover, Jesus raises the level of all that builds up and enhances the family. He increases union of hearts, mutual respect, attentiveness to others, signs of forgiveness, mutual assistance in trials, etc.

Jesus takes up residence in the home along with all His celestial followers such as angels and saints that are welcomed by the family in its prayers. He occupies the premises, takes His place within it, and the house is filled with the fragrance of His holiness. When Satan and his fallen angels, always on the lookout for new residences, approach this house to destroy it, they see that Jesus resides there, and they flee in terror! They are disarmed! Their power is gone! Since Jesus defeated Satan on the cross, His simple presence drives the enemy away. For the devil it is a burning that he cannot endure. Satan is disarmed not only against us but his power also diminishes over other families who do not yet know Jesus. In other words, if we are diligent in inviting Jesus each day into our homes, He will be our ever-watchful guardian, the protector of our peace. A family that prays is a family that is building a fence against the destroyer. But for a family that does not pray, where is the fence? [1]

A lot of couples think, 'everything is going well for us. We love each other, we have everything—a home, work, good health, leisure, children who do well in school; there's no need to pray.' But there's nothing there to frighten Satan! Our goods or our feelings do not terrify Satan! Jesus terrifies him! Jesus alone has the power to disarm the enemy, by the blood of His cross. Why is it that so many young couples, who are full of good will and endowed with a sincere desire to start a family that will stay together, break up after a few years, or even a few months of married life and file for divorce? What was wrong in their plan? They thought they had

---

[1] At this point some parents will say, "So we got everything wrong! What can we do for our adult children? They have been formed in atheism, since we weren't yet converted during their childhood, and now they don't want to hear anything about God and the Church!" It's not too late to act, far from it! The Blessed Virgin responds clearly to this question. She says, "Do not enter into arguments. You can change the hearts of your children through your love, your prayer, and your example." There is also the precious assistance of our Guardian Angels! Send your angel with the mission to be near your children, and pray to their angels! They have the power to whisper things of God into the hearts of their charges, because they know God's plans for them. So they, along with the saints, are your best ambassadors to your children!

everything, but without Jesus at the center of their lives, what did they really have? What we are witnessing today is a terrible epidemic!

"Let parents pray with their children. Let children pray with their parents," Mary tells us. To Vicka in 1982 she said, "When you are united in prayer, Satan can do nothing against you!" She also said, "Dear children, do not think that you will have peace in your families if you do not put my Son Jesus in the first place." Jesus is the keystone of our homes!

Times have changed. Before, natural common sense helped families to refuse whatever could do them harm. Today, evil no longer asks permission to enter into households or into schools, but it moves in and imposes itself through the media, through the new laws imposed by our atheist governments, through the internet and through all the electronic devices that young children have at their disposal very early in life. Happy are those parents whose children of six, seven or eight years old haven't already been contaminated at school or elsewhere by disastrous programs of pornography or Satanism! And we won't go into *gender theory*—that takes the cake! It's a scandal that makes us understand why the Mother of God insists so much in giving us weapons that are adapted to the battle of faith, before it's too late.

There is one major obstacle to prayer in the family and that is time. Very often, I hear from pilgrims, "We don't have time to pray, we're too busy!" An Italian priest told me that a man once maintained that he didn't have time to pray. "If you don't have time to pray," the priest advised him. "Then take your lunch hour to pray! You will always find the time to eat!" That quip says a lot. Fr. Jozo Zovko, the former pastor of Medjugorje asked a group of American pilgrims, "When did your families start breaking up?" A deep silence followed his question, so he gave the answer, "When you declared that you have no time to pray!" Father Slavko Barbaric, a holy Franciscan of Medjugorje who prayed, and taught his parish to pray liked to say, "When there is love in the heart, one finds the means. When there is not love, one makes excuses." That's wisdom! To think that one will gain time by eliminating prayer is a bad calculation that deserves a zero in math!

Let me explain. If Jesus dwells in a house, thanks to the faithful prayers of the family, He pours out His blessings there, and this includes peace. Now everything that is done in peace is done better and faster. Jesus also pours out the spirit of mutual help, and when we do things together with everyone's skills, everything is done better and faster. Besides, Jesus does not come alone. His Mother is constantly with Him. The two of them have never been separated since the day of the Annunciation. When Mary accompanies her Son, she accomplishes her part of the work also. With a skill that is unique to her she extends her maternal mantle over that dwelling and thus protects its members from many accidents and illnesses that are so costly in time and money. Moreover, she opens some doors before us into diverse arenas, such as work or relationships, doors that would not open without her care. This spares us so much trial and wasted time! She goes before us along our path and keeps our soul from evil, because God has chosen her to crush the head of the Evil One.

Jesus comes also with the Holy Spirit. "May the Holy Spirit reign in your families," says the Blessed Mother. She also said, "Begin to invoke the Holy Spirit every day. When the Holy Spirit descends upon the earth, everything then becomes clear and everything is transformed." The action of the Holy Spirit, then, is infinitely precious, for in our decisions and in the choices that need to be made, He enlightens us. Thus we are spared from going off on a tangent, which would cost us dearly if we go without his illumination. Need we mention here the assistance of the angels and saints who accompany Jesus and Mary?

Mother Teresa of Calcutta often said, "If we don't have the time to do what we have to do, it's because we haven't prayed enough!" In fact, those who pray a lot and pray with all their heart are not stressed. Their life is well ordered, since God is taking the lead! As one Franciscan priest used to say, "If your prayer doesn't change you, change your prayer!"

Mary insists that our prayer should be full of life and should not be boring. To this end she recommends that families, and that everyone, be steeped in the Bible and the lives of the Saints. Let the father of the family explain the life of Jesus to his children. That way, they will assimilate the divine wisdom and the light that emanates from Sacred Scripture. The lives of the Saints are among the best means of sowing the seeds of faith in the hearts of children. How many have received their vocation while reading the life of this saint or that, or while watching a good movie! Parents can help their children to have a deep and personal encounter with God through their own example and their love. These treasures of faith will remain with them always, even through the inevitable crises.' Let prayer, Sunday Mass, and the reception of the sacrament of Reconciliation, be familiar to the child as an integral part of life.

To give an example, let's say that one day your little four-yearold says to you, "Mom, I don't want to eat!" Your response is, "But, sweetheart, you have to eat! You can see that everyone is eating. It's important!" The child understands that he has to eat and that it's part of life. One evening, the child says to you, "Mom, I don't want to go to sleep!" Your response is, "But you have to sleep. See? Even Daddy goes to bed. You can't live without sleep!" The child understands. One day, he says to you, "Mom, I don't want to pray!" And you answer, "Oh, that's alright, you can pray tomorrow. You can go out and play!" What does the child understand? That eating, drinking and sleeping are the essential things in life, one can't do without them, but God, well, one can do without Him, He's not important. That is how you raise an unbeliever, because by the time he is twelve he will no longer see why he should go to Mass and be bored just to be with someone who is not important, when his friends have invited him to do something else.

On the other hand, if parents live out their connection with Heaven in a joyful and vibrant way, if they talk about it between themselves quite naturally, if they manifest their wonder at the graces they receive, if they cite episodes in the lives of the saints, the child will grasp very quickly that God exists and that Jesus is a wonderful friend. Of his own accord he will begin to speak to Him in his heart. If the child sees his parents getting down willingly on their knees before God, if he hears them pray, then from an early age he will develop in his own soul, a spiritual dimension that will be an enormous help to him later. If someone has prayed as a child they are different from others; they carry within themselves this openness to things of the Spirit that a child with no Christian formation will have greater difficulty developing. By virtue of their fundamental innocence, little children are closer to God than we are, and their spiritual "antennas" can surprise us in their acuity. Their little inspirations can make us melt.[2]

---

[2] See chapter 50.

Daniel-Ange Speaks

"Dear children! I invite you to reflect about your future. You are creating a new world without God, only with your own strength and that is why you are unsatisfied and without joy in the heart. This time is my time and that is why, little children, I invite you again to pray. When you find unity with God, you will feel hunger for the word of God and your heart, little children, will overflow with joy. You will witness God's love wherever you are. I bless you and I repeat to you that I am with you to help you. Thank you for having responded to my call."

(MESSAGE OF JANUARY 25, 1997)

The voice of Father Daniel-Ange has been resonating these last few years, especially in its advocacy for the protection of children, adolescents, and families, at a time when they are the target of diabolic plans, to put it bluntly. With his permission, I would like to quote here several excerpts from his recent writings that help us to be aware of the battle that is going on, and how urgent it is to arm ourselves accordingly.

Speaking about particular school programs, this is how he denounces the situation, "Isn't this viper's venom being injected into our children's fragile veins? Aren't they already bombarded from every angle by the invasion of pornography, including on their ipods and iphones—and even (this beats everything) in certain "sex education" classes? How can one deny the connection between pornography, and the promotion of various sexual orientations and practices?

"In many of these *sexual education* classes, videos are shown containing *information,* that, in fact, *incentivizes* having sex, polluting the memory and infesting the imagination of children and adolescents. But this is just one more assault, verging on psychological rape, and is outside the bounds of school education!

"In this new system, one must expose children to every possible sexual deviation, and to every imaginable form of marriage. Then we have the adolescent, who is already so perturbed, required to choose his or her gender from among multiple possibilities, in the same way that he must also choose by which precise experience he will be initiated into exercising his physical sexuality. Will it by participating in an orgy? Sodomy? Rape? Will it be with girls, or boys, or children, or teenagers? Will the adolescent's first sexual experience be with an adult, or maybe even an animal? The menu is a la carte and we just have to choose something.

"Have we lost our minds? This indoctrination is provoking a dichotomy between school and family. At home, the child hears this, 'Great! You're a girl, you're super-beautiful, be proud of it!' At school she hears, 'You wish you were a boy? You can be both woman and man at the same time. You can choose your gender. You can even become a transsexual, no problem.'

"Yes, but how are they to choose? Using what criteria, since we no longer even know what it means to be female and/or male, and it's possible to be one after the other or both at the same time? It's enough to make the poor kid schizophrenic! Schizophrenic because we are separating anatomy and psychology—the bodily from the spiritual, the physical from the psychic, the real from the virtual. 'You're a male, but feminine. You're female, but masculine.' Of course, from the ripe old age of 5, the child understands all this. It's so obvious, so simple! How can it have taken us so many millennia to discover it!

"And even in nursery and kindergarten, there is already the practical application. Is this science fiction? In some Scandinavian schools every allusion to the masculine or the feminine has been eradicated. They incite boys to wear skirts and play with dolls and girls to box and play with toy machine guns (as yet in plastic). The children cannot be left alone, because, if they are, they revert spontaneously to the hobbies of interest to their sex. In Sweden, they want to forbid little boys from urinating standing up, which is seen as an intolerable discrimination against girls. 'Why should he be able to do that and not me?' In the USA, some parents make sure that no one can guess the biological sex of their child, dressing them one time as a girl, another time as a boy. 'That way, he/she is free to choose.'

"Logically, this injection of the gender virus will end sooner or later in transsexual surgeries for children. We already have pediatric and adolescent transgender health clinics or sex-reassignment clinics for children, which have actually created a new category of children called 'transkids.'[3] In Sweden, some families are refusing to send their children to public schools. Some are even taking refuge in Norway, which has abandoned gender theory in schools.

"At such a vulnerable age, when children and teenagers struggle so much to find their way, to find their identities, to structure their lives, to become themselves, how can we inject them with this venom of doubt as to their sexual identity? How, when they are already made so unstable by the eroticism that surrounds them, and wounded by parents either

---

[3] www.transkidspurplerainbow.org.

not living out the complementary graces specific to women and men, or living them out badly, could anyone take advantage of their inner shipwreck in order to push them down into quicksand, from which they will perhaps never be able to extract themselves?

"When one knows the degree to which homosexuality is proven to be a wound that is experienced painfully by the great majority, (and I know what I'm talking about having received so many secret confidences from young people) how can anyone dare to consciously and willingly encourage them to go in that direction? How does one dare to present homosexuality as an equivalent alternative to heterosexuality? Homosexuality as an alternative lifestyle dooms the child to be frustrated forever, both in his state of being different than other children, and in his lack of fruitful procreation, (unless, of course one resorts to artificial procreation, thereby breaking any filial bonds)?

"I dare to shout it out loud: all of this is a violation of the child's soul, deceiving their intelligence, falsifying their innate common sense, perverting their conscience, destroying their instinct for what is real, distorting their reason, breaking down their ultimate reference points! They are being massacred in their innocence, and in the end, their entire existence is wrecked.

"No, no, and no. You don't play with the life of a child, just as you don't play with his body. You do not deceive his intelligence, just as you do not arouse his senses. No, no and no. You do not inject them with mortal poison. No, no and

no. They are not guinea pigs.[4] You do not use them for
psychological experiments the way people were used for
medical experiments in Nazi camps. You do not use them as
a social experiment either, the way we carry out drug trials to
see if there are any bad long-term effects, which usually
become the basis of lawsuits anyway, because of their deadly
secondary effects.

"In Spain, the government is re-thinking the teaching of
gender at school. 55,000 families have made an objection of
conscience, refusing to send their children to school and
initiating 2,300 lawsuits. In 9 cases out of 10, tribunals have
condemned the government for infringing on the rights of
parents.

"In Russia, a law aims "to protect minors from homosexual propaganda and information which endangers their
health, and their spiritual and moral growth."[5]

"In Norway, where there has been a complete failure of
asexual education, neutralizing the sexual differences, they
are at the point of renouncing the program …

"All of these examples show that reality, the truth of who
we are as male and female human beings, wins over fiction."

[4] This word has been used by Pope Francis on April 12, 2014,
   after he mentioned the totalitarianism of today saying, "children
   are not guinea pigs in a laboratory."

[5] Text vote in the Duma on January 25, 2013 resulted in 388 for,
   1 against, 1 abstention.

Venerable Marthe Robin Speaks to Yannik Bonnet

In her messages to Mirjana, Mary speaks to us often about the Heavenly Father. Now, Marthe Robin had a profound knowledge of fathers of families on earth, who work for their family in concert with the Heavenly Father. In my interview in the spring of 2013 with Father Yannik Bonnet, the priest shared another aspect of his dialogue with Marthe Robin.[6] At that time, Yannik had just had his 7th child.

"Martha, he asked her. "Do you believe it's useful for Christians to engage in politics?" (John Paul II had not yet stated it clearly.)

"Of course! But for you, not before 10 more years!" Martha answered him.

"Why?" asked Yannik.

---

[6] See chapter 26 on France.

"Because you've just had your last little one, and she needs her father's guidance for 10 years."

These are luminous words if ever there were any for our generation! Yannik added to the story, "Marthe spoke to me a lot about education and the role of the father, since that's what I had come to hear. She was very clear on the importance of the role of the father, who prepares the child for autonomy and gives him inner structure, while the mother gives him all the love he needs to love life. Because children who are not loved by their mothers often have strong temptations towards suicide."

"In fact, the young of today are not structured," continued Yannik. "They can't stay the course. Among my companions in the Seminary of Rome, there are some who have already left the priesthood. They couldn't hold on. They are centered on their own feelings, and they are not structured. In our seminaries I can easily see that we have good teachers for my young friends while in seminary; but the students lack fathers, in the strongest sense of the word."

In Medjugorje, Mary reveals the path to healing. She says, "My children, through prayer hearken to the will of the Heavenly Father. Converse with Him. Have a personal relationship with the Father, which will deepen even more your relationship as a community of my children—of my apostles. As a mother I desire that, through the love for the Heavenly Father, you may be raised above earthly vanities and may help others to gradually come to know and come closer to the Heavenly Father," (Message of November 2, 2013).

49

Don't Damage One Another!

IN THE UNITED STATES, Kim is part of the *Diaspora-Medjugorje*. She lived for almost two years at our house, and when she returned to her home in California, an avid follower of the Virgin's messages, she never stopped witnessing to her faith. Her joy is contagious, and she attracts a lot of young people to the Lord. In her parish, she is involved in the formation of catechumens. One day, she met a certain Mona Gallia.

Mona is very beautiful. Originally raised by her parents as a Seventh Day Adventist, she stopped all religious practice during her adolescence. Fond of fiestas, happy hours, and evenings at clubs, she led a carefree life, without troubling herself with too many rules. She was very popular because of her great beauty and loved attracting the attention of friends and simply having fun, although not without watering everything down with healthy doses of alcohol.

Then, at the age of 21, she found herself pregnant and decided to keep the child. Did this choice come out of some religious conviction that Mona might have developed? Certainly not. But she did know deep inside that her baby was a human being, even before it was born. Today, delighted at her decision, she does not hide her joy in seeing her child alive and well, even if it has been difficult to raise him alone.

She continued to go out with other men and finally found one, Martin, who made her very happy. True love was born between them. She moved out of her home to live with him. When their relationship became more serious, they talked about marriage. However, Mona's friend imposed one condition: since he was Catholic, he couldn't imagine marrying a woman who didn't share the same faith. He suggested that she look into his faith, to see if she wanted to be baptized and enter the Catholic Church. Very open by nature, Mona had nothing against this. "Why not?" she said.

In 2012, he brought her with him to Easter Mass, and there, Mona was very touched by the splendid liturgy of this parish. During the course of the celebration, she felt more and more deeply moved. Not long afterwards, wanting to know more, she asked to register for the RCIA (Rite of Christian Initiation for Adults) formation program and began her formation to become a Catholic.

It was at this time that she was put into the hands of our friend Kim. Mona's profound experience during the Easter Mass had kindled in her such a love for the Mass that she began to go there often. In contrast, Mona's Catholic friend was content to go only at Christmas and Easter! With a great deal of wisdom and tact, given Mona's past, Kim explained to her in depth the points of our faith, without trying to move more quickly than Mona's heart.

When Mona learned that Catholics attend Mass every Sunday, she was not content to go by herself, and only on Sundays. She wanted to take her friend along with her, and attend Mass sometimes during the week. After all, it was he who had demanded that she become a Catholic! However, each week, while she was getting ready to go to church, Martin always found an excuse. Either he didn't want to leave the house, or he couldn't miss a certain sporting event, etc. She was surprised and saddened but continued going alone to Mass.

Everything that she discovered about the teachings of the Catholic Church enthralled her, and she found in them, more and more, a meaning to her life. Endowed with a curious mind, and a very open heart, she willingly took in every facet of these teachings. The time came when she discovered God's plans for the family, for the human couple, for the beauty and grandeur of that particular creation. With a great deal of delicacy, Kim informed her about the sexual morality advocated by the Church and how it was important to remain chaste before giving oneself to one another in the sacrament of marriage, so as to live under God's blessing. When Mona questioned her boyfriend on that teaching, he said, "But nobody follows those rules anymore!"[1] However, all that she had discovered as a catechumen about the value of the human person and the sacred character of the sexual act had the effect of a bomb! A bomb so powerful and ines-

---

[1] Fortunately, many people follow these guidelines from the Church, and not only Catholics. Most Christian churches teach the same thing, as does the Orthodox Jewish religion and many others. May they be blessed for that! The Mother of God says in Medjugorje, "Dear Children, I cannot help you if you don't live by the commandments of God, if you do not fully live the Mass." In North America, a movement called "Pure Hearts" has been formed, a gathering of young people who dedicate themselves to living in chastity until marriage. Some wear a bracelet inscribed with the words 'Pure Hearts.' In Italy, a similar movement was born with Ania Goledzinowska, "Cuori Puri,"—www.facebook.com/cuoripuri. These young people recite a prayer of consecration and a promise of chastity with sexual abstinence in the presence of a priest who gives them a blessing. Then they receive a ring as a sign of their belonging to a family. Many countries are missing founders of such movements. They have not yet emerged. May they rise up without delay!

capable that she wanted to be part of it. So, she made the decision to leave Martin's house and to live with her mother until the marriage. It all took place with the greatest of ease without crises or tears. While packing her bags, Mona explained to Martin that if he wanted her to be a Catholic, then she was going to become a real Catholic!

To her great joy Mona was baptized at Easter time in 2014! She is anxious to continue her formation in the Christian faith, conscious that God is so great that she will never finish learning about Him. As for her marriage, she put it off. She said, "because now that I am a believer, I can't see myself married to a man who prefers to stay in bed on Sunday morning rather than answer the invitation of God!"

What can we take from this story of Mona in the Church of Christ? I think back to the words of the Curé of Ars, "The saints didn't always begin well, but they all ended well!"

Marthe Robin had the Answer

In her dark little room, this great mystic with the stigmata saw people from every walk of life streaming in and out of her room. Familiar with her profound union with God, and with her gifts of wisdom and prophesy, they came to ask her advice and entrust their burdens to her powerful prayer. Marthe listened, prayed, and from her childlike voice let out a simple word, which changed the direction of an entire life. (This was my case and that of many of my friends.)

One day, a man and a woman arrived at her home. They had been married in the Church, but not to each other. In reality, both converted late and married too quickly. They suffered terribly in those marriages. They had the opportunity to work together in an apostolate among the destitute and fell in love with one another, strongly and deeply. But, because they were already linked to others in the sacrament of marriage, they did not live together, despite the enormous temptation, which was at work within them. That magnificent harmony that they were experiencing together, a harmony they had never known before, made them think that they had been made for one another, if only they hadn't made those single errors of direction. But were they made for one another now? They laid open to Marthe both their suffering and their love, hoping to receive from her some light about their future.

Marthe was known for her profound admiration for the human couple and for the love, which could live between them. She saw in a couple one of the most beautiful gifts the Creator has for the children He created in His own image, through love and for love. Deep within the sentiment of deep love in these two beings, she could see the presence of God and the inestimable potential, which had been accorded to them, to know the God of love better and to serve Him, together. Because they had married in the Church and separated without an annulment, she gave them this admirable response, "Love one another, but don't damage one another!"

In other words, Marthe invited them to go into the deep and reach a more profound degree of love. She encouraged them to love each other much more, to challenge their love for one another through the sacrifice of chastity, without damaging one another by falling into sin, and remaining under the blessing of God.

50

The Prayer of Children, a Wonder!

"Today bring to me the meek and humble souls and the souls
of little children, and immerse them in My mercy. These
souls most closely resemble My Heart. They strengthened Me
during My bitter agony. I saw them as earthly Angels, who
would keep vigil at My altars. I pour out upon them whole
torrents of grace. Only the humble soul is able to receive My
grace. I favor humble souls with My confidence."

(JESUS TO SR FAUSTINA, §1220)

L ITTLE JAKOV WAS 10 years old when the apparitions
began in Medjugorje in June of 1981. Since his father
had died, he was left with only his mother as family, and he
lived with her in a tiny house of stone and clay not far from

Mirjana's. Like all the children of Bijakovici, one of the five hamlets of Medjugorje, Jakov was familiar with hunger, cold, uncertainty about tomorrow, and the need to fight hard to survive.

One evening, during an apparition, Our Lady asked him to pray constantly, that is, always to remain open to the presence of God in his heart. She advised him to say little prayers often, when he was going to school, when he was walking down the street, when he was playing with his friends, when he sat down at the table, etc. She gave the example that he could say, "Oh, Jesus, I love you!" or "Lord, may Your name be blessed!" or "Virgin Mary, my Mother, help me, I need you!" or "My God, I adore You!" or "Glory be to God the Most High in Heaven!" or "Jesus, I trust in You!" or "My Father, I give myself completely to You!" In short, little words that spring from the heart! Jakov understood the request very well and decided to put it into practice.

The next day he had a soccer game with his friends. (I will point out here that Jakov was passionate about soccer.) He was getting ready, running towards the field, when he suddenly realized he had forgotten to pray on the way there. Truthfully, he didn't remember to pray because he was concentrating on the soccer game and the joy that awaited him! But since he loved the Blessed Virgin so much, he stopped and recited a Hail Mary to her very quickly before joining the other players.

That evening, at the time of the apparition, Our Lady said to him, "Thank you, Jakov, for the prayer you offered to me, even if you said it very fast."

Then, during the apparition, she showed him a scene in China, a country that was very strange to him. Jakov saw a house, and in one of the rooms there was a bed. On the bed, a man lay inanimate. The Blessed Mother said, "You see this man, Jakov? He is dead. He was a very bad man and he was going to go to Hell. But thanks to your prayer, I was able to grant him a special grace, and he regretted all his faults at the last minute. So, he is saved!"

It goes without saying that Jakov was blown away by this! A simple prayer and a man changes direction for all eternity? What power prayer has! Mary has said, "Dear Children, if you knew the value of the least of your prayers, you would pray unceasingly!"

Have Your Children Attend Adoration!

On August 16th 1988, our friend, Thérèse Stoop, received a word in her heart during the evening Mass in Medjugorje, "Go to the children. It is through their prayers that the adults and the powerful will convert!" Since then, with the spiritual help of Father Slavko, she has founded a group of child who adore the Blessed Sacrament in Belgium. She is convinced that it will be through childrens' adoration that the world will be saved. As a matter of fact, a great many vocations and holy families are born from these beautiful initiatives. Father Poppe, a Belgian priest currently in the process of canonization, had little ones brought to adoration, and he used to say, "Have your children do adoration and the churches will be full!"

When Thérèse first started to create this team of little adorers, she began very poorly—she had only three children the first year, and her pastor thought she should stop. "These little ones have their whole lives to do adoration later," he said! She accepted this decision with sadness, but Jesus Himself took things into His own hands in an unexpected way. He incited a strong reaction in the hearts of the little ones, who sent a letter to the pastor saying that they wanted to continue to have adoration! Jesus won!

Two years later, a first miracle occurred through the prayer of the little ones. They had been asked to pray for a young person afflicted with leukemia who had only a few hours to live. The children prayed and fashioned a flower out of paper, which they placed in front of the house of the young person. A year later, that same young man, whom they did not know, arrived during their prayer time to say that he was studying at the university. He was moved to find the children, and to thank them because, on the day he should have died, he felt blood flowing through his veins. He was able to sit up in his bed, and the next day, to the astonishment of the professors of hematology, he returned home. That young man had come to ask if he could pray with the children, because he had stopped praying a long time ago! All the children cried with joy at this enormous gift from Heaven.

Another time, several days before Christmas, Thérèse said to the children, "This evening, it is you who will lead adoration, and I will help you." Invited with other adults and parents of the children, a young man named Joël came to that adoration. Six-year-old Nicholas prayed in this way in front of the Eucharistic Jesus, "Forgive me, Jesus. You speak to me often, and I don't listen to you!" At that moment, Joël began to cry his heart out. Later, he confided to Thérèse, "When I was 12, 16, 20 years old, Jesus called me to the priesthood, and I wouldn't listen to Him. I ran away from Him. Today, I'm going to follow Him!" Now Joël has been a priest for 12 years, and he's a very good one!

A young person who is now 24 years old shared with Thérèse an experience he had in Medjugorje. He had come to Medjugorje for the first time with a group of child adorers at the age of six. Thérèse recounts, "While he was praying the Stations of the Cross, a girl who was older than him took

him by the hand to the 10th station, and there, she left him.
Angry and upset, he picked up a stone and announced to me
that he was going to throw the stone at the girl. Not knowing
what to do, I said a quick 'Our Father.' The Lord interrupted
me to whisper in my heart, 'Say it slowly with all your heart,'
which is what I did. Then I rejoined my group of 53 children
at the 11th station. There, to my great astonishment, the Lord
showed me the importance of praying with the heart. That
child put his stone down, behind the bronze relief. He had
taken off his shoes and continued in bare feet, even though it
was March and very cold outside. While going back down
Krizevac, I saw him make the sign of the cross before the
cross at each station. When he reached the bottom, he told
me, 'Jesus told me to make the sign of the cross before each
cross, because it's a prayer.' The next year, he participated in a
pilgrimage following the life of Don Bosco. During adoration he saw Jesus, who was lighting seven candles. When
leaving the chapel, he confided to me, 'You know, Jesus told
me, *you see these candles? Look, I am blowing them out one by
one, and I'm taking away all your fear of the dark.*' And actually," continued Thérèse. "Several weeks later, I ran into his
mother, who told me, 'It's strange. He's not afraid of the dark
anymore. I don't have to leave a light on in his room at night
anymore.' And finally, following another pilgrimage, he told
me very calmly, 'Jesus spoke to me again, but he asked me
not to say anything about what He told me.'A number of
children brought their friends to our adoration, and after
that, a number of families returned to the Church. Some
have even become teachers of religion!"

Thérèse also reported to me that she picks up a little girl
of three on Wednesdays after school. This little girl's parents
no longer prayed, but the little girl never stopped saying,
"Me, I love Jesus, Mary and Joseph!" The little one often tells
Thérèse about her life. Once she said, "Sometimes I sing to

Mary, full of grace, in my bed for my little brother Anatole." Anatole is 18 months old.

Thérèse testifies that 25 years of adoration each week, with little ones from age two and a half to eleven, have already resulted in many religious vocations, missionary priests, and holy families. There must be so many beautiful things to tell! All those "thank yous" that the children give to Jesus each week, and those many "forgive mes" that burst out with no fear or shame: "Forgive me, Jesus, because I am jealous. My big sister received a beautiful dress, and I didn't." "Forgive me, Jesus, because my dad asked me to open the door of the garage, and I said 'shit' to my dad." "Thank you, Jesus, for having food to eat every day and for being able to go to school."

"Forgive me, Jesus, because I didn't obey my mom when she asked me to set the table."

"Thank you, Jesus, for making it possible for me to come to adore You every Wednesday."

May the Holy Spirit give rise to many Thérèses in our parishes, because so many children will jump at the chance to be able to adore Jesus!

Children's Cute Words

It is beautiful to see how close Heaven is to children, how much their angels, "who contemplate the face of God without ceasing," inspire them sometimes in magnificent ways. Their spiritual antennas, still fresh, receive in a privileged way the anointing of the Holy Spirit, and deliver us unexpected treasures. Should we be surprised? After all, Jesus said, "Whoever receives this child in my name receives me, and whoever receives me receives the one who sent me. For the one who is least among all of you is the one who is the greatest," (Luke 9:48). Here are a few vignettes from children around the world who have been touched by Heaven in a very special way!

Friends of ours from Rome bring their children to Medjugorje every year to recharge the whole family's spiritual batteries. They live out, as best they can, the messages and pray every day together. Here are some pearls taken from the mouth of their son, who is still very young: "Mom, when you go to heaven, can you tell me if Mary has blue eyes or brown?"

"But, my little one, if I'm dead, how can I tell you?" "You'll tell me in my heart!"

The mother wrote me, "It's very beautiful to see that the Blessed Mother is a real person in the lives of children and that for them there exists a language of the heart. Recently, we were expecting Father Antonello at our house, and the children love him very much.

'Mom, is Father Antonello coming today?' 'Yes!'

'Is he going to pick me up from school?'

'I think so, Francesco.'

How great it would be if he gave a blessing to all the children in the school!'

"At this news, Fr. Antonello wanted to go right away to that school. We were able to speak with the nun in charge, who was surprised and very touched by the request of Francesco. The next day, as a group, all the children of that school received a blessing!"

A four-year-old child was afflicted with a severe lung infection. Since he had already suffered painful procedures conducted by the medical staff, he was afraid of them. The radiologist tried to reassure him saying that he would carry out a painless examination. He explained to the four-year-old that a scanner would help the medical staff to see everything that was inside of him, and this would allow them to be gentler with him. The child was astonished. He said, "You'll see everything that's inside of me?"

"Yes," said the radiologist.

After the examination, the doctor explained the diagnosis to the parents in very complex terms, and the child became more and more impatient to know what the doctor saw. When he could stand it no longer, he interrupted the doctor and asked him, "If you saw everything that was inside me, then did you see the Blessed Mother who is in my heart?"

In Slovakia, in a village where a priest from the Family of Mary is the pastor, a child of seven was excited about everything that concerned the Church and the liturgy. He loved to watch the priest, and to be around him. He also loved to help with little tasks within his reach. One day, the priest was preparing to lead an hour of adoration with Jesus exposed on the altar. In the sacristy, he asked the child to prepare everything on the altar while he changed and put on his chasuble. The child, very happy, went into the church, prepared everything, and waited for the priest to come. When the priest arrived, he found everything perfectly in order, and Jesus was even placed in the monstrance!

A mother lost her child when she was 6 months pregnant. She explained to her little Sara, who was four, that her little brother would not see the light of day, and that he was not born as she had been born. This mother's little Sara cried out, "Well, then, Mom, he remained in Heaven!"

In Mzorsko Gonica, a little village in Slovakia, a sister from the Family of Mary Community was teaching the Catechism, and she was wearing a habit, which indicates that she is consecrated to Christ. A little girl of five asked her why she was wearing a ring on her finger since she is not married. The Sister explained she is not married to a man, but she is the spouse of Jesus. The little girl exclaimed with admiration, "Oh! Then you go every night to sleep in Heaven!"

Praying as a family is the most beautiful gift parents can offer their children, in this world and for all eternity!

51

Tony Daud, the Sorcerer of Java

"My dear children, tonight your Mother warns you that in this time Satan desires you and is looking for you! A little spiritual emptiness in you is enough for Satan to work in you. For this reason your Mother invites you to begin to pray. May your weapon be prayer. Prayer with the heart you will overcome Satan. Your Mother invites you to pray for the young people throughout the world."

(Message to the prayer group, September 5, 1988)

It happens sometimes that, before having *the last word,* the peace of God follows a path that is as strange as it is unexpected. This next story took place in Indonesia on March 19, 2014.

My dear friend from Jakarta, who had prepared my mission to Java and Sumatra, invited me into his office, and it was there that Tony Daud sang to us, over the telephone, the song that he had learned from angels on a particular day that was crucial in his life.

Tony Daud, otherwise known as Anthony David, was born in Indonesia, in the center of the long, thin island of Java. He was half Indonesian, half Chinese. On the date of this story he was 39 years old. His great-grandfather was not only a famous sorcerer but also the head of all the sorcerers in the country. Here is a bit of his story:

"I was born on a certain Saturday of the year which, according to the Javanese calendar, corresponded to the D day" established by the codes of sorcery, a day which designated the elect, the ones who would be worthy of receiving powers.

"In the world of black magic, sorcerers cannot die without first transferring their powers to carefully and properly selected people. In fact, there is no possibility for such powers to be lost!

"I was only 9 years old when my great-grandfather became my master, and transmitted to me all his powers. My great-grandmother, who belonged to the group called *Devil Fire,* also initiated me. Like her husband, she couldn't die without first transferring her powers. She was the quickest killer of all, one who never left a trace when exercising her sorcery. At the end of her life she had a very difficult death."

Tony Daud went on to describe for me a series of powers that he received after his first lesson. It was a striking list! I will not be specific about these powers, except for one particularly amazing faculty. He could disappear from everyone's sight without leaving any trace, or changing places. To keep his powers, several stipulations were placed on him. His hair was never to be cut, and he was to remain single. He told me, "When I was 12 years old and in middle school, I received a new magical power from my master. To have this power, I could not fall in love or get married. I had to remain single. After I received the last power, my master said to me, 'I am going to die at 2:30 this afternoon. Before I die, I would like to tell you the secret of your destiny: on your 18th birthday, you will see a very brilliant light. At the age of 19, you will meet a *king who has come from the Orient.* That's your destiny.' My great-grandfather died at 2:30 exactly.

"After his death, I found myself disoriented, without direction, and lost. Then I did some research on other people with special powers, so that I could challenge them. Deep down, I wanted to compare my powers with other sorcerers' powers, especially those who claimed to have the same powers that I had. I challenged many people and brought back victories against the most powerful magicians of Java. After I easily defeated everyone within my society of sorcerers and magicians, I challenged a Protestant minister, the Reverend Gilbert Louis, from the city of Solo.

"This pastor had given a testimony on television, declaring that no true Christian, Protestant or Catholic could be destroyed by the practices of sorcery, because Christians had received from God the seal of the Holy Spirit, and the blood of Christ protected them from all evil.[1] He also spoke about faith, by which a Christian carried within him the power of Christ. Such declarations challenged me. I was unnerved and sought to know if this was true. I went to ask the pastor what his powers were and from whom he had received them. But the pastor, like little David against the giant Goliath, stood before me with no other weapon except his faith in Jesus. He explained to me that he didn't have any power in himself and that no magic power had ever been transmitted to him.

"This language was new for me, so I asked the pastor to have a battle, a kind of mental duel to see which of us would conquer the other. The Reverend had no desire to fight, but, faced with my insistent threat, he had to take up the challenge. His sole weapon was the power of Jesus Christ, his Master, whom he loved with all his heart and whom he served with great faith. Armed with the Divine Word (like so

---

[1] 1 Peter 1:1–2 Peter, an apostle of Jesus Christ, To those who reside as aliens, scattered throughout Pontus, Galatia, Cappadocia, Asia, and Bithynia, who are chosen according to the foreknowledge of God the Father, by the sanctifying work of the Spirit, to obey Jesus Christ and be sprinkled with His blood: May grace and peace be yours in the fullest measure.

many Protestants), he knew his Bible very well! He knew that God would not abandon anyone who placed his trust in Him with humility, the way a child places his trust in his father.

"For three days, from morning until noon, we stood at a distance of one meter from one another in a dramatic face-to-face. I tried with all my might to destroy this pastor. During this entire trial, the Reverend never stopped praying to his God, the Living God, praising Him and giving Him thanks. As for me, I got nowhere. For the first time in my life, someone had resisted me!

"Towards the end of the 3rd day, I saw in front of me a strong light. Inside it was the pastor, completely surrounded and protected by this light. I knew in my spirit what prayer the pastor was saying. I could hear the "Alleluia" that he kept repeating constantly in his heart. Then I used my most devastating powers to try to destroy the pastor. Then the pastor shouted, "In the name of Jesus, depart!" At that moment, I was projected back a distance of twelve meters. I was defeated. I immediately lost consciousness, and, for an entire year, was deprived of my intelligence and all memory. I didn't even know who I was, nor from where I came. I wandered about on my two legs like an automaton, like a man deprived of all sense. My brain seemed empty. It was later revealed that the one from whom I had received my powers was Lucifer himself. When the pastor cried out, "In the name of Jesus, depart!" he saw Lucifer depart from my body while pronouncing his own name, Lucifer, in an atrocious and inhuman howl, like a signature on his action before leaving.

"In 1993, a year after this had taken place, I turned 19. It was on that day that a blinding light came upon me and within me, and I heard these words, 'I am the Alpha and the Omega. I am who am.'[2] The light then became Jesus, and I saw Jesus in person. 'Look at me!' He said. 'I was dead and I am resurrected. Do you wish to believe in Me?' I replied, 'Yes, I believe! You are the power, and this makes me believe in you.' In a very great outpouring of the Holy Spirit, I saw my sins, and I was seized with a profound contrition when faced with the evil I had committed. Jesus gave me the strength of the Holy Spirit to guide me and to help me realize in what ways I had sinned. I confessed to Jesus each new sin that I saw in my past. I had to admit to my sin of using black magic. The moment that I repented and confessed all my sins to Jesus, I immediately lost my magic powers.

"I could not see the face of Jesus, and I never saw it later, because it was more brilliant than the sun, and my eyes couldn't stand such clarity. I only saw the robe of Jesus, which was itself very luminous. However, I saw angels singing all around Him. Later, I wrote these songs down, remembering the words that I heard from the angels. At the end of this life-changing encounter, Jesus said to me, 'Preach the Gospel!' For me this moment with Jesus was very short and very intense."

During my conversation with Tony Daud, he sang some of the angels' songs to me, in their original melodies, just as he had heard them in *Baasa,* the local language. Of course, I didn't understand their meaning, but my Indonesian friends expressed admiration when they heard the splendor of those words. Tony said that the angels came down from Heaven

---

[2] These are the same words that Adonai addressed to Moses in the episode of the burning bush, (Exodus 3:13–14). The following quotations are found in the book of Revelation 1:8.

bearing treasures, and that they sang these hymns with unparalleled voices.

Tony Daud searched for Reverend Gilbert, who welcomed him warmly into his parish in Solo, in the heart of Java. He became like a father to Tony. As one might expect, the experience they went through together profoundly marked them both, and established a very strong link between them. At the beginning of his conversion, Tony wavered a little, because he knew nothing about the Christian faith, but he understood that he had to let himself be guided by the pastor, and simply obey him.

He enrolled in the School of Theology in Solo, in central Java, and, in 1996, he obtained his diploma. Today, Tony is an evangelical pastor in Reverend Gilbert's parish, which is called *Glow* (a word that expresses flamboyance, brilliance, blazing color, and ardor).

Thanks to the knowledge he gained from his former background in sorcery, Tony Daud is also capable of foiling actions of magic, which could be damaging to faithful Christians, or to anyone among his people. He knows how to identify where black magic is practiced, and he is currently fighting against it. Basically he merges his faith as a disciple of Jesus, with knowledge of his past techniques. By doing that, he has become a powerful instrument in the hands of God.[3]

Today, Tony is married and is the father of a family! He travels across all of Indonesia to preach the gospel and to

---

[3] This can be compared to drug addicts who understand one another on a deep level, and after recovery are able to help their fellow addicts through the steps of healing.

testify to his experience.[4] When I asked him why, in his opinion, he hadn't been able to destroy the Pastor, and what major obstacle in the man prevented Tony from doing it, Tony answered me simply, "His faith!"

And here you have the key to the event! The powerful faith of Reverend Gilbert allowed God to act through him. So, Tony confirmed the words of St. Paul, cited by the Reverend on television! In truth, he who belongs to Christ and lives in him need not fear magicians and sorcerers; he carries within him the divine seal which protects him from Evil.

May this testimony encourage all the humble souls who pray and make sacrifices every day in monasteries or out in the world, in the secret of their solitude, those who undoubtedly never see such conversions take place around them to persevere! May these souls rejoice and be glad! One day—and it is near—the Lord will tell them that it is thanks to their profound Christian life and to their merits that his dear lost son, Tony Daud, came back to life and that, for him also, peace prevailed over death!

---

[4] Tony Daud has written a book about his experience. Currently, it only exists in the Indonesian language.

52

The Medal That Attracts Miracles

"Today bring to Me the pagans and those who do not yet know Me. I was thinking also of them during My bitter Passion, and their future zeal comforted My Heart. Immerse them in the ocean of My Mercy."

(JESUS TO SAINT FAUSTINA, §1216)

FIVE MEN WERE BORED to death in their narrow prison cell in Vicksburg, Mississippi. One of them, Claude Newman, noticed, hanging around the neck of his cellmate, a little oval medal attached to a cord. He asked him what it was. The man was annoyed: "It's a medal!" Claude asked again, "What's that medal?" The man became even more annoyed and, cursing, threw it at Claude's feet, "Just take the stupid thing!"

Claude Newman (1923–1944) was a black American. Separated from his mother, Florette, at the age of five, he grew up with his grandmother, Ellen Newman, and his older brother in Bovine, Mississippi. There he joined the difficult and heavy labor of the cotton plantations, where Sid Cook, his grandmother's second husband, was also employed. Claude, now nineteen years old, was a daily witness to the cruel treatment and numerous beatings inflicted by Sid on his dear grandmother. One day in December of 1942, unable to stand it anymore, Claude got hold of Sid's weapon and killed the malicious man. He attempted to flee but was quickly spotted and condemned to death in the electric chair for murder. He waited for his day of execution in prison.

The day that he picked up the medal thrown by his cell-mate, Claude put it around his neck. He was far from knowing the marvelous origin of that medal![1] But he had no time to waste finding out. During the night, while he was sleeping on his rudimentary bed, he was awakened all of a sudden by someone who brushed him delicately on his wrist. He would later say, "There, right in front of me was the most beautiful woman God had ever created."

Frightened and unsettled, Claude didn't know what to do. But before disappearing, the Lady reassured him, "If you want me for your mother, and if you want to become my child, have a priest come from the Catholic Church." Alone

---

[1] On November 27, 1830 on the Rue de Bac in Paris, the Virgin appeared for the second time to Saint Catherine Labouré, a Sister of Charity. Catherine could see on two fingers of Our Lady "rings covered with stones, each one more beautiful than the next, and which emitted rays of light. At the end of the apparition, the Virgin disappeared to be replaced by a medal, and Catherine heard these words, "Have a medal made that looks like this model. All persons who wear it will receive many graces just by wearing it around their necks. The graces will overflow for those who wear it in faith." A little time later, the Virgin appeared again to Catherine. She presented a globe, which represented the world, and especially France. Our Lady was still wearing her rings, and Catherine noticed that certain stones were not giving off light. Then Mary explained to her, "These stones which emit nothing are the graces that people forgot to ask me for." Two years later, the medal, called from that time forward the Miraculous Medal, was created, and with it, and its hundreds of thousands of copies, miracles have multiplied.

again, Claude began to shout so loudly that all his cellmates woke up. He yelled, "Get a Catholic priest!"

The next morning, young Father O'Leary came to Claude, who confided in him what had happened during the night. To the great surprise of Father O'Leary, Claude and the other four prisoners asked to be instructed in the Catholic faith. The priest remained skeptical. However, these cellmates, while never having seen or heard the voice of the Lady, vehemently confirmed Claude's tale. The missionary promised to give them some catechetical lessons.

The following day, he came to the prison for the first lesson right on time. Once there he noted with surprise that Claude Newman knew neither how to read nor write, because he had not gone much to school. His ignorance about the faith was abysmal. In reality, he knew nothing, absolutely nothing. He was unfamiliar with Jesus. He was totally ignorant that God could even exist. Father O'Leary began with the fundamentals. The ABCs for Claude, and surprisingly, his cellmates helped in his initiation.

Several weeks went by, and during his catechesis, the priest declared, "Well men, today we're going to talk about the sacrament of Reconciliation!" Claude quickly responded, "Oh, on this point, I'm up to date! The Lady told me that when we confess, we don't kneel in front of the priest, but in front of the cross of His Son. And when we truly repent from our sins and we confess them, the blood which he shed for us flows within us and purifies us of our sins."[2] Father O'Leary was stupefied. He didn't say a word. He needed to recover from the shock. "Oh, don't get angry," Claude apologized. "I didn't mean to cut you off."

"Oh no, I'm not angry. I'm just surprised. So, you've seen the lady again?" the priest asked him. But Claude waited to be alone with the priest to tell him in confidence, "The Lady told me that if you have many doubts or hesitations, I had to recall for you the promise that you made to the Virgin Mary in 1940 in Holland, lying in a trench, because she is still waiting for you to fulfill it." Later, Father O'Leary felt obligated to testify, "Claude described to me the exact contents of my promise. That unbelievable revelation succeeded in convincing me that Claude was telling the truth about those apparitions."

When he came back to the group of catechumens, Claude continued to encourage the four men who had really become his students in a way. "Don't be afraid of confession! Really, you tell your sins to God and not to the priest. You know,

---

[2] Jesus to Saint Faustina: "Tell souls that they must look for consolation at the tribunal of the Divine Mercy. There, the greatest miracles will keep repeating without ceasing. It is sufficient simply to cast oneself in faith at the feet of the one who is taking my place and tell him his wretchedness, and the miracle of the Divine Mercy will manifest itself in all its fullness. Even if that soul is like a decomposing cadaver and even if, humanly speaking, there is no longer any hope of returning to life and all seems lost, it is not that way with God. The miracle of Divine Mercy will bring that soul back to life in all its fullness. Oh! Unhappy are those who are not profiting now from this miracle of the Divine Mercy. In vain will you call; it will be too late!" (Saint Faustina, §1448).

Our Lady explained it to me, through the priest, we speak to God, and God, through the priest, speaks to us."

A week later, Father O'Leary prepared a teaching on the Eucharist for his five prisoners. There again, Claude let him know that the Blessed Mother had instructed him on this point as well. "Our Lady told me that the Host only has the appearance of a piece of bread, but in reality, it is Her Son. She even explained that Jesus remains only a short time inside me, just as He stayed only a short time inside her before His birth in Bethlehem. So, I have to spend my short time with Him the way she did during her lifetime: in loving Him, in adoring Him, in praising Him, in asking for His blessing, and in thanking Him. During those few minutes, I should not think about anyone and be occupied with nothing except spending that time with Him alone."

On January 6, 1944, at the end of the catechesis, the five prisoners were baptized and received into the Catholic Church. Claude's execution was to take place four days later. The day before, Sheriff Williamson asked him, "Claude, you can make a last wish. What would you like?" The prisoner responded, "You are all agitated. Even the guards are upset, but you don't understand that only my body will die. I'm going with her. So, I would like to plan a party."

"What do you mean by that?" asked the sheriff.

"Well ... a party!" answered Claude calmly. "Can you ask the priest to organize a party with cake and ice cream and allow the prisoners on the second story to roam freely in the main room, so we can all enjoy the party?" "Someone might attack the priest," one of the supervisors warned.

Claude addressed his jail companions and asked, "Boys, you won't do that, okay?" The priest then went to pay a visit to a rich benefactor in the parish who could provide desserts and ice cream. Can you imagine this party of prisoners? To finish it, Claude wanted all the invited prisoners to be allowed to have a Holy Hour in the same room. Father O'Leary helped them meditate on the Stations of the Cross. Then they prayed for Claude and for the salvation of their souls.

The prisoners went back to their cellblock, and Father O'Leary went to the chapel to get the Blessed Sacrament. He gave Holy Communion to Claude; both of them knelt and prayed together with all their hearts. Claude was happy!

But 15 minutes before the execution, there was a change in the program! Sheriff Williamson climbed the stairs four at a time and began to yell, "Adjournment, adjournment! The governor has issued a stay of two weeks!" As a matter of fact, the sheriff and the lawyer of the district had done everything possible with the relevant authorities to save Claude's life. But when Claude learned about it, he began to cry! Were those tears of joy and relief, as Father O'Leary and Williamson believed? Not in the slightest! Shaking and sobbing, Claude stammered out, "You didn't understand anything! If you had even one time seen her face, if you had looked into Her eyes, you wouldn't want to live a single day more! What stupid thing did I do this week?" He asked the priest. "That God is refusing to call me to Him? Why do I have to spend two more weeks on this earth?"

Father O'Leary had a brilliant idea. He recalled for Claude the case of James Hughs, another detainee, who, although he had once been educated in the Catholic faith, had led a totally immoral life and had also been condemned to death for murder. (We have to state here that this Hughs nourished a profound hatred of Claude Newman.) "Maybe Mary wants you to offer the sacrifice of not going right away to Heaven for the conversion of Hughs," the priest said. "Why not offer up to God each minute you are away from

Our Lady, so that this prisoner won't be separated from God for all eternity?"

That struck a chord in Claude, and he accepted the deal immediately. He asked Father to teach him some prayers he could say to offer this sacrifice to God. The priest helped his protégé, who confided, "Father, here in prison, Hughs hated me from the very beginning, but right now it's 100 times worse!" Claude, who had had his twentieth birthday two weeks previously, generously offered up each vexation, sacrifice, and prayer for the intention of James Hughs.

Two weeks later, Newman was granted his greatest wish. He was executed and his soul went to God. Later, Father O'Leary commented, "I have never seen anyone go to his death so serenely. Even the official witnesses and journalists were dumbstruck. They could not fathom how the face of someone condemned to death in the electric chair could express such serenity."

Claude's last words were for Father O'Leary, "Father, I will remember you, and when you have an intention, resort to me, and I will transmit it to the 'beautiful Lady.'" That was February 4, 1944. But the story doesn't stop there!

James Hughs, the mortal enemy of Claude Newman, was supposed to be executed three months later, May 19, 1944. Father O'Leary recounted, "This was the most dishonest and immoral man I had ever known. There are no words to describe his hatred towards God and towards everything spiritual." Several minutes before the sheriff came to get him in his cell to take him to the place of execution, the district doctor, Dr. Podesta, asked the detainee insistently to at least kneel and recite the Our Father.

But the condemned man swore and spit in the face of the doctor. The minute Hughs was positioned in the chair, the sheriff made one last try, "If you have anything left to say, say it now!" The answer was another swear word. But, all of a sudden, James became mute, staring at a corner of the room, his eyes wide open. He was terrorized! He cried out in a loud voice to the sheriff, "Bring me a priest!" Since the law in Mississippi prescribed the presence of a priest in that era, Father O'Leary was already present in the room, but hidden behind some journalists. As a matter of fact, James Hughs had threatened to spew a torrent of curse words if he saw any "little priest" near him. Father O'Leary then approached the condemned man, who said to him, "I'm a Catholic, but at the age of 18, I pulled away from the Church by living immorally."

At that moment, everyone left the room except the priest and the prisoner. James Hughs confessed like a child, with profound remorse. When the confession was finished, the sheriff came back into the room with his men and asked with curiosity, "Father, what provoked that change in Hughs?"

"I don't know," answered the priest. "I didn't ask him."

"Oh," said the sheriff. "If I don't find out, I won't be able to sleep a wink tonight!" So he addressed the condemned man, "What changed your mind?" It was a totally transformed Hughs who answered him, "Do you remember that black man Claude Newman, who was so disgusting to me? Well, he was there in the corner of the room! I saw him! And behind him, with her hands on his shoulders, was the Virgin Mary! Then Claude said to me, 'I offered my death in union with Christ on the cross for your salvation. Our Lady obtained for you the grace to see the place in Hell which is destined for you, if you don't repent.' That was when I yelled for a priest."

A little later, James Hughs was executed. He was converted at the last minute![3]

Still today, Our Lady tells us, "Dear children, I am with you ... If you knew how much I love you, you would cry with joy," (Message of March 18, 2009).

MEDJUGORJE, MAY 31, 2014,
ON THE FEAST OF THE VISITATION.

---

[3] See the magazine Triumph of the Heart, November/December 2013, No 69.

APPENDIX 1

For Your Bread at Fasting Time, Some Suggested Recipes

AFTER BEGINNING TO fast, in response to the call of Mary in Medjugorje, some people have become tired of the bread and abandoned this good practice. Changing the bread is often the best remedy! Since it's very difficult to fast with bread that is of poor quality (the simple white bread of today doesn't contain much nutrition), we invite the "fasters" to use a whole grain bread, fairly rich, and with no artificial ingredients, in order to be sufficiently nourished for those days. The ideal way would be to bake the bread yourself, that way a dough that suits all the different health considerations of the household can be prepared. The Blessed Mother baked her own bread, like most mothers of families in past centuries.

Here are seveal recipe ideas.

Marie-Line's recipe

For 1 ½ lbs (650 gr) of whole spelt flour

1. In a small bowl, place 1 tsp. (5 ml) of dry yeast in 5 ½ tblsp (80 ml) of water at 98.6°F (37° C). Add 1 tsp. (5 ml) of sugar. Let it stand for 10 min or until the volume doubles.

2. Put 1 ½ c. (350 ml) of warm water in a large bowl.

3. Add 1 ½ teaspoons of salt and 4 tsps (20 ml) of
    coconut or olive oil. Mix.

4. Gradually add the flour while kneading.

5. Cover with a damp cloth and let it rise for 60 min in a
    warm place at 77–86°F (25°-30° C.)

6. Remove the cloth, punch down the dough and let
    stand 30 more minutes covered with the damp cloth.
    Let it rise again in a warm place, at around 82° F. (28°
    C.)

7. Grease a loaf pan.

8. Remove the cloth and shape a loaf of bread using a
    little flour on a flat surface.

9. Leave to rise for about 20 minutes in a warm place.

10. Bake in the center of the oven at 175° C (350° F) for
    50 minutes.

Many people make the mistake of putting the dough into the
oven at low temperatures in order to let it rise better. However, the oven is too hot and the bread falls. The dough must
rise slowly, at room temperature. Putting it into the oven to
rise with just the light on is the right technique.

Note: There are low-cost bread machines that will allow you
to make bread in two or three hours depending on the
appliance. Just put in the ingredients and the bread will come
out ready to be eaten. This allows those who are fasting to
choose their flour and have real "home-made" bread without
spending too much time on it. (This is also a good gift idea
for your friends!)

Sister Sarah's recipe for fasting bread

For 10 cups (1k or 2.2 lbs) of cereal flour

o 3Tb instant baker's yeast

o 1.5 tsp salt

o 2 Tb oil (olive, sunflower or other)

o Knead flour with yeast, salt and oil

o Add a little warm water at a time until the dough comes off the hands

o Let rise near source of heat

o Put into bread pans (3 pans for 1k)

o Let dough rise longer

o Bake in oven at 375º F (190ºC or gas mark 5) 25 to 30min Watch!

Flavia's Recipe for Fasting bread,
Made without yeast, like chapattis in India.
Ingredients for about 6 servings:

o 2 ½ cups of whole wheat flour

o ¾ cup of white flour

o ½ tsp salt

o 2 ½ tabs olive oil

o 1 ½ cup of water

o ¼—½ cup of ground almonds (or other nut); optional

o 1/3 cup of raisins soaked in a cup of very hot water; optional

Instructions

- ○ Soak the raisins in a cup of very hot water to become plumb, about 15 min.

- ○ Preheat oven to 400 degrees F (or 200 degrees C).

- ○ Then combine all ingredients in a bowl. The mixture should be very wet.

- ○ Add mixture to a non-stick pan or grease a glass baking dish.

- ○ With hands or spoon, pat and smooth the mixture evenly on the bottom of the pan. Bake for 15 min on the top rack, then remove and place on the bottom rack for another 15 min.

- ○ When firm to the touch, and the sides are crispy and pulling away from the pan, it is done. Leave to cool slightly. Remove from pan and serve immediately.

Gluten-Free Fasting Bread Recipe, From a bakery, in Italy. Makes approximately 1 ¾ lbs (800g) of bread.

- ○ 1 cup (250 g) light brown rice flour

- ○ ½ c. (100 g) chestnut flour

- ○ ½ c. (100 g) corn flour

- ○ ¼ c. (50 g) potato starch

- ○ 1 ounce (20 g) fresh Baker's yeast or ¼ ounce (7 g) dry yeast

- ○ 1 ½ ounce (50 g) honey

o   1 ¼ c. (300ml) warm water

o   2 tbsp olive oil

o   1 pinch fine salt

Instructions

o   Mix your different types of flour and the salt

o   Mix water, yeast, honey and oil

o   Add your liquid mix to the flour mix and stir vigorously with a wooden spoon!

o   Leave to rise for one hour in the bowl, then place the dough in a loaf pan

o   Leave to rise at room temperature for 50 min

o   Bake in a hot oven 410°F (210°C) for 25 minutes, then lower the temperature and continue baking for 20 min!

APPENDIX 2

FROM THE VERY FIRST days of the apparitions, Our Lady recommended that we all go back to using holy water. In the town of Medjugorje, there is already a strong tradition among the Catholic families: Every Saturday, the mother of the family goes in to each room of the house and walks around the property outside, while praying and sprinkling holy water and blessed salt everywhere. It would be good to adopt this practice, because it uses "sacramentals" offered by the Church, so powerful for the protection of persons in homes, fields, offices, etc. Many wonder how to protect themselves from the influences of the evil spirits. Well, here is a simple and efficacious way! Only or a Priest or a Deacon has the ability to bless the water and salt; a simple lay person cannot do it in their stead. You can find the rites of benediction and exorcism offered by the Church today in books available on the internet. What follows are formulas that were used before the Second Vatican Council. They are more difficult to find, but they are very powerful. After a Mass or other liturgy, you can bring these formulas to a priest and have him bless the water and salt.

RITES OF BENEDICTION AND EXORCISM FOR SALT
AND WATER FOR PRIESTS AND DEACONS

Exorcism of Salt

P: Our help is in the name of the Lord.

ALL: *Who made heaven and earth.*

P: God's creature, salt, I cast out the demon from you by the living + God, by the true + God , by the holy + God, by God who ordered you to be thrown into the waterspring by Eliseus to heal it of its barrenness. May you be an exorcised salt, a means of health for those who believe, a medicine for body and soul for all who make use of you. May all evil fancies of the foul fiend, his malice and cunning, be driven afar from the place where you are sprinkled. And let every unclean spirit be repulsed by Him who is coming to judge both the living and the dead and the world by fire.

Let us pray.

Almighty everlasting God, we humbly appeal to your mercy and goodness to graciously bless + and sanctify this creature, salt, which you have given for mankind's use. May all who use it find in it a remedy for body and mind. And may everything that it touches or sprinkles be freed from uncleanness and any influence of the evil spirit; through Christ our Lord.

ALL: *Amen.*

Exorcism of the Water

P: God's creature, water, I cast out the demon from you in the name of God + the Father almighty, in the name of Jesus + Christ, His Son, our Lord, and in the power of the Holy + Spirit. May you be a purified water, empowered to drive afar all power of the enemy, in fact, to root out and banish the enemy himself, along with his fallen angels. We ask this through the power of our Lord Jesus Christ, who is coming to judge both the living and the dead and the world by fire.

ALL: *Amen.*

P: Let us pray. O God, who for man's welfare established the most wonderful mysteries in the substance of water, hearken to our prayer, and pour forth your blessing on this element now being prepared with various purifying rites. May this creature of yours, when used in your mysteries and endowed with your grace, serve to cast out demons and to banish disease. May everything that this water sprinkles in the homes and gatherings of the faithful be delivered from all that is unclean and hurtful; let no breath of contagion hover there, no taint of corruption; let all the wiles of the lurking enemy come to nothing. By the sprinkling of this water may everything opposed to the safety and peace of the occupants of these homes be banished, so that in calling on your holy name they may know the wellbeing they desire, and be protected from every peril; through Christ our Lord.

ALL: *Amen*

*Now the Priest pours the salt into the
water in the form of a cross, saying:*

P: May this salt and water be mixed together; in the name of the Father, and of the Son, and of the Holy Spirit.

ALL: *Amen.*

P: The Lord be with you.

ALL: *May he also be with you.*

P: Let us pray. God, source of irresistible might and king of an invincible realm, the everglorious conqueror; who restrain the force of the adversary, silencing the uproar of his rage,

and valiantly subduing his wickedness; in awe and humility
we beg you, Lord, to regard with favor this creature thing of
salt and water, to let the light of your kindness shine upon it,
and to hallow it with dew of your mercy; so that wherever it
is sprinkled and your holy name is invoked, every assault of
the unclean spirit may be baffled; and all dread of the serpent's venom be cast out. To us who entreat your mercy grant
that the Holy Spirit may be with us wherever we may be;
through Christ our Lord.

ALL: *Amen.*

"I have told you this so that you might have peace in me. In the world you will have trouble, but take courage, I have conquered the world."

(JOHN 16: 33)

OTHER PUBLICATIONS
BY SISTER EMMANUEL

Medjugorje,
Triumph of the Heart

The Hidden Child

The Beautiful
Story of Medjugorje

Freed and Healed
Through Fasting

Maryam of Bethlehem

The Amazing Secret of
the Souls in Purgatory

RETREAT WITH
SISTER EMMANUEL

Set in the beautiful Rocky Mountains, Sr. Emmanuel led a
retreat focused on the messages of Our Lady in Medjugorje.
This DVD set includes all six lessons:

- ○   Take the Hand of your Mother
- ○   Make Peace
- ○   Embrace Suffering
- ○   Pray with your Family
- ○   Respond to Our Lady

Order online at:
www.childrenofmedjugorje.com

Printed in Great Britain
by Amazon